# METAPSYCHOLOGY FOR CONTEMPORARY PSYCHOANALYSIS

*Metapsychology for Contemporary Psychoanalysis* is a complete revision of the theoretical underpinnings of psychoanalysis and psychodynamic psychotherapy. It seeks to replace the traditional *drive–defence* model of Freudian tradition with an *information processing* model of the mind. This book argues that the central human need is for *self-knowledge*, and that drives are best understood as means towards this end.

Richard Sembera begins with a close reading of Freud's own metapsychological writings, isolating the many unresolved difficulties and inconsistencies which continue to burden psychoanalytical theory today. By returning to the actual observable clinical phenomena in the analytic situation, it is shown that an alternative interpretation is possible that eliminates the theoretical difficulties in question. In the analytic situation, Sembera argues that clinicians do not in fact see individuals struggling against the expression of biological drives, rather they observe individuals struggling to clarify their experience of themselves in the presence of the analyst and put this experience into words. When this process is formalized and expressed in theoretical terms, it is found to consist of three distinct aspects: *objectification, imagination*, and *symbolization*. This process as a whole – ascent towards the other, relationship with the other, disclosure of self in the light of the other – is termed the *dialectical structure of the self.* It is conceptualized as the main accomplishment of the core mental process, the *process of contextualization*.

This work is distinguished from other attempts at theoretical revision by its fundamental commitment to coherence and clarity as well as its determination to challenge accepted psychoanalytic dogma. It argues for the complete irrelevance of biology and neuroscience to the psychoanalytic enterprise and rejects the theory of drives in its entirety. Instead it affirms the centrality of the *traumatic response* to mental functioning, emphasises the social matrix in which drives are embedded, re-examines the concepts of free will, accountability, and responsibility, and concludes with an attempt to understand waking life as a creative product analogous to the *lucid dream*.

Drawing on major psychoanalytic thinkers including Bollas and Benjamin, and current philosophy of mind, this book provides readers with a clear, updated model of metapsychology. *Metapsychology for Contemporary Psychoanalysis* will appeal to psychoanalysts and psychotherapists, as well as philosophy scholars and anyone with an interest in the philosophy of psychoanalysis.

**Richard Sembera** is a Registered Psychotherapist and a Canadian Certified Counsellor. He is also a Training Candidate of the Canadian Institute of Psychoanalysis (Québec English). He presently works in the area of psychosocial emergency preparedness and response.

# METAPSYCHOLOGY FOR CONTEMPORARY PSYCHOANALYSIS

## Mind, World, and Self

*Richard Sembera*

Routledge
Taylor & Francis Group
LONDON AND NEW YORK

First published 2017
by Routledge
2 Park Square, Milton Park, Abingdon, Oxon OX14 4RN

and by Routledge
605 Third Avenue, New York, NY 10017

*Routledge is an imprint of the Taylor & Francis Group, an informa business*



*British Library Cataloguing in Publication Data*
A catalogue record for this book is available from the British Library

*Library of Congress Cataloging in Publication Data*
A catalog record for this book has been requested

ISBN: 978-1-138-24221-0 (hbk)
ISBN: 978-1-138-24222-7 (pbk)
ISBN: 978-1-315-27889-6 (ebk)

Typeset in Bembo
by Taylor & Francis Books

Therefore for the man who is guided by reason, the final goal, that is, the highest Desire whereby he strives to control all the others, is that by which he is brought to an adequate conception of himself and of all things that can fall within the scope of his understanding.

(Baruch Spinoza, *Ethics* Part IV, Appendix, para. 4)

# CONTENTS

# ACKNOWLEDGEMENTS

The cover image is of a painting by Rosemary Carson, titled *A Walk Down the Corridor* (Banstead Hospital), oil on board, 18 × 20 ins. Image courtesy of Henry Boxer Gallery, London, http://www.outsiderart.co.uk/carson.html.

The epigraph at the start of this book is taken from Baruch Spinoza (1992). *The Ethics. Treatise on the Emendation of the Intellect. Selected Letters* (S. Feldman, Ed., & S. Shirley, Trans.), Indianapolis and Cambridge: Hackett Publishing Company (Part IV, Appendix, para. 4; p. 196). Reprinted by permission of Hackett Publishing Company, Inc.

# INTRODUCTION

## I

The present book is the result of an attempt on my part to reformulate the fundamental conceptual basis of psychoanalysis and in so doing to provide a metapsychology for contemporary psychoanalytical practice. It is the third complete revision of a manuscript begun in February 2007. In its original form, the book was a straightforwardly philosophical treatise on the nature of reality that attempted to combine the language of Western metaphysics with insights from Eastern philosophical systems as well as from my own meditation experiences. It had reached a length of 220 handwritten pages by October of the same year when I decided that I could no longer continue the project in that form and broke off the writing of the manuscript. In late 2009 I completely rewrote the text, which had now taken the form of a tightly focussed essay on group dynamics. This draft was finished in the summer of 2010, but my dissatisfaction with the results led me to abandon this version of the project. Finally, in 2010, I began the initial drafts of the text that would become the present book. Although I think I can say the book has benefited as a whole from having been completely rewritten twice, and that it has preserved the best of the two previous drafts while avoiding their shortcomings, I nonetheless find myself wishing that the path to its completion had been somewhat less tortuous; but that is a story for another time and place.

## II

Broadly speaking, most disciplines outside philosophy lack the necessary conceptual tools to construct adequate theoretical foundations of their own practical enterprise; this is unfortunately often enough true within philosophy as well. Yet if philosophers fail to attain adequate theoretical insight into the foundations of their own systems and fail to give them adequate theoretical expression, as a rule no one is harmed (generations of exasperated philosophy students notwithstanding). Psychoanalysts, on the other hand, are supposed to be able to take responsibility for other people's mental health, which is a tremendous obligation. This makes the relative lack of attention given to adequate theoretical foundations for psychoanalysis all the more puzzling. Where attempts at theoretical revision have been made at all, they usually fail through too rigid an adherence to a classical framework, or else by neglecting the importance of clarity and intelligibility.

Insofar as the shortcomings of psychoanalytic theory are discussed within psychoanalysis itself, this discussion usually takes the form of a condemnation of theoretical plurality and an attempt by one means or another to secure some sort of monolithic body of "correct" doctrine – in other words, an attempt to separate the wheat from the chaff. I cannot agree that this is a productive approach. It seems to me that the ultimate basis of every psychoanalytic theory consists of a definite individual perspective that is valuable in itself, even where the enshrinement of this perspective in the foundational concepts of the theory along with their theoretical elaboration are deficient. In other words, I have a fundamental commitment to theoretical pluralism (more on this in Chapter 3). At the same time, I think that the ideal of a single overarching theoretical system that makes all other partial systems redundant has a definite pragmatic value. Striving for this ideal encourages us to take other theoretical perspectives into account, to think about them and understand them, to integrate them into our own way of thinking, and to experiment with rephrasing their valuable if limited insights in what is hopefully a more stringent and more transparent language. In Leibnizian terms, it encourages us to balance economy of basic principles against richness of content. The bottom line: I highly doubt that there will ever be one single universal psychoanalytic theory that adequately explains every psychoanalytic observation it is possible to make. Nevertheless, I think there is nothing lost, and much gained, in aiming at such a theory.

## III

If asked to explain the essential difference between classical metapsychology and the new and hopefully improved system of *Metapsychology for Contemporary Psychoanalysis* while standing on one leg, I would simply answer that classical metapsychology is based on a *drive–defence* model of mental activity, while my own system is based on an *information processing* model. After being allowed to seat myself again, I would continue by adding that Freud believed that a theoretical construct called a "drive" was the fundamental explanatory unit of psychoanalysis; that a drive is a mental expression of a biological chemical process; that it exerts an influence on the mind comparable to the effects of another, extra-psychoanalytic theoretical construct, namely a "force"; that it could be opposed by another force in the act of "repression"; that the effect of repression is wholly or partially to prevent the expression of a drive; and that mental conflict is ultimately best understood as the inability to muster sufficient force to keep the offending drive in check. This line of thought necessarily leads to the inescapable theoretical conclusion that there are two paths to mental health and two alone: either to undermine repression and bring the offending drive under conscious control, or else to buttress the activity of repression through submission to the established social order. Healthy people are content with pedagogy; for the disaffected neurotics, there is psychoanalysis. They differ with respect to the means, but not the goal, which is identical in both cases: self-control.

*Metapsychology for Contemporary Psychoanalysis* rejects all of these beliefs. In their place it asserts the following: the fundamental unit of the mind is *experience*. An experience is neither material nor mental; it is a unit of information from which the experience of a material and a mental world can be derived through a process of interpretative elaboration. Furthermore, it is not possible to occlude an experience – to stop thinking something – by opposing a "force" to it, no matter how metaphorically this force is conceived. An experience cannot be obliterated, confined, or rendered harmless by any means except by thinking it; so long as it remains unthought, it is always active. Thus mental conflict can under no circumstances be understood as a failure of "repression"; repression *always* fails as a control strategy. In the absence of knowledge there is *never* any successful outcome, i.e. one in which the activity of a "drive" would be rendered completely inoperative or even be mitigated to any real extent. Experience can be misunderstood, and it can be integrated into the self in a variety of ways both simple and complex, but it is always eternally present in an eternal unending now unless and until it is *contextualized*, i.e. successfully thought. Mental conflict can thus best be understood as *a failure of the mind to think its own experiences*. This necessarily leads to the inescapable theoretical conclusion that there is one path to mental health and one alone: that one should be able to have one's own thoughts about one's own experiences, and in this way arrive at authentic self-knowledge, by whatever means enable one to do so. That is to say: with the assistance of both pedagogy and psychoanalysis where possible; and in defiance of them both where necessary.

## IV

I have sometimes been told that my writing style is more reminiscent of a philosopher than a psychoanalyst. I am not entirely sure what this is supposed to mean. If we consult Freud's own metapsychological writings, they are clearly philosophical in character, even if their style is nowhere near as accessible as one could wish. It may be, however, that my critics had something else in mind, namely my disagreement with the widespread belief that clinical vignettes are the basic building blocks of psychoanalytical argument. The epistemological weaknesses of the case history are well known, and I can only mention them in passing here: selection bias is impossible to eliminate, and the requirement to preserve confidentiality requires biographical details to be altered, with the result that in virtually every single case the story no longer rings true. The material in such vignettes is so highly distorted that there is no way for the reader to get at the truth of what actually happened in session and thus no way to evaluate the writer's claims. Furthermore, in our modern Internet age, when practically everything is accessible to everyone else, I think it is unconscionable to publish case histories without client consent. This creates additional problems for psychoanalytic writing that I cannot address within the limited scope of this Introduction. I will state only that for my own metapsychological enterprise – the specifically psychoanalytical study of the mind qua mind – I do not require any particular clinical observations over and above the fundamental observations available to every analyst in every case, to wit: the observations that give rise to the theoretical concepts of repression, the unconscious, and transference. More on this in Chapter 4.

Much of the territory that I am going to explore in this book has been charted by other authors, though I think I can say that this has generally been done in an unsystematic and largely unsatisfactory way. If one's goal is to draft a reliable map, one does not generally do so by compiling information from a vast quantity of existing unreliable maps; and yet the officially approved techniques of academic research all too easily amount to precisely this, particularly when too much emphasis is placed on demonstrating a familiarity with the popular authors of the day instead of with the territory that is being mapped out. In this book I have tried to return to the bedrock of experience, using other authors largely for illustration and emphasis. My aim is to chart the most direct and most reliable path through the jungle of metapsychology, and to do this one has to begin at the beginning, not jump into the middle of tangled thickets where others have already gotten stuck. Some readers may find this unnecessarily tedious; perhaps such readers can be compared with musicians who complain that they simply want to play the works of their favourite composers without having to care about the complex history and origins of all this equal temperament stuff. I cannot follow them in this. Ultimately, perhaps, it all boils down to a question of personal style.

## V

In this book I have found myself in the position of having to challenge and ultimately reject some of the most fundamental and most cherished assumptions of psychoanalysis as it is traditionally conceived. I have tried to do this in the spirit of chivalrous disagreement to the greatest extent possible in the hope that my theoretical innovations will be accepted in the same spirit. Unfortunately, experience suggests that chivalrous disagreement and academic discourse often do not exactly go hand in hand. In psychoanalysis there are some good reasons for this; as I discuss in Chapter 3, metapsychological systems necessarily have a very personal meaning for their adherents, so a criticism of a metapsychological assumption can often feel like an attack on the mind. In point of fact this is frequently true, owing to a pervasive confusion of levels of discourse among psychoanalytic communities that I have attempted to address in Chapter 2. Many analysts, in practice, act as if they believe that to interpret is to refute. If they hear an argument to which they have no real answer, this type of analyst will instead interpret the motive of the speaker in putting forth the argument. I know that analysts are supposed to be aware of the difference, but at the pragmatic level this often enough seems not to be the case, at least in my own personal experience of psychoanalytic training. Since this experience tends to lead me to expect such a response to my book, I have proceeded to examine the logical fallacies involved in some detail. I apologize if anyone finds this tiresome, but I think it is important to expose fallacies as fallacies, and that understanding exactly why they are fallacious is an important intellectual contribution as well as a strong remedy against the temptation to indulge in them.

## VI

In formulating the theoretical position here put forth I have been influenced principally by the works of the following authors: Piera Aulagnier, Wilfred R. Bion, W. R. D. Fairbairn, Sigmund Freud, Erich Fromm, Martin Heidegger, Edmund Husserl, Immanuel Kant, G. W. Leibniz, Joyce McDougall, Alice Miller, Friedrich Nietzsche, Plato, Arthur Schopenhauer, Baruch Spinoza, and D. W. Winnicott. Their influence is evident on every page I have written, even where I have not explicitly referred to any of their writings. I disagree with all of them on major issues, but I have found their writing for the most part both stimulating and inspiring.

I think it is important to remember that psychoanalytic writing is still in its infancy; there may well come a time when the entire corpus of presently extant psychoanalytic texts will seem as fantastic and chimerical to us as the fragments of the Presocratics now seem to contemporary philosophers. It may also be, however, that a worse fate awaits them. Owing to some peculiarity of the subject that is difficult to elucidate, a certain affinity with the arts perhaps, great philosophical works have an eternal character: with the exception of minor factual inaccuracies, the works of Plato are quite as relevant to our century as they were to the century in which they were written. Psychoanalytical works do not seem to have this character. Like mainstream scientific works, they gradually show their age and become obsolete, eventually becoming of merely historical interest.

By and large I feel that most people would agree that the best and most respectful tribute one can bring before great teachers is an equal devotion to the truth, which entails a persistent effort to discover and remedy their mistakes: *amicus Plato, sed magis amica veritas*. Unfortunately, it is difficult to discover this attitude in the orientation of many psychoanalytic writers – perhaps even most – towards Freud. In reviewing the extant corpus of psychoanalytic theories one is often forced, however reluctantly, to the conclusion that their true motto is *amica veritas, sed magis amicus Freud*. This is a strikingly odd trait for a discipline with scientific ambitions.

## VII

For a number of different reasons, I find much of the classical English vocabulary of psychoanalysis problematic. I divide this problematic vocabulary into five principal categories as follows.

(1) Terms that were translated with a view to creating a scientific vocabulary in English where none exists in Freud's original German. These terms include "cathexis," "ego," "id," and "super-ego"; compare the French *investissement, moi, ça, surmoi*. This is the category of mistranslations against which Bruno Bettelheim's criticism is primarily directed in *Freud and Man's Soul* (1984).

(2) Terms whose selection was influenced by Freud's own need to phrase things scientifically even when the matter under consideration really does not warrant it, e.g. "object," which invites confusion at all semantic levels with "thing," or the use of "affect" instead of more commonplace options such as "emotion" (*Emotion, Empfindung*) or "feeling" (*Gefühl*). To some extent "cathexis" (*Besetzung*) and "counter-transference" (*Gegenübertragung*) fit into this category as well.

(3) Terms that fail to capture an essential nuance of Freud's original German, yet to which there seems to correspond no really adequate translation. For example, "repression" fails as an accurate rendering of the German *Verdrängung*, which literally means "driving off" or "fending off." Another example is *Übertragung*, "carrying over," rendered into English via Latin as "transference."

(4) Terms such as "libido," a Latin word to which Freud resorted because there was no German equivalent capable of doing the same work, but to which there corresponds a perfectly good English word, namely "desire."

(5) Terms that, in both English and German, have an inescapably pejorative connotation and are derived from the names of historical or mythological persons, and for both these reasons cannot be used in a purely descriptive sense or even defined with any real precision, e.g. "masochism," "narcissism," and "sadism." They give rise to the further inconvenience that to obtain a neutral term one has to resort to oxymorons, e.g. "healthy narcissism."

After much consideration and a fair amount of soul-searching, I have decided by and large to retain the traditional vocabulary of psychoanalysis, despite its many shortcomings. I do not wish to overburden the reader with a bewildering array of neologisms. Clarity and comprehensibility are my main concerns. Where I feel it is necessary, I will introduce new definitions of old terms that I think are particularly problematic, and I will also introduce new ways of talking about things. I will also resort to the creation of new terms where I think it really necessary to do justice to the subject matter. For the most part, however, I have tried to integrate the traditional and the novel as seamlessly as I could.

One major change I have made is in the word that I use to refer to the people who are actually undergoing analysis. The problem with calling them "patients" was recognized fairly early on: people who need help are not necessarily "sick" in the sense in which a medical patient is "sick" (Bettelheim, 1984, p. 39 ff.). For this reason the inelegant neologism "analysand" is employed by some authors, a term that in addition to being inelegant also suggests a falsehood. No one comes to us for analysis; people come to us for help. Analysis is a means towards this end. I think we can agree that something along the lines of "fellow sufferer" would be far closer to the truth; but this too would make for stilted writing. The only word that I have found to be reasonably serviceable is a word borrowed from my own profession as a counsellor: "client." Not only does this word avoid the undesirable connotations of "patient," it also reminds us of a very fundamental truth that analysts would do well not to forget: analysts are at bottom paid professional consultants and therefore the employees of the persons who are paying their fees. I think that keeping this in mind is a helpful corrective against certain psychic hazards of the mental health profession, some of which I address in Chapter 4.

Turning to the other end of the therapeutic relationship, I have decided to retain the term "psychoanalyst" (or "analyst," for short) largely because no elegant alternative suggests itself, but I will take a moment to clarify the sense in which this word will be used in the present book. If the word "psychoanalyst" be taken to mean a practitioner of psychoanalysis, then it should be kept in mind that the vast majority of "psychoanalysts" earn their living through some other form of clinical work than "psychoanalysis" strictly defined, so that in this respect there is little to differentiate the analyst from the non-analyst. If, however, the word "psychoanalyst" be taken to indicate someone who has undergone a certain course of formal psychoanalytic training, then I feel obliged to comment that I am not at all sure that successful completion of this formal psychoanalytic training, in its present dominant forms, is a necessary condition of being able to practise analysis effectively. I will add that I am quite certain that it is *not* a sufficient condition of the same.

Generally speaking, then, the somewhat inelegant phrase "psychoanalytic psychotherapist" would be more accurate as a designation of all practitioners of psychoanalysis in whatever form, but other considerations than its inelegance led me to avoid its use. In my experience the phrase is often used pejoratively by those with an interest in maintaining the prestige of the "psychoanalyst" as well as by those who, for similar reasons, feel the need to maintain a rigid and artificial distinction between psychoanalysis and psychoanalytic psychotherapy. I have therefore decided to stick to the traditional term "psychoanalyst," although I underline that in the present book it is not meant to be understood in any narrow or rigid sense, but rather as a convenient abbreviation of "psychoanalytic psychotherapist."

A third important respect in which I have deviated from tradition is that I do not cite Freud according to the *Standard Edition*. I believe the Strachey translations to be most unsatisfactory and unusable for all practical purposes; their ideological bias is so patent and distortions in meaning are so evident that no German-speaking scholar could cite them with an entirely clear conscience. Accordingly, in the vast majority of cases I have simply cited and translated Freud directly from the *Stu-di-en-aus-ga-be* published by the S. Fischer Verlag, since this is the best readily available edition of Freud's works in German.

Translations of French, German, and Greek texts are either my own, or translations by others that have been compared with the original and altered according to my own best judgement. For a time I considered including original language citations in footnotes, but in the end my dislike of footnotes outweighed my dislike of translations. In any case fluency in the three main European languages – English, German, and French – is increasingly rare in our post-modern world, so the average reader will not be served by including original language citations, and those who are fluent in these languages no doubt have the wherewithal to verify my translations without my assistance.

Although by and large I quote from original language source texts, I have done what I could to make it easy for readers to locate the corresponding passages in the translation of their choice by giving additional information regarding the position of the passage in question in the structure of the text as a whole. I cite according to standard paginations where such standards exist, e.g. Plato and Aristotle are cited according to the Stephanus and Bekker paginations respectively, or else by Book and Section; Nietzsche is cited by section (§), Spinoza's *Ethics* by Book and Proposition, and so on.

I have made an effort to make my writing gender-inclusive while avoiding any unnecessary distortions of English style, not because this is the fashion, but because I prefer not to leave anyone out.

## VIII

In the preface to the first edition of *The World as Will and Representation* Schopenhauer compared Kant's philosophy with a cataract operation, and his own philosophy with a set of spectacles especially prepared for someone who had undergone the operation. I see the relationship of my work to Freud's differently. I see myself as a mechanic who has completely rebuilt the engine of the automobile that Freud assembled. Not much difference is evident from the outside, but the real difference makes itself felt when you get in, start it up, and step on the gas. In other words, I do not expect to make much of a difference to the way analysts speak, but I hope to make a significant difference to the way they think, which is, after all, the main thing. For this purpose I have tried to ensure that the vast majority of technical terms are more or less compatible with their existing use by analysts. They should still know how to operate the vehicle, even if the drive itself is very different from anything they are used to.

In training new mental health professionals, established practitioners seem to be determined to communicate an impression of how difficult it supposedly is to understand clients' problems; it seems to me that this is as true of counsellors as it is of psychoanalysts. In any case I, for one, have had the opposite experience. It is a very, very rare opportunity to be seated before someone who is speaking freely and without conscious self-censorship, and despite all the pain and tragedy my training brought with it, I still feel privileged to have had the opportunity to work with clients in this way. For what is strikingly obvious to anyone who knows how to listen, who is curious, who asks questions, who wants to learn, and who likes people and wants to help them, *is how startlingly clear the true nature of their problems is when they speak in this way*. I am at a loss to explain the dichotomy between the crystalline clarity of these primeval experiences and the apparent confusion in the literature on mental health, including psychoanalytic literature.

A similar state of affairs exists with respect to the significance of trauma. In my opinion, mental health professionals as a whole seem determined to give the impression that trauma is difficult to understand and difficult to treat. Psychoanalytic writers too seem to have struggled with the issue of trauma since the very inception of psychoanalysis. It would not be an exaggeration to say that psychoanalysis proper begins with a certain view on the nature and origin of trauma, to wit, Freud's abandonment of the seduction theory. It would be superfluous to enter into the wearisome debate surrounding this issue. In any case, I certainly concur that trauma is difficult to treat, but I cannot agree that it is difficult to understand. Accordingly, the present book not only contains a complete theory of trauma (Chapter 15), but also postulates the traumatic response as the fundamental mental operation (Chapter 16), and thus restores trauma to its rightful place in psychoanalytic theory: at the very core of the mind.

This theoretical approach also has another advantage: as I have already indicated, it allows us to replace the classical psychoanalytical drive–defence model with an *information processing* model of the mind. To be sure, this tendency is already present in contemporary psychoanalytic theorizing, perhaps nowhere more prominently than in the work of W. R. Bion. It is, however, commonly overlooked by his interpreters that Bion himself draws directly from the philosophy of Kant without due acknowledgement and without true understanding. I would go so far as to say that without a prior in-depth knowledge of Kant what is of value in Bion is largely unintelligible to the reader. What is still worse, Bion's important insights are almost completely buried beneath an obsessive and Byzantine style of writing that is more reminiscent of an alchemist than a psychoanalyst. The present system of metapsychology corrects these defects by going back to the source, namely Kant, and combining all the important and fundamental insights of the thinkers I mentioned in section VI of this Introduction into a synthesis that I hope is both reasonably original and reasonably useful to the clinician.

## IX

The aim of psychoanalysis is clarity. The fundamental insight of psychoanalysis is that clear thinking heals. It follows from this that, all other things being equal, those who are most capable of clear thinking are also most capable of functioning as psychoanalysts. No one's interests are served by theoretical writings that are deliberately obscure or badly written. Despite any and all assertions to the contrary, obscurity does not necessarily entail depth, and vice versa. For my part, I believe that what is worth saying at all can be said clearly and comprehensibly, and this book is itself an attempt to demonstrate the essential truth of that proposition.

# 1

# WHAT IS METAPSYCHOLOGY?

The word "metapsychology" is a neologism introduced by Freud in imitation of an older philosophical term, namely "metaphysics." According to tradition, "metaphysics" is a word that originated in antiquity. An early editor of the works of Aristotle[1] found a group of writings that seemed to belong together, yet whose place in the rest of the Aristotelian corpus was unclear. As such, the editor simply called them "the books that come after the books on nature," and positioned them according to this description. In Greek, this phrase is *ta meta ta phusika*, which over time was contracted, via Latin, to "metaphysics."

Aristotle's books on metaphysics are distinguished by their peculiar subject matter. They contain reflections that Aristotle himself referred to as "first philosophy." For Aristotle, first philosophy is a universal discipline that examines the basic principles of all other particular disciplines such as medicine, grammar, and mathematics. While each particular discipline studies one particular type of thing, first philosophy studies what all things have in common insofar as they are things at all. In Aristotelian terms, first philosophy is the investigation of the existent qua existent (*Metaphysics*, IV.2). The details of Aristotle's inquiry do not concern us here; suffice it to say that in the end, Aristotle is led to assume the existence of an atemporal, non-spatial, and unperceivable entity completely absorbed in self-contemplation (*Metaphysics*, XII.7; XII.9). Because of the obviously transcendental character of this investigation, the term "metaphysics" began to take on a different significance. The Greek preposition *meta* is ambiguous and can mean both "after" and "beyond." As a result, "metaphysics" began to be understood as a discipline that inquired into whatever lay beyond the natural world.

Freud, who was well acquainted with ancient Greek, was at least partially aware of the etymology and meaning of the word "metaphysics," as his various uses of the word suggest. According to an editorial note in Vol. III of the German *Studienausgabe, Psychologie des Unbewußten* (1997, pp. 9–10), Freud first used the term in a letter to

Wilhelm Fließ dated February 13, 1896. There Freud states that "metapsychology" could be used as a name for his own system of psychology, since it "leads behind" consciousness to the unconscious. Freud's first use of the term in print dates to 1901, in *The Psychopathology of Everyday Life* XII *C) b)* (p. 292). There, Freud suggests that the mythological and religious view of the world is "nothing but *psychology projected into the external world*" (the emphasis is Freud's). Freud speculates that his system of psychology, the psychology of the unconscious, might well succeed in tracing mythology and religion back to their ultimate origins: endopsychic perceptions that are misconstrued as perceptions of the real world, giving rise to "the construction of a *suprasensual* [übersinnlich] *reality*."[2] In so doing, the psychology of the unconscious, according to Freud, would "dissolve" traditional religious myths and so also ultimately "transform *metaphysics* into *metapsychology*" (p. 289). Freud's meaning is that once the fundamentally "paranoid" projective mechanism behind traditional religion and metaphysics is completely understood, both religion and metaphysics will simply disappear as cultural phenomena, like any other neurotic symptoms that have been properly analyzed. Their place will then be taken by the critical discipline that brought about their end: metapsychology.

Freud did not refer to metapsychology again in print until 1915, in section IV of "The Unconscious" (Freud, 1915b/1997). Here, Freud revives the term "metapsychology" in a slightly different context: "I suggest that we call it a *metapsychological* exposition when we succeed in describing a mental [*psychisch*] process according to its *dynamic, topographical,* and *economic* relationships" (p. 140). This represents "the way of seeing things [*Betrachtungsweise*] that is the perfection of psychoanalytical research." The reader familiar with Leibniz' theory of definitions – see section 24 of Leibniz' *Discourse on Metaphysics* along with his "Meditations on Knowledge, Truth, and Ideas," both in Leibniz (1989) – will immediately recognize these formulations as attempts at nominal, not real, definitions. In other words, they tell us how to recognize metapsychology, but not what it is, or even what it is supposed to accomplish. The "metapsychological descriptions" that follow these definitions are of little help. They are highly speculative and at some considerable remove from concrete experience, and serve merely to underline Freud's conception of metapsychology as a transcendental discipline, i.e. one willing to go far beyond what is indicated with relative certainty by the observable clinical material in order to speculate about occurrences in the furthest reaches of the mind.

If we turn for assistance to Freud's three criteria, we come upon several points of interest. The economic point of view, we are told on the same page, "strives to follow the destinies [*Schicksale*, more freely: "vicissitudes"] of quantities of excitation and to attain at least a relative estimation of the same." Five years later, in 1920, the very first paragraph of *Beyond the Pleasure Principle* (1920/1997) repeats the nominal definition of a metaphysical exposition but informs us that the economic point of view consists of understanding mental [*seelisch*] processes in terms of the pleasure principle: mental processes are directed towards the avoidance of displeasure [*Unlust*] and the pursuit of pleasure [*Lust*]. Freud then begins a rather uninformative tirade against philosophy, apparently taking it for granted that the reader knows what the dynamic and topographical viewpoints are supposed to be. He seems unconcerned with the fact that his explanation of the economic viewpoint is not entirely compatible with the earlier explanation in "The Unconscious." The earlier formulation appears to focus on the process of repression understood in terms of a struggle of opposing mental forces. While this process may indeed be motivated by the operation of the pleasure principle, it is clearly not identical with it (compare Chapter 5). In the later formulation there is an obvious shift of emphasis, and perhaps a narrower focus as well.

We have an easier time figuring out what is meant by the topographical viewpoint. In chapter II of "The Unconscious" we are told that the topographical viewpoint attempts "to specify, for any given mental [*seelisch*] act, inside of which system or between which systems it is taking place" (p. 132). The two (or three) mental systems whose existence Freud recognizes at this time are consciousness, the unconscious, and (possibly) the preconscious.

On the same page we are told – and this is also all we are told – that the dynamic viewpoint is what distinguishes psychoanalysis from psychology. While this allows us to make an educated guess, if we want a firm textual basis for a sure opinion, we have to turn to a paper of 1912, "A Note on the Unconscious in Psycho-Analysis" (1912a/1997). Here Freud briefly discusses the phenomenon of post-hypnotic suggestion: a subject is ordered to carry out a certain task at a certain fixed time after the end of the hypnotic state, and does so without initially being able to explain why. Freud suggests that the results of such an experiment lead us "from a purely descriptive conception to a *dynamic* conception of the phenomenon" (p. 30). This consists in the view that certain thoughts can simultaneously be both unconscious and "active," i.e. capable of influencing the conduct of the individual at a conscious level.

If we attempt to summarize all these remarks in as concise a definition as possible, it seems that for Freud metapsychology is a discipline that acknowledges the influence of the unconscious, that sees the mind as consisting of several distinct yet interacting systems, and explains the interaction of these systems in terms of the pleasure principle. While this is a slightly better definition than any we can find in any one place in Freud's writings, it is still a nominal definition. It does not tell us what metapsychology actually is, or why it should do precisely those three things that Freud says it does.

In place of Freud's nominal definition I would like to suggest the following real definition: metapsychology is the investigation of the fundamental processes, structures, and components of the mind insofar as these are accessible to study within the analytic situation. Put differently, we could also say that metapsychology is the specifically psychoanalytic study of the mind qua mind. By the phrase "mind qua mind" I mean that we focus on the mind insofar as it is a mind at all, and not the mind of any particular person: the mind is considered independently of personal history or personal psychopathology with a view to identifying universal characteristics and features. I consider both the above definitions as conceptually equivalent real definitions of metapsychology.

It follows from both of the definitions in the previous paragraph that the ultimate role metapsychology plays is to specify the *fundamental explanatory units* at the disposal of the analyst when attempting to account for the workings of the mind. Metapsychology specifies the fundamental inventory of entities and principles in terms of which psychoanalytical explanations can be framed; and it thereby also sets a limit to the scope of these explanations.

It is common knowledge that Freud's own attitude towards metapsychology was highly ambivalent. On the one hand, in the second paragraph of section III of "Analysis Terminable and Interminable" he derided it as a "witch" to whom he turned for magical solutions when clinical experience posed apparently insoluble problems (1937/1975, p. 366); on the other hand, he appears to have regarded it as a seductive indulgence with no real scientific substance. One occasionally has the impression that for him metapsychology was the ultimate guilty intellectual pleasure.

Theories, however, should not, in my view, merely consist of pleasurable indulgences. Metapsychology should also have a definite real contribution to make, just like any other part of psychoanalytic theory. I would like to outline briefly the criteria that I think a system of metapsychology should have to meet in order to be of practical use. I will also add some remarks on criteria that I think a metapsychological system should not have to meet, either because a misconception of its task is involved, or because the nature of metapsychology has been misunderstood. Finally, I will explain what I think the specific contribution of philosophy to metapsychology should be, and define my conception of a system of philosophical metapsychology.

In the first place, I understand metapsychology as the psychoanalytic study of the mind qua mind, i.e. the mind as such, not the mind of any one individual. At the same time it is important to remember that the internal landscape of each particular individual may vary to such an extent that no overarching description of the architecture of the mind might be possible or even desirable. Metapsychology must leave room for exceptions to the rule and for future revision and innovation. I consider the use of metapsychology as a navigational and heuristic tool to be of prime importance.

I will now identify four qualities that I think a system of metapsychology must exhibit in order to be useful. A metapsychology should be *accurate*, that is to say, within the limits of an investigation of this sort, it should describe typical mental elements and structures along with all their likely variations across different individuals. It should also be *compact*, i.e. simple and as easy to learn and use as possible. It should not, for example, be constructed with a view towards the display of erudition for its own sake. It should be *open-ended*, and so leave room for discovery, expansion, assimilation of new material, and contributions from other theories. It should be able to resist any attempt at forced identification with any particular school of thought, and should not be usable as a rallying point for the same. Finally, it should be *practical*: its clinical applications should immediately be evident. It should be a system of concepts that helps us get work done.

One criterion that I think a metapsychological theory should not have to meet is compatibility with the sciences in general, and with biological science in particular. Other writers, for example Jean Laplanche (2008), have criticized Freud's biological bias at length, and for our present purposes some very general comments regarding this issue will suffice. I think that it was clear from the beginning that psychoanalysis is not, and cannot be, concerned with the biological basis of mental suffering for the simple reason that the analyst, qua analyst, is not occupied with the body but with the mind. Put differently, we could say that the proper object of study of psychoanalysis is not the body, but fantasies involving the body. This should have been clear to Freud from his earliest work on hysteria and hysterical paralysis, in which the lack of correspondence between manifest physical symptoms and the actual layout of the nervous system is obvious.

While Freud's attempt to see mind and body as one indivisible unit is laudable – if one is willing to leave aside the obviously reductionistic aspect of his program – there is no question that mere biological metaphor cannot do the real work of bridging the gap in our understanding of the interaction of mind and body. It is clear, I think, that much of Freud's scientific language is quite simply just that: biological metaphor. It is as if Freud, in attempting to explain the subjective experience of tension, took as his basis the muscular "tension" present in the muscles in a state of anxiety, along with the electrical "tension" across certain neuronal gaps, and then identified the first type of psychological tension with the latter two physical types. We cannot exploit the multiple meanings of words to escape the work of thinking. Metaphors cannot do the work of concepts, and the use of scientific metaphor does not constitute a science.

I have no particular objection if individual analysts wish to combine their interest in psychoanalysis with an interest in neurophysiology or other similar disciplines, but I think it should be clear that these *are* two different interests. Until we know exactly how a chemical event becomes an experience – if this is indeed what happens, which is not at all clear – there can be no real conceptual bridge between the biological sciences and the academic disciplines that study the mind. The client's physiology is not accessible to the analyst through free association, but the client's feelings and fantasies are, and it is therefore these that are the proper objects of study of psychoanalysis (Guntrip, 1971). To quote Kant, "It is not enrichment but deformation when one allows the boundaries of the sciences to flow into each other" (*Critique of Pure Reason*, B VIII–IX). When physiology becomes involved, the role of the psychoanalyst ends, and the neurologist should be called in. The best, I think, that can be hoped for from neuropsychoanalysis is the eventual discovery that "neuropsychoanalysis" is an oxymoron.

Although as a rule I dislike analogies that compare human beings with machines, I have sometimes found the following illustration helpful. A computer is a machine that stores and manipulates information electronically. The machine as a whole can be conceived as consisting of two broad aspects: hardware and software. Hardware is the totality of the physical aspects of the machine, while software refers to the totality of the various instructions that the machine obeys in the course of its functioning. Hardware exists in the physical world; software is information carried by a variety of symbols. Now if there is a problem with a certain computer program, it is certainly true that the problem in question must have some sort of presence in the hardware. But would we then conclude that we should call in a hardware engineer to solve the problem? Hardly: the physical states of the hardware are not open to direct physical manipulation, and even if they were, the information is stored in such a complex series of electronic states that manipulating them directly would be impractical. Rather, if there is a problem with a program, one calls in a software engineer to fix the bug in the program's instruction code. Of course what the software engineer does ultimately will result in a change in the hardware as well; but is that a matter of particular importance? The computer, being a product of human engineering, shares this, and this alone, in common with humanity: it exists on two different levels, a physical level and a level of meaning or significance; the two levels are in constant communication; a change of state in one level effects a corresponding change of state in the other level; and physical problems are fixed by physical means, while problems with meaning or significance are fixed by someone who can disentangle that type of problem. As analysts, we are concerned with *meanings*. We are called in when there is nothing wrong with the hardware, but the software is buggy. When there is really something wrong with the hardware, then another type of specialist has to be called in, not because there is a sharp distinction between the mind and the body, but because one chooses the direction of approach that is likely to cause the greatest productive change with the least effort; and this usually does not involve taking a screwdriver to the hardware.[3]

I want to underline that I do not intend a criticism of the scientific enterprise or scientific methodology as such, only its extension into areas of the humanities where it can only obscure matters of fundamental human concern. It is obviously useful for a psychotherapist to know, for example, that many of the symptoms of an anxiety attack are physiological concomitants of hyperventilation, or that alcoholic intoxication can make rage feel like euphoria; and it is also useful to know that fear can often produce physiological sexual arousal – in fact, I think that these topics should be discussed far *more* than they currently are in the education of mental health professionals in general and of psychoanalysts in particular. My objection is simply that psychoanalysis studies a domain of human experience that cannot be reduced to or even correlated with physiology in any simple or straightforward way, and that this must be respected in order to do justice both to the discipline as such and to the people we see in analysis. We are interpreters, not bookbinders or typographers; and these *are* distinct and conceptually unrelated disciplines.

Now it is clear that I do think that philosophy is a discipline that, unlike biology, can be fruitfully combined with psychoanalysis. This is largely because I see metapsychology as an essentially philosophical enterprise, and I think that Freud's own antipathy towards philosophical inquiry blinded him to the many important contributions that a properly articulated philosophical viewpoint can make to psychoanalytical theory. I do not wish to burden the reader with unnecessary technical details; I can refer those with a special interest in the subject to an earlier work of mine (Sembera, 2007, pp. 1–32). What I have to say about philosophy in general and about phenomenology in particular can be found there. I will simply add some informal explanations of what philosophical and phenomenological approaches to psychoanalysis mean to me.

Broadly speaking, the aim of traditional philosophy is certainty regarding matters that transcend the limitations of human experience, and its chief instrument is argument. By contrast, the aim of phenomenology is finding meaning within the limitations of human experience, and its chief instrument is descriptive investigation. Traditional philosophy, in other words, is inclined to transcend the boundaries of experience by means of argumentative inference from the known. Thus when Plato argues in favour of the immortality of the soul, he begins with familiar features of our mental life: that the mind is non-extended, that it has no parts in any spatial sense of the word, that only the physical can be broken up into pieces. From these evident facts Plato then infers that the mind cannot suffer dissolution, that it is therefore immortal, and that our mental life will continue after death.

With regard to the same issue, a more phenomenological approach would be to consider the question of the survival of the soul after death to be a matter for faith rather than for philosophy. Heidegger, for example, in his main work *Being and Time* (1927/1977), completely ignores the question of whether there actually is life after death. Instead, he focusses on the question: what is it like to be aware of the inevitability of your own eventual non-existence? A phenomenologist would also be intrigued by these questions: if the mind is non-extended and non-spatial, then where is it? Can it really be in the body or in the brain? How do we know about it? How do we experience it, and if we experience it as lasting and enduring, and incapable of dissolution, what is it about the mind that gives us that impression? The focus of phenomenology is on questions that open up new aspects of our experiences and their sources; traditional philosophy, if I may say so, has a focus on shutting out aspects of our experiences, making them simpler and offering a firm base for conviction. Plato wants consolation through certainty. Heidegger wants a richer life through inquiry.

It is, I think, precisely because metapsychology has hitherto been more sympathetic to the aims of traditional philosophy than to the aims of phenomenology that the subject can benefit from a phenomenologically informed critique. Nevertheless, so that my own position is entirely clear, I wish to stress that phenomenology is *one* approach, and by no means the only approach, to metapsychological investigation. In the present book I have combined both phenomenological and traditional philosophical approaches depending on which seemed to be most appropriate to the immediate needs of ongoing exposition.

## Notes

1 Possibly Andronicus of Rhodes, 1st century BCE.

2 Parenthetically: this "projective" theory of religion did not originate with Freud. It is present in all essentials in Ludwig Feuerbach's *Das Wesen des Christentums*, first published in 1841.

3 We shall see in Chapter 18 that this is a woefully inadequate metaphor for the true relationship between mind and body, but this is the closest approximation possible with the conceptual instruments presently at our disposal. An adequate discussion of the issue presupposes our metapsychological system in its entirety, for which reason I beg my readers' patience until we are in a position to return to the subject.

## References

Aristotle. (1978). *Aristoteles' Metaphysik. Erster Halbband: Bücher I (A) – VI (E).* (H. Seidl, W. Christ, Eds., & H. Bonitz, Trans.) Hamburg: Felix Meiner Verlag.

Aristotle. (1980). *Aristoteles' Metaphysik. Zweiter Halbband: Bücher VII (Z) – XIV (N).* (H. Seidl, W. Christ, Eds., & H. Bonitz, Trans.) Hamburg: Felix Meiner Verlag.

Feuerbach, Ludwig. (1841). *Das Wesen des Christentums.* Leipzig: Otto Wigand.

Freud, S. (1912a/1997). Einige Bemerkungen über den Begriff des Unbewußten in der Psychoanalyse. In S. Freud, *Psychologie des Unbewußten* (pp. 29–36). Frankfurt am Main: S. Fisher Verlag.

Freud, S. (1915b/1997). Das Unbewußte. In S. Freud, *Psychologie des Unbewußten* (pp. 125–164). Frankfurt am Main: S. Fisher Verlag.

Freud, S. (1920/1997). Jenseits des Lustprinzips. In S. Freud, *Psychologie des Unbewußten* (pp. 217–272). Frankfurt am Main: S. Fisher Verlag.

Freud, S. (1929). *Zur Psychopathologie des Alltagslebens. Über Vergessen, Versprechen, Vergreifen, Aberglaube und Irrtum* (11th ed.). Vienna: Internationaler Psychoanalytischer Verlag.

Freud, S. (1937/1975). Die endliche und die unendliche Analyse. In S. Freud, *Schriften zur Behandlungstechnik* (pp. 357–392). Frankfurt am Main: S. Fischer Verlag.

Freud, S. (1997). *Psychologie des Unbewußten* (8th ed.). Frankfurt am Main: S. Fisher Verlag.

Guntrip, H. (1971). *Psychoanalytic Theory, Therapy, and the Self.* New York: Basic Books.

Heidegger, M. (1927/1977). *Sein und Zeit.* (F.-W. v. Herrmann, Ed.) Frankfurt am Main: Vittorio Klostermann.

Kant, I. (1996). *Kritik der reinen Vernunft 1.* (W. Weischedel, Ed.) Frankfurt am Main: Suhrkamp.

Laplanche, J. (2008). *Nouveaux fondements pour la psychanalyse.* Paris: Quadrige/Presses Universitaires de France.

Leibniz, G. W. (1989). *Philosophical Essays.* (R. Ariew, & D. Garber, Trans.) Indianapolis & Cambridge: Hackett Publishing Company.

Sembera, R. (2007). *Rephrasing Heidegger. A Companion to "Being and Time".* Ottawa: University of Ottawa Press.

# 2

# THEORIES AND FANTASIES

I think it is fair to say that there is a reasonably strong anti-philosophical undercurrent in psychoanalytical thinking and, by extension, also a reasonably pronounced bias against metapsychology. Psychoanalysts come by this honestly; the same traits are markedly present in the original writings of Freud. Insofar as objections to metapsychological investigations are rooted in something other than mere ideological habit, they tend to cluster around one central issue that can be paraphrased in the following way: theories are fantasies about facts; fantasies are subjective; therefore all theories are subjective fantasies; therefore we should avoid theories and stick to facts. In order to clarify what is wrong with this thesis it will be helpful to inquire more deeply into the relationship between fantasy and fact in theoretical systems. I am sorry if anyone finds this tedious and if I at times give the impression of someone mashing the elevator button in the hopes that it will make the elevator arrive sooner, but I encountered such initial difficulties in making my thinking clear to my acquaintances in psychoanalytical circles that it seems absolutely necessary to me to clarify the rules of the game at length before we sit down to play. My apologies to those who already know the rules.

To begin at the beginning: it is an open secret that Freud's metapsychology is in essence an intellectual elaboration of his own fantasies about himself. In my view, chief among these are the fantasies that 1) the mind is a nation at war with itself; 2) the currency of this nation is "libido"; 3) the mind is not really a nation, but in fact a machine. That these fantasies are biographically motivated and largely defensive in nature is clear. Now the point I would like to stress – and it is a point that I think has been insufficiently stressed by the literature on the subject – is that the subjective origin of these fantasies is in no way an argument against the usefulness of the theories of which they are the inspiration. The fact that the compiling of a dictionary may be at once an expression of and defence against oral and anal-sadistic fantasies of various sorts tells us nothing about the quality of the finished product, tells us nothing about the accuracy of the definitions that the dictionary proposes.

This is a simple enough point, yet it seems to be little acknowledged in the area of psychoanalytical criticism. Psychoanalysis in general seems often to blur the distinction between intellectual and analytical discourse, and it tends to regard the discovery of an unconscious motive as a valid objection to an intellectual argument. There is some limited clinical validity to this approach: from an analyst's perspective, calling attention to the unconscious subject matter of a given intellectual argument is generally more therapeutically effective than countering the argument. However, outside the consulting room this approach has a very limited application. Calling attention to your opponent's unconscious fantasies about chess pieces is not likely to help you win the game, at least not if your aim is to win by the rules. It is unfortunate that much of the acrimonious debate between different schools of analytic thought amounts to precisely this.

Parenthetically, I want to underline that the quest for unconscious motivation can be abused even within the consulting room. The fact that a client is rationalizing does not mean that there is no truth to the rationalization. It may well be that the truth is being exploited for unconscious purposes, but that does not mean that the rationalization, qua argument, is wrong. And the fact that clients sometimes abandon their rationalizations when they are no longer needed also does not entail that the original rationalization, qua argument, was wrong.

For the sake of clarity, I want to outline two elementary logical fallacies to which we can easily fall prey when there is confusion between appropriate verbal interaction in the consulting room and appropriate verbal interaction in the wider world. These fallacies involve the belief that a person's character can, in and of itself, guarantee the truth or falsity of that person's statements:

1. If, for example, X makes the statement *S* and we assert that *S* must indeed be true simply because X said so, we have committed the fallacy known as the *argument from authority*.
2. If, on the other hand, X makes the statement *S* and we assert that *S* on the contrary must be false simply because X said so, we have committed the fallacy known as the *ad hominem argument.*

Both the argument from authority and the *ad hominem* argument boil down to believing that, independently of any other evidence, the character of a particular person is sufficient guarantee of the truth or falsity of that person's statements; or, put even more simply, they are arguments based on people instead of on facts. It is easy to see that believing that the subjective sources of inspiration of a theoretical system can in and of themselves entail the correctness, or lack thereof, of the theoretical system in question, is closely related to this type of logical fallacy. Here is a particularly crude yet typical example of this mistaken way of thinking:

> when I once made the attempt to shed a critical light on the contemporary way in which science is produced, I had to assume that science, if it is to remain really objective, must alternate between working purely psychologically and purely in conformity with the physical sciences [...] which corresponds to an oscillation between pro- and introjection. I called this the *utraquism* of every correct way of doing science. In philosophy, ultraidealistic solipsism means a falling back to an egocentric infantilism, and the purely materialistic, psychophobic conception is a regression to the exaggerations of the projection phase, whereas Freud's adherence to dualism does perfect justice to the utraquistic requirement.
>
> *(Ferenczi, Das Problem der Unlustbejahung, 1926/2014, p. 206)*

Against this point of view I would assert that the psychological state of a given individual tells us nothing in and of itself about the correctness, or lack thereof, of a given individual's point of view. It is like claiming that Gödel's incompleteness theorems must be wrong because he suffered from paranoia. And yet precisely this line of argument is not uncommon among psychoanalytic critics. For example:

> In the metapsychological manner of speaking one could say that these [i.e. unconscious liars] are people with *several super-egos* the unification of which was unsuccessful. As well, those among the learned who do not at the outset reject the possibility of there being a "plurality of truths" regarding the same subject would have to be people whose scientific morality has not blossomed into a unity.
>
> *(Ferenczi, 1928/2014, p. 228)*

One could hardly find a more pristine specimen of begging the question combined with character assassination; and yet this particular writer, for all his usual perspicacity, seems completely blind to the elementary logical fallacies in which he has permitted himself to indulge. Furthermore, although I have drawn on a relatively early source text, I think that everyone will have come across numerous similar examples of faulty reasoning in contemporary psychoanalytical literature, suggesting that this is a persistent problem that still needs to be addressed within psychoanalytic circles. There seems to be a general lack of awareness regarding the scope and limits of psychoanalytic criticism and I think ultimately this goes back to Freud's habit of "nothing but" thinking: whenever he unearthed an unconscious motivation for a particular belief, he assumed that the belief in question could simply be reduced to its unconscious motivation and consisted in nothing else. Thus, as we saw in Chapter 1, to Freud religion and metaphysics were "nothing but" fantasies projected onto the external world; similarly, art was "nothing but" getting through fantasy what artists are unable to get through action; civilization was "nothing but" the struggle against biologically rooted drives; criticism of psychoanalysis was "nothing but" resistance to its truth, and so on. It is as if we should claim that a book is "nothing but" wood pulp and pigment, forgetting entirely that the wood pulp and pigment has been given a certain structure and organization for reasons that may ultimately have little to do with wood pulp and pigment, and that these two materials may simply be what it has been most convenient to use at a certain point in time in order to make the message of the book accessible to others. The whole "nothing but" approach is founded on a fundamental misapprehension of the relationship between manifest and latent content. To be fair, understanding this distinction is tricky, but failing to make it leads us to a Pandora's box of confused dialogue where it becomes impossible to distinguish between the medium and the message – and there *is* a clear distinction between the two that we need to keep in mind both inside and outside of the consulting room, at least if we want to do right by our clients and to be fair to those who disagree with us.

All of this to say that there are some psychoanalytical critics who reject metapsychology altogether because they think they can find unconscious biographical motivations underlying every theoretical position. To these critics, the all-pervasiveness of unconscious motivation makes metapsychology a hazardous enterprise whose risks outweigh its potential benefits. I believe this view to be fundamentally mistaken; after all, what *else* would we expect to find underlying a theory? A pristine devotion to reason for its own sake? One could well imagine mathematicians who have an unconscious fantasy of coitus whenever they see binary numbers and who are for this very reason fascinated with the subject; and yet, so long as their calculations are correct and they aren't running into any personal issues, why should anyone care? And if they do have personal issues and happen to have analysts, would it necessarily be a sign of the success of the treatment if the mathematicians gave up working on binary mathematics altogether? I'm sure that all my readers would say it wouldn't; and yet I suspect that a significant number of them, perhaps even a small majority, have all at some time mistaken interpretation for refutation, so pervasive is this habit among analytically oriented psychotherapists.

The indulgence in "nothing but" thinking has of course had a significant impact on the reception of metapsychology in psychoanalytical circles. To begin with a first example, the authors of the book *Faces in a Cloud* (Stolorow & Atwood, 1979) undertake a "phenomenological" analysis of four major analytically oriented personality theories, those of Freud, Jung, Reich, and Rank. Having identified the major personal motivations of all four theorists, they then conclude that the metapsychological theories in question are irremediably compromised by the personal interests of their founders, simply because their founders *do* have personal interests, and that therefore metapsychological pursuits are to be avoided altogether. But surely this is to confuse critical biography with critical reasoning. It seems to me that if, for example, I consult a map or dictionary, or similar reference tool, what is of interest to me is the accuracy of the reference tool in question, and not the biography, conscious or unconscious, of the person or persons who assembled the tool. In fact, the question of accuracy has to be settled by entirely different means than by the discovery of significant biographical factors. Is it that surprising to find out that compilers of maps and dictionaries and similar reference tools often have a certain obsessional streak? Should that discourage us from compiling maps and dictionaries?

Biographical criticism and the verification of the reliability of a tool are two entirely different things. One cannot do the work of the other.

Granted, Stolorow and Atwood do have a valid concern, namely that the personal issues of influential theorists may compromise the theoretical integrity of the systems they put forth, leading to psychological blindness, faction-building, and the exploitation of theoretical systems for defensive purposes. However, this is a problem inherent in creative intellectual work in general. It is not solved by a refusal to create, but by striving for transparency, by not dismissing others' views out of hand, by incorporating constructive criticism, and by the use of appropriate means for the evaluation and criticism of intellectual systems. The ultimate criteria for the value of a metapsychological system are its productivity and richness. I should hardly need to argue that Freud's metapsychology, despite its many shortcomings and its obvious biographical motivations, has in fact made an enormous contribution to our understanding of human nature, both at the purely intellectual level and at the level of the practical clinical work of analysis.

Stolorow and Atwood continue their program in the volume *Structures of Subjectivity* (1984), in which they attempt to formulate a "psychoanalytic phenomenology" that avoids the risk of contamination through unconscious personal agendas by eschewing metapsychological speculation. The result, in my view, is a metapsychology that is a metapsychology in all but name. Throughout the volume, theorists' supposed personal motivations are consistently used as arguments against the validity of their theories. I find the section on Edmund Husserl particularly disappointing, as it repeats all the old platitudes about Husserl's life and attitudes and summarily dismisses the results of his philosophical inquiries with counter-assertions of Stolorow and Atwood's own personal philosophical convictions. I am not entirely sure how to explain their apparent confidence that their own system is largely free of the same type of personal agendas that they claim to discover on the part of the theorists they discuss, and the existence of which they consider grounds for the dismissal of the ideas of the said theorists.

In everyday life, of course, we often find that people do use *ad hominem* arguments in abundance, for example in courts of law, though they are called by a rather more polite name, to wit: "establishing the credibility of the witness." It must be conceded that in certain very specific circumstances there is a limited validity to this style of argument. If, for example, there were to be a legal dispute regarding violent assault in which two people, X and Y, each claim that the other initiated the assault, and X has a documented history of repeated acts of violence while Y does not, in the absence of any other reliable evidence it is reasonable to conclude that X is more likely to be guilty than Y. This is, however, by no means certain, and it is not in itself sufficient to justify disregarding other evidence that might be presented at the trial.

In any case, it seems obvious to me that theoretical debate, particularly in psychoanalysis, cannot be conducted according to the manner of the law courts; furthermore my concern is not with the *ad hominem* argument as such, but with the specific abuse of it that is characteristic to psychoanalysis and that leads to many evident absurdities. For example, we should have to discard the physical sciences entirely, because they are a product of the psychotic fantasy that the living is the dead (Bion, 1962/1977, p. 14). Furthermore, we would have to discount the success of the theory of relativity because it was inspired by Albert Einstein's phallic-omnipotent fantasy of riding alongside a beam of light. Finally, it is clear, as Anthony Stevens discusses in his book *Private Myths* (1996), that much of René Descartes' philosophy is a rationalization of his own profoundly schizoid experience of the world. It seems, then, that according to the logic of the supposedly psychoanalytic *ad hominem* argument, we shall have to reject the Cartesian system of co-ordinate geometry as being inescapably compromised by Descartes' own personal schizoid agenda. We shall also have to reject the arguments of the *Meditations* entirely, since, as analysts, we have identified Descartes' personal pathology and can therefore summarily dismiss Descartes' conclusions. What need is there for a creative assimilation of Descartes' arguments? What need is there to take the trouble of understanding Descartes' points and evolving sophisticated counter-arguments in reply?

Now in my view a properly psychoanalytic view of the issue is something like the following. Although Descartes did indeed suffer from a profoundly crippling personality disorder, the remaining healthy part of Descartes' personality, a part endowed with unparalleled and truly enviable genius, was able to use his disorder creatively as no one before or since in order to formulate powerful and unsettling arguments that to this day pose major challenges to philosophical thought. And they are able to do this precisely because Descartes' own sickness forced him to experience fundamental truths about human nature that the healthy part of his personality was able to seize upon and articulate, truths that most of us are not able to experience because of our own fear of the loneliness, isolation, and unreality that Descartes experienced for most of his life. Though of course the disturbed part of his personality was able to twist Descartes' achievement to serve its own purposes, the healthy part of his personality was also able to use his sickness in the service of astonishing creativity. While we can find his personal motives deplorable, this cannot in any way invalidate the greatness of his achievement, which, at both the personal and the purely intellectual level, deserves both our acknowledgement and our profoundest respect.

To make the point one last time in a way that I hope will convince everyone and put the issue permanently to rest: the fact that you can analyze an astrophysicist's irrational fear of an asteroid crashing into the earth does not mean that you know anything about astrophysics, or about the real probability of an asteroid crashing into the earth. One needs to acknowledge one's own limitations, even – and especially – as an analyst.

In conclusion, I would not wish to say that uncovering the unconscious motivation for a theoretical position *never* has any legitimate use – I employ an argument of this type myself once in this book, and only once, in Chapter 14 – but it should be used rarely, judiciously, and only after more powerful arguments have made it reasonably clear that the theoretical position that is being subjected to criticism is fundamentally in error. In other words, it can be used after it is clear that there is an error, in order to explain the subjective origin of the error, but intellectual integrity precludes its use at any point before that.

Now to return to my principal theme. In my view, all analytic experience is shaped by the analyst's own personality and therefore also by the analyst's own fantasies, and this is as it should be. Analysis is not, and cannot be, the dispassionate investigation of a third party. All human inquiry, as all human experience, is necessarily shaped by fantasy, without which experience itself is impossible. This thesis is already suggested in the works of Bion (1962/1977), but it will be further developed and explored in later chapters of the present book. Analysts, in my view, understand their clients by understanding their fantasies about their clients; and that means by understanding themselves. To eliminate the analyst's subjective contribution by suppressing metapsychology, as Stolorow and Atwood propose, is to put out the analyst's eyes for the sake of ensuring that the analyst never takes a wrong turn.

Another well-known critic of metapsychology, Roy Schafer, has undertaken to provide a "reconceptualization of psychoanalysis in terms of an action language" in the volume *A New Language for Psychoanalysis* (1976). Schafer's project is a consequence of his deeply held theoretical commitments to the linguistic and philosophical doctrines of Ludwig Wittgenstein. Although I can do full justice neither to Wittgenstein nor to Schafer in such a restricted space, I will do my best to explain why I can agree neither with Schafer's basic premises nor with the conclusions he reaches, and why I therefore consider his "new language for psychoanalysis" unsuitable for use.

Although I agree with Schafer that metapsychology is a philosophical enterprise (1976, p. ix), I disagree with Wittgenstein's thesis that doing philosophy consists in formulating a set of language rules. This is to confuse music theory with performance. In fact, theory emerges as a *post hoc* attempt at an explanation of successful performance and quite clearly is not itself performance. Nevertheless this confusion, acquired through a particular reading of Kant's epistemology, is endemic throughout the writings of Wittgenstein and his school. While I agree that Freud's metapsychological language is "eclectic" in a negative sense, I do not agree that it is necessary to stop using it altogether, nor that Kleinians have "carried the reifications of metapsychology to a grotesque extreme" (p. 3). What is needed, in my view, is not a campaign against "reification," but a convincing demonstration that the elements of the mind are not sufficiently articulated through Kleinian conceptualizations. Such a demonstration is not furnished by assuming that Wittgenstein's conclusions are correct and then rewriting the language of metapsychology in conformity with these conclusions. This is an ideological programme, not a philosophical one.

Furthermore, I agree with Schafer that the appeal of metapsychology stems "from its being congruent with the archaic bodily language of infancy" (Schafer, 1976). Schafer, however, characterizes this language as "concretistic," "deficient," "inconsistent, diffuse, and unstably, if at all, differentiated." This is in line with his fundamentally Wittgensteinian conviction that there is something wrong with language that needs to be fixed. It is also, analytically speaking, a gross injustice to children.

Schafer, in short – I begin to paraphrase – seems to think that it is the analyst's task to empty the mind of its contents by replacing talk about mental agents by talk about actions. This, again, is in line with the ideological agenda of another of Wittgenstein's disciples, Gilbert Ryle (1949/2000). It seems to me, however, that the actual results of implementing Schafer's action language during analysis would not be to empty the client's inner object world of its contents, but to deprive the client of the vocabulary that is necessary for talking about that inner object world. An object relations theorist, who in contrast to Shafer does not consider the purging of the client's inner world as a legitimate goal of analysis, might therefore expect a lessening of insight, reduced therapeutic efficacy, and increased feelings of shame when clients do feel the need to talk about their internal objects. I would grant, however, that clients who are particularly tormented by their inner objects may well experience an initial sense of relief, but I think that over the long term Schafer's action language is likely to do more harm than good, since it would also tend to interfere with acquiring new and better internal objects in general, and in particular with the introjection of the relationship with the analyst as a new object. I have no way of knowing whether Schafer or anyone in his immediate circle has actually observed these effects, but for what it is worth, the fact that Schafer's new language has not achieved widespread adoption may well suggest that very few analysts find Schafer's approach helpful. To me at least, the linguistic doctrine of Wittgenstein, especially when it is implemented within a psychoanalytic idiom, is uncomfortably reminiscent of a "Newspeak" that is supposed to make "thoughtcrime" impossible (Orwell, 1949/1990). I would be far happier if analysts saw their role as one in which they and their clients evolved their own mutually personalized idiom for talking about their shared experiences of analysis – a normal enough occurrence among intimates, family members, and members of other closely-knit groups. I do not consider it the place of analysts to impose their own linguistic conventions and convictions upon their clients, regardless of their intentions in doing so.

I find Schafer's chapter on "Internalization" particularly disappointing. In this part of his book he identifies "fantasy" with "mere fantasy"; the creative, life-affirming potential of fantasy is not acknowledged or addressed in any way. While Schafer may well be correct in stating that the theory of introjects has always had a "spooky" quality, one wonders whether this does not belong to the actual experience of introjection itself, and therefore to the experience of being human. In any event it would make more sense to subject the theory to closer examination than to discard it entirely. If it be true that "an introject can only be a fantasy, that is, a special kind of daydream which, in a more or less clearly hallucinatory experience, the subject takes for a real-life event" (pp. 163–164), is it not rather more appropriate to ask why this experience is virtually universal and what purpose it serves rather than to formulate an entirely new language in which this experience becomes impossible to articulate, though it may very well continue behind the scenes? It is of course not at all uncommon for clients to become able to continue the experience of analysis outside the consulting room by fantasizing that the analyst is "with" or even "in" them in a fantasized internal dialogue. This is one sign that what is being learned in analysis is also being applied to daily life. It may well be that there is an archaic aspect to the adult personality that *needs* this type of fantasy in order to be healthy, and that the needs of this archaic aspect of ourselves are far more important, in the long run, than any particular philosopher's intellectual zeal for language reform. I suspect that Schafer may simply have taken Freud's metaphor of draining the Zuider Zee in the *New Introductory Lectures* at the end of lecture 31 (1916; 1933/2007, p. 516) far too literally.

In my view the task of the analyst is not to drain or deplete the internal world of the client in any sense. The task of the analyst is to help clients understand what they experience as their internal world, to help them evolve a personal idiom for speaking about it, and to help cultivate that world – or not – as clients themselves see fit in the light of their experience of analysis. One strongly suspects that in practice Schafer is unable to use his action language very consistently, and I would wonder about clients who are able to tolerate its use for long periods of time.

In conclusion I would like to quote a passage from William Blake: "The Imagination is not a State: it is the Human existence itself" (Milton, 1977, p. 586). Presumably Schafer and Wittgenstein would maintain that Blake is philosophically confused. As I will endeavour to demonstrate throughout the rest of this book, however, I am of the opinion that Blake has intuitively grasped something of vital importance about the human condition that cannot be ignored or suppressed, but only acknowledged, respected, and, circumstances permitting, developed to its fullest potential.

## References


Bion, W. R. (1962/1977). Learning From Experience. In W. R. Bion, *Seven Servants*. New York: Jason Aronson, Inc.

Blake, W. (1977). Milton. In W. Blake, & A. Ostriker (Ed.), *The Complete Poems* (pp. 513–607). London: Penguin Books.

Ferenczi, S. (1926/2014). Das Problem der Unlustbejahung. In S. Ferenczi, *Schriften zur Psychoanalyse II* (pp. 200–211). Frankfurt am Main: S. Fischer Verlag GmbH.

Ferenczi, S. (1928/2014). Das Problem der Beendigung der Analysen. In S. Ferenczi, *Schriften zur Psychoanalyse II* (pp. 227–236). Frankfurt am Main: S. Fischer Verlag GmbH.

Freud, S. (1916; 1933/2007). *Vorlesungen zur Einführung in die Psychoanalyse Und Neue Folge*. Frankfurt am Main: S. Fischer Verlag.

Orwell, G. (1949/1990). The Principles of Newspeak. In G. Orwell, *Nineteen Eighty-Four* (pp. 312–326). London: Penguin Books.

Ryle, G. (1949/2000). *The Concept of Mind*. London: Penguin Books.

Schafer, R. (1976). *A New Language for Psychoanalysis*. New Haven and London: Yale University Press.

Stevens, A. (1996). *Private Myths. Dreams and Dreaming*. London: Penguin Books.

Stolorow, R. D., & Atwood, G. E. (1979). *Faces in a Cloud. Subjectivity in Personality Theory*. New York and London: Jason Aronson, Inc.

Stolorow, R. D., & Atwood, G. E. (1984). *Structures of Subjectivity: Explorations in Psychoanalytic Phenomenology*. Hillsdale and London: Lawrence Erlbaum Associates.

# 3

# THE PRACTICAL USES OF METAPSYCHOLOGY

It is important to underline that my attitude towards theories parallels Winnicott's attitude towards mothers: they do not need to be perfect, they only need to be good enough. The fact of the matter is that everyone is different, and even if we assume that some metapsychologies are really more correct than others, i.e. more accurate descriptions of a given client's internal landscape (or of the analyst's fantasies about that landscape, to give Schafer his due), it does not follow that any particular system of metapsychology among the more correct ones will be an equally accurate description of *every* client's internal landscape. In a way, every individual client requires an individual iteration of a metapsychological system. A tailor, though working from general patterns, must tailor each suit to the individual client's fit. As well I think we can assume that, within reason, analysts working with less correct systems of metapsychology that they are personally more comfortable with will, all other things being equal, be happier and therefore better analysts than those working with more correct systems towards which they feel dislike or even antipathy.

At the same time, I think that it is a mistake to see the personal element, whether on the client's or on the analyst's side, as the decisive factor. Clients cannot be so different from each other that no theoretical generalizations about human nature are possible; and there surely is something to be learned from theory that cannot simply be supplied at will from the analyst's personality when it is missing from the analyst's personally espoused theoretical framework. As well, although it is, I think, reasonably clear that psychoanalysis is not, and cannot be, a "science" in the sense in which this term is commonly used in the English-speaking world, if there is to be any concern for truth at all in psychoanalysis, there has to be an acknowledgement of the fact that some theories are likely to be better than others insofar as they are more accurate and more useful, and there also has to be a corresponding effort to distinguish one group of theories from the other. This effort cannot, however, be based on ideology or on a personal commitment to a particular school within the psychoanalytic movement. It must be based on clinically observed facts as well as on the fundamental rational principles common to every systematic mode of inquiry. Psychoanalysis cannot claim the right to an exceptional position simply because its subject matter is so often exceptional.

Every particular system of metapsychology proposes a certain model of the mind and its functioning. We must, however, distinguish between two uses of a metapsychological model. A model can be used in such a manner that it is a model *of* the mind, and again in such a manner that it is a model *for* the mind. A model *of* the mind is a model in the usual sense. It attempts to anticipate the most likely variations in the structure of any given individual's internal landscape so as to facilitate both assessment and treatment. A model in this sense can be compared to a map. But there is, however, another sense in which a model can be compared not to a map but to a blueprint. In this case the model functions as a model *for* the mind. It is, in short, an outline of what a healthy mind is supposed to look like. In the first place, every metapsychological model, by its very nature, must contain not only a diagnosis of the human condition, but also a prescription for its cure. And though we hope that analysts are objective enough to prevent their personal needs from interfering with their theoretical commitments and thus with their analytic work, we can hardly expect them not to have some major emotional investment in both certain diagnoses and their corresponding cures. I am not as confident as Freud was that metapsychological models can so neatly be separated from personal world-views (1933/2003). In the second place, it must not be forgotten that by the very nature of the analytic situation, the analyst's own subjective experience necessarily acts as a model *for* (in our technical sense) the client's own subjective experience. I mean by this quite simply that the material the client provides is filtered through the analyst's mind, and it is this modified result, ineluctably bearing the personal stamp of the analyst's personal perspective and character, that the client can use for good or ill, to change or to remain the same, to improve or to become worse. The analyst's communications are never, and can never be, neutral and objective statements. They represent a deep level of sharing and of community between two human beings.

Metapsychological models also have a special technical purpose that is intimately linked to the use of *constructions* in analysis (1937/1997). The developmental aspect of a model contains, or at least suggests, an inventory of possible constructions. A particular model will, therefore, decisively influence the manner in which the analyst understands the influence of the past upon the client's present. The classical treatment of the subject can be found in Serge Viderman's book *La construction de l'espace analytique* (1982), although the particular metapsychological justification for the use of construction that he suggests does not concern us here. From the clinical point of view, there are certain feelings and states of mind that are extremely subtle, even ephemeral, and that cannot be traced back with any certainty to definite events in the client's early life history. Yet it is vitally important that the analyst be able to articulate these shadowy half-feelings and half-memories in words, for the therapeutic effect, and even the sense of relief reported by the client when such a construction is successful, is quite pronounced. Thus, to a client whose recollection is being flooded by scene after scene from infancy, the analyst might say something along the lines of, "It seems that your early home atmosphere was one in which you were constantly overstimulated." No one single memory can possibly correspond to an interpretation of this sort, and yet the subjective feeling of "rightness" that the client may report is too remarkable to be ignored.

Not every construction is equally successful, of course, but the point is that there are some feelings and states in the client to which no definite memory can correspond, and so cannot be worked through unless they are given some sort of name or description by means of which the client can take hold of them. And the point is also that they *can* be worked through when they are given an appropriate name, even though the name in question be merely provisional. As Viderman stresses, this particular type of interpretative construction always has an indeterminate truth value. I mean by this simply that constructions are tales told in the mode of "as if." Although these "just so stories" are historically unverified and typically also unverifiable, they nevertheless enshrine some important aspect of the client's subjective truth, and they have an obvious therapeutic effect. It seems that, like mothers, interpretative constructions too need only be good enough.

Since the entire area of interpretative constructions is an area of nebulous, vague, historically indeterminate material, its very vagueness invites a wide variety of interpretative perspectives. How many ways must there be of pronouncing the ineffable? It is clear that in this realm the results of analysis are, in a very real sense, a co-creation of the analyst and the client. This is why any model is better than no model at all: any language that provides clients with some vocabulary for the elaboration and articulation of previously formless thoughts and feelings allows them to gain at least some inkling of what is happening inside them. This is also why some models may be more appropriate than others for use with certain clients and by certain analysts.

This sheds yet another light on the error of Stolorow and Atwood. As previously said, the material that clients provide is filtered, as it were, through the mind of the analyst and returned to the mind of the client for the client's personal use. The analyst's subjective imprint can be found in everything that transpires during the course of an analysis. We will be studying this in more detail at a later point in our investigations, but the important point is that it is as important for a model to describe the mind of the analyst as it is for it to describe the mind of the client. In technical terms, models are tools for understanding and interpreting both transference and counter-transference. It is only by seizing upon what is happening in themselves that analysts will be able to improvise a vocabulary, tailored to the needs of the client, for what is also happening in the client. This vocabulary will inevitably also bear the personal, subjective stamp of the analyst's personality. Without a model suited to the analyst's own personality, no analytic work can be done, just as without an essential compatibility between client and analyst (i.e. a resemblance of internal structure, or at least the ability to grasp the geography of the client's internal landscape by analogy with one's own) no meaningful joint analytic undertaking is possible.

Metapsychological odysseys are clearly not to be embarked upon lightly, for the consequences of mistakes and omissions are far-reaching. As I have underlined above, a metapsychological model provides a basic vocabulary for analysts to talk about their own minds as a starting point for the co-creation of a joint vocabulary along with their clients for the purpose of talking about their clients' minds. This is why no truly scientific (in the sense of objective and dispassionate) metapsychology is possible. This is also why analysts tend to become so personally attached to particular systems of metapsychology: a criticism of a particular metapsychological viewpoint can, for a number of different reasons, be experienced as an attack on the analyst's own mind, or as a criticism of one's mother tongue.

For all these reasons, then, an analyst's metapsychological commitments must be treated with respect, but as I hope to have made clear, there is such a thing as respectful criticism. Analysts should be free to choose their own idiom, but not to make up entirely new dialects, at least not if they truly desire to help their clients, to be understood by the wider community of analysts, and ultimately, if it is important to them to be honest with themselves. I do not see that it is my place to dictate the characteristics of an ideal metapsychology any more than it is my place to formulate criteria for an ideal language, but I think that I can at least emphasize the disadvantages of a dialect spoken by a community of one, and the superfluity of re-inventing the wheel. We should also keep in mind that metapsychology being what it is, very often different metapsychological systems say precisely the same thing in idiosyncratic ways. While a sense of personal identity is important, one generally hopes that it is not bought at the expense of a wider sense of community.

There is no reason why a basic commitment to truth in psychoanalysis should not be completely compatible with a basic commitment to theoretical pluralism within the discipline. The field of psychoanalytical inquiry is so vast that it is highly unlikely that any two analysts could study exactly the same thing in exactly the same way. There is no reason why analysts cannot both appreciate the necessity for a multiplicity of models while concurrently hoping for an ultimate convergence of their differing theoretical perspectives at some unspecified point in the future. The concept of absolute truth is useful as an ideal and as a final goal, but it is an ideal that we can probably not expect ultimately to attain, and a goal that we can probably never finally reach.

Psychoanalysis is much like philosophy in that we almost certainly cannot expect to arrive at absolutely final answers to any of our questions. This is so not merely because of the inherent limitations of all human modes of inquiry, but because of the peculiar nature of the subject matter of psychoanalysis. Each individual analyst studies the same subject matter, but what they learn can only be articulated from each analyst's individual point of view and in fact only has value when it is expressed in this way. Imagine the subject matter of psychoanalysis, the unconscious, to be an invisible, infinitely small and dimensionless point. Now imagine that each analyst performs a circumambulation about this point. It is possible to draw an infinite number of straight lines that connect the centre of the circle with the current position of the analyst on its circumference. Each line represents one unique individual point of view from which the unconscious can be seen and understood. Each line has value in itself. The early analysts could complete one or even several circumambulations during a lifetime, so that the whole could be seen, but without very much detail. But as individual psychoanalytic knowledge increases – as individual perspectives multiply, and the centre can be seen from more and more points of view – the circle widens and the distance from the centre increases, increasing in turn the length of the arc along the circumference, so that an individual analyst is no longer able to complete a circumambulation of the whole because there is simply too much to learn. The reward is that the detail revealed from the points of view that are accessible within the angle of the traversable arc – the lifetime of the analyst – becomes so much greater. We see less; but we also see it less myopically. There is no progression of psychoanalytic knowledge in a straight line. There is, instead, an eternal and ever-widening circumambulation about an eternal invisible point that individual analysts eternally must rediscover in their own individual ways.

Now I want to add one last observation about the nature of metapsychological systems that seems to me to be of fundamental importance. I want to introduce a distinction between what I call *third person theories* and *first person theories*. The inspiration for these terms, of course, comes from the grammatical concept of person as an aspect of the conjugation of verbs. In the case of a third person theory, the point of view is that of someone speaking about a real or fantasized other, while the hearer is a second real or fantasized other who is not involved in the relationship between the first two. This perspective is the norm in traditional academic prose. It tends to convey a sense of theoretical objectivity. It is the basic perspective of all Freud's technical metapsychological writings. The danger that I think is involved in using a third person theory to gain access to the mind is a confusion of perspective. One sometimes hears people speaking of "my ego" or "my super-ego," "my libido," "my id," "my defences," and so on. But in so doing, what is really happening is that a third person perspective is being illegitimately imported into the mind. One cannot experience oneself as a third person, except defensively, and even then this cannot actually be an experience of oneself as a third person. The agencies id, ego, super-ego and so on only become accessible to an outside person using a theoretical, third person perspective to describe what is being seen. What is important for any given individual is not a theoretical description of ego, id, super-ego, but access to the experience of what it is like to *be* these three agencies; and this is a perspective that cannot straightforwardly be extracted from third person theories. In the words of Bion (1965/1977, p. 148): "Reality has to be 'been': there should be a transitive verb 'to be' expressly for use with the term 'reality'."

Following this line of thought, we might be inclined to conclude that first person theories would be more appropriate. A theory with a first person perspective is articulated from the point of view of someone who is speaking about himself or herself to a real or fantasized other (e.g. the reader). A first person theory thus involves a dyadic relationship in contrast to the triadic relationship in a third person theory. The silent listener's supportive presence makes it possible for the talker to investigate the contents of his or her own mind. This type of perspective is dominant in the *Meditations* of Descartes; it is also important for traditional systems of phenomenology. It is also commonly found in those of Freud's works that involve considerable amounts of self-analysis, e.g. *The Interpretation of Dreams*. Unfortunately, here too we run into a problem. The phenomena that are properly the objects of psychoanalytic study are not really accessible through any form of introspection, even with the most benign possible hearer. A different type of relationship is required to get at the objects of psychoanalysis.

In analogy to first and third person theories, we can conceive of theories that are distinguished by a *second person* perspective. In first person theories, the dyad involves an unequal relationship: an active speaker, and an essentially passive listener whose presence serves no other purpose than to facilitate the task of the speaker. The perspective of a second person theory again involves a dyad, but it represents a dialogue between a speaker and some other person who is essentially viewed as a peer and an equal. A second person perspective conveys a perspective from *inside* the relationship, while a third person perspective conveys a view of someone else from *outside* the relationship. In short: a second person perspective is a narration not of someone else's supposed experience (third person), nor of your own experiences (first person), but of your experience of someone else. The first person perspective implies a monologue in the presence of a quietly sympathetic listener. It represents your own understanding of yourself. It cannot reflect the distinguishing feature of a second person perspective, which is a creative assimilation of and reaction to another person's opinions. A third person theory is not addressed to you at all. In other words: a second person theory is a model not of your own experience (first person), nor of another person's experience (third person), *but a model of your experience of the other.*

To sum this all up: the point is that the unconscious is not accessible from a first person perspective any more than you can see the back of your own head. The unconscious is also not accessible from a third person perspective because it is not a thing but the inmost, most alive essence of a living individual. The unconscious is only really accessible in a second person relationship because it is only given to you in and through someone else's perspective of you (see Chapter 13). The issue in question is how to preserve the unique features of a second person perspective in writing, which is by nature more suited to monologues (first person) or lectures (third person) than actual dialogue (second person).

It is clear that the basic form of writing as such makes it difficult or impossible to communicate in the second person, since one does not know the other who is going to be reading. In some cases perhaps, where the target audience is well defined, it may be possible to address the reader in the second person with some degree of stylistic success, as in Winnicott's guide for expectant mothers (1964/1987); however, we can hardly expect the target audience of metapsychological theories to be as clearly defined. Good metapsychological writing will probably always sound like a third person theory at the purely textual level even if its intent is to present a second person theory. In any event, I personally have not found a way of communicating a second person perspective in writing in a way that I think would be stylistically acceptable considering the task that I wish to accomplish. I do think, however, that the underlying fantasy makes a difference. Historically speaking, the best examples of second person theories known to me are the dialogues of Plato and the works of Schopenhauer. While I cannot realistically hope to equal the style of these two luminaries, I can, I think, at least approach closely enough to their excellence in order to have reasonable prospects of success at communicating the fundamental perspective of the metapsychological theory that I have in mind.

## References

Bion, W. R. (1965/1977). Transformations. In W. R. Bion, *Seven Servants*. New York: Jason Aronson, Inc.

Freud, S. (1933/2003). Über eine Weltanschauung. In S. Freud, *Vorlesungen zur Einführung in die Psychoanalyse Und Neue Folge* (pp. 586–608). Frankfurt am Main: S. Fischer Verlag.

Freud, S. (1937/1997). Konstruktionen in der Analyse. In S. Freud, *Schriften zur Behandlungstechnik* (pp. 395–406). Frankfurt am Main: S. Fischer Verlag.

Viderman, S. (1982). *La construction de l'espace analytique*. Paris: Éditions Gallimard.

Winnicott, D. W. (1964/1987). *The Child, the Family, and the Outside World*. Cambridge, MA: Perseus Publishing.

# 4

# A DESCRIPTION OF THE ANALYTIC SITUATION

The analytic situation is by nature of virtually limitless complexity, and it is important to keep this in mind. If we do not, we may begin to think that it is possible to grasp it in its entirety, to reach some absolute certainty about it, and this is most unlikely. Some measure of doubt and uncertainty is a constant concomitant of the analytic process, and this is another reason why the use of artificially scientific standards of certainty in an analytic context should be discouraged. Nevertheless we should not despair of saying something meaningful and essential about the analytic situation, even if what we say is never entirely complete. By convenience we may call the note produced by a certain vibrating string a C, but this note contains overtone upon overtone, so that in fact we treat a complex chord as a single note for the sake of convenience. In the same way the analytic situation contains nuance upon nuance, layer upon layer of meaning, and while it is impossible to exhaustively catalogue them all, it is possible to give them names that are good enough to do analytic work, just as we *can* call the note of a vibrating string by a certain single-letter name, and still make music.

The aspect of the analytic situation upon which I now wish to focus is one single strand of a complex tapestry: the client's speech. Freud tended to see this in a rather stilted way, calling it "free association," but what is decisive is just that clients be able to relax the usual attention they give to establishing coherence and context in everyday conversation and to speak freely and flowingly about whatever they feel like talking about at the moment. Free association is not an exercise in intellectual introspection, nor is it a game of word association. It is just freely flowing speech.

In my view, regardless of the specific technical limitations that are adopted, interaction between the two parties involved in the analytic situation should resemble an everyday social interaction as much as possible, with one all-important difference, namely that the focus of the relationship is on both parties getting to know one of them as well as possible. This is, I think, the only really necessary asymmetry in the analytic relationship, and it should go without saying that I do not see this as entailing an imbalance in the distribution of power, but simply as a necessary renunciation of the usual pleasure in social interaction on the part of both the client and the analyst.

Outside of an analytic relationship it is exceedingly rare for us to hear another human being speak really freely. Even within the analytic relationship we unfortunately do not always have ears to hear what is being said, even when clients are able to speak it. Nevertheless, if our concern is to lay a solid and reliable foundation for a system of metapsychology, we must first descriptively isolate the clinical phenomena that are in need of explanation. I have identified four striking features of free association that, in my view, are essential:

1. Sooner or later, in every analytic relationship, it becomes obvious that clients' present difficulties are rooted in problematic and conflictual relationships with important figures of the past, typically close family members. This is so much the case that clients' problems appear almost as a caricature of their past relationships as clients report them, and this is ultimately true even of symptoms that do not appear at first sight to have any relational aspect (de Mijolla, 1981/2003). Thus the first metapsychologically significant clinical phenomenon disclosed by free association is that *all symptoms without exception are rooted in fantasies about other people* (the word "fantasy" is here being used in a technical sense that will be made clear in Chapter 11). There are, let it be noted in passing, clients who flee to the past to avoid the present, e.g. clients who prefer to talk about their personal biographies in order to ignore significant current events that require their immediate attention (Laplanche, 2008, p. 117), but in this case the defensive aspect of the return to the past is clear, and I am not now speaking of defence but of symptom aetiology.
2. All individuals, including analysts, will, to a greater or lesser degree, fail to make connections between present difficulties and the past relationships that function as their prototype. They will also fail to notice significant omissions, contradictions, and absurdities in their free associations. There will also be evident inconsistencies when different statements or trains of thought are compared and contrasted. These phenomena, to which I assign the technical phrase *failures in contextualization*, are typically of such a nature that they would be noticeable even to someone with no special training, while clients, as a rule, fail to detect them, and often have some difficulty recognizing and acknowledging them even when they are explicitly pointed out. Their own emotionally charged nature makes it clear that errors in contextualization are facilitated by, but cannot directly be explained by, the relaxation of the conscious attention given to establishing coherence and context in conversation outside of the analytic situation. They are clearly motivated by deeply personal concerns.
3. Given enough time, the failures in contextualization described in (2) above will lead to a clinical situation in which significant pressure is placed upon the

analytical relationship to conform to the template of the client's past conflictual relationships. Clients apparently strive to reproduce what they fail to contextualize.

4. Free association has a definite structural organization that can be briefly described in the following way. I distinguish between three *registers* in which free associations can be understood. (i) There is a *first register* of communication that is represented by the client's speech taken by both parties at face value. It is whatever the client happens to be talking about or intends to communicate, and it is what one's attention would be focussed on if the speech were occurring in an everyday context. In traditional terminology we could call this the *manifest content* of the client's speech. (ii) There is, furthermore, a *second register* in which a verbal and conceptual processing or formulation occurs whose eventual product is the manifest content of the client's speech. Often this becomes evident when the client is groping for words, hesitates, backtracks, or decides to say something else. It also becomes evident through failures in contextualization. It also takes place when none of these happen, but in this case we are dependent on inference. In analogy with the traditional term for the corresponding process in dreams, the "dream work," we could call this the register in which we listen for the *work of association*. (iii) Finally, there is a *third register* that consists of the basic material or the fundamental topic of the free associations, independently of any changes that the work of association may have made to their substance in order to produce the manifest content of the client's speech. For convenience I will again rely on traditional terminology and refer to this register as the *latent content* of the client's free associations.

I would like to take a moment to further clarify these distinctions with a number of examples. For the sake of simplicity we will focus on individual statements, ignoring the context that is so important to actual interpretation in the analytic situation, and ignoring the further complication of transference meanings. I will also choose examples with the same latent content in order to make the role of the work of association particularly clear. Finally, it should be noted that X in the examples refers to the name of a person.

1. Suppose that a client says, "I hate X." The manifest content of this statement is an assertion of the client's hatred of X, the work of association involves affirmation, and the latent content is hatred of X.
2. Suppose alternatively that a client says, "I do not hate X." The manifest content of this statement is a denial that the client hates X, while the work of association involves negation, and the latent content is the same as in the first example, namely hating X.
3. Finally, suppose that a client says, "I hate X, but X is really not all that bad." In this case the manifest content may be something like a denial that there are

> real reasons for the client to hate X, while the work of association involves something like toning down, or perhaps taking back with one hand what one has just given with the other, and the material is, once again, hatred of X (because of X's badness).

Now it cannot be emphasized strongly enough that identifying the latent content and the work of association of a certain strand of free association *does not in and of itself tell us anything about either the correctness or the incorrectness, or the accuracy or inaccuracy, of the manifest content.* Information regarding correctness or its opposite has to come from other sources: the analyst's consideration of failures in contextualization, comparisons with other client statements, material from the client's biographical reports, and so on. In fact, in all but the very simplest cases, the proper identification of the latent content also requires a careful consultation of all these additional sources of information. This demands the use of all aspects of the analyst's training and personality, and it is yet another reason why analysis is perhaps best regarded as an art and not a science – which is neither to deny the legitimacy of science nor to minimize the validity of analytic inquiry.

There is a second complication that is often overlooked, namely that it is impossible to express any negative statement without the prior thought of the corresponding positive statement. Thus the very nature of negation requires us to have the prior thought of liking green jellybeans in order to express the thought "I *don't* like green jellybeans." It would obviously be a mistake to conclude from this that whenever people say that they *don't* like green jellybeans they really mean that they *do* like green jellybeans; and yet this is the precise error that Freud comes perilously close to committing in his (in)famous paper on denial or "Negation" (1925/1997).

Finally, it is of course common knowledge that when careful attention is paid both to the context and the latent content of the client's speech, statements about third parties may well appear to be disguised references to the analyst. But there is, one might say, a very fine line, if not a razor-thin line, between transference interpretations and ideas of reference. Analysts cannot rely on intuition, but must make full use of their critical intellect. Without critical reflection transference interpretations in particular are nothing more than shots in the dark at best, and at worst they rapidly devolve into ideas of reference.

I would like to add a last example taken from the works of Joyce McDougall, since it illustrates a more complex type of communication involving a similarly more sophisticated work of association:

> That reminds me of something. I was maybe three years old. I drew near to my father, fascinated, to watch him eat. Then he offered me a mussel. I still see him separating the two little … uh … parts. I almost said 'the two little lips'! Yes, and once they were separated he put a drop of lemon inside. I swallowed it with delight.
>
> *(McDougall, 1989, p. 298)*

The manifest content of this anecdote is clear enough; the client is recounting an episode from her childhood. The latent content is probably something along the lines of a fantasy of intercourse with the client's father. This fantasy, as McDougall makes clear, had a central role to play in the client's symptom formation. The work of association has, in this case, taken on a level of sophistication rivalling that of a dream, giving credence to Bion's claim that we are constantly "dreaming," i.e. constantly translating latent content into manifest content, even while awake (1962/1977, pp. 15–16). It is worthy of note that the memory in all likelihood is more or less accurate, but is still invested with a latent content. Fantasy is able to make use of reality and of real memories in a way that suits its own purposes. McDougall also underlines the need to make use of further associations and context to work out the latent content, though educated guesses based on the analyst's own associations are also frequently helpful.

To return to our concern with the starting point of our system of metapsychology: I take the four clinical observations listed above as the experiential bedrock on which the foundation of any successful system of metapsychology must be laid. It is relatively easy to show that the majority of Freud's own metapsychological conceptualizations can be traced back directly to the same four sources. For Freud, (1) is the justification for the *analysis of the past*; (2) is the clinical basis for the concepts of *repression* (or *defence*), *resistance*, and the *unconscious*; (3) is the basis of the concept of *transference*, while the analyst's failure to deal adequately with the transference leads to the concept of *counter-transference*; and finally, (4) is the clinical basis for the division of the mind into *ego* (the source of manifest content) and *id* (the ultimate source of latent content). Furthermore, the observable aspects of the work of association are the clinical basis for what Freud called *preconscious* mental activity, and insofar as the work of association exhibits a clearly defensive function, the motive of this defence can be understood as the fear of a punitive *super-ego* or as the narcissistic investment in a certain *ego-ideal*.

It may now be found helpful to outline certain characteristic features of the Freudian conceptualization of the analytic situation in order to better understand both the strengths and limitations of his system of metapsychology. In the first place, it is obvious, as many critics have pointed out (though perhaps none with as much vehemence as Schafer) that Freud had a tendency to assume that every discrete type of mental process was initiated by a definite mental agency. Sometimes, when Freud used a lens of spatial metaphor, these were referred to as "systems" or "places"; at other times, when Freud wanted to underline the independently functioning nature of the mental processes in question, he spoke of them as "authorities" or "agencies" [*Instanzen*], almost as if they were homunculi, or little selves within the self. This has uncomfortable parallels with popular demonology and is in any case obviously unsatisfactory. Furthermore, the exact nature of these entities is most unclear. Are they physical areas within the brain? If so, which ones? How do they work together to produce a coherent functioning self? Or are they something else entirely?

Other problems are raised by Freud's implicit notion of the relationship between client and analyst. In his published writings at least, even if he did not always act this way in practice (Ellman, 2002), Freud tended to depict the analyst as a friendly yet detached observer, while the client was seen as a friendly but detached laboratory assistant. Analytic work was seen as a joint project undertaken on behalf of the client, with the analyst as a paid professional consultant. Freud was strongly inclined to see any departure from this idealized presentation of analysis as irregular and undesirable. If it was the client who departed from the idealized norm, the ensuing interactions were considered to be manifestations of "transference," whereas similar departures initiated by the analyst were called "counter-transference." Both these manifestations of "transference" were considered to be pure repetitions of past relationships with the ulterior motive of sabotaging the progress of the joint undertaking. This in turn led to the theoretical stance that any feelings in the analytic relationship other than feelings appropriate to a friendly business partnership were in some sense unreal and in need of elimination through analysis. Thus according to the classical view taken at face value, neither a client nor an analyst could, for example, ever justifiably feel hate or love for each other so long as the appropriate relationship boundaries were observed.

Experience on both ends of the therapeutic relationship as well as much reflection have convinced me of the essential correctness of this view – within certain limits that I will discuss in the paragraphs below; at the same time they have also convinced me of the fundamental inadequacy of Freud's theoretical foundation. Complicating matters is the fact that the whole analytic situation is so unusual, so without precedent in our everyday experience, and so artificial, i.e. in need of so many complicated arrangements to hold it together – the prone position on the couch, the method of free association, the studied reticence of the analyst – that it is very difficult to understand precisely why it is structured in this way. One has the impression that Freud, with some uncanny instinct, hit upon one type of right environment for psychotherapy without ever being able to give a coherent and satisfying explanation of why precisely these parameters are necessary. One looks, I think, in vain for any situation in early childhood that parallels the analytic situation; I think it is best understood as an entirely novel type of interaction without any real precedent in human experience, an artificial construct intended to take advantage of the psychological constitution of the mind in order to further the development of self-knowledge and thus effect therapeutic change.

In short, it seems to me that Freud understood the fundamental importance of *fantasy* in the psychogenesis of mental conflict and that in a shadowy, instinctive manner he designed the analytic situation in such a way as to permit privileged access to his clients' unconscious fantasy lives. I emphasize that for me the analytic situation is an entirely *novel* situation. There can be no question of analysis "making up" for something that the client didn't get as a child; by the time you seek out an analyst it is far too late to have had the type of childhood you would have liked to have had. Analysis creates an entirely new type of mental structure, one that approximates the functions of the mental structures possessed by those who have had reasonably good childhoods, but is at the same time a structure that is not possessed by those who have not had the experience of analysis. In this respect it can perhaps be compared with a coronary stent. A stent approximates the functioning of a healthy coronary artery, but is not possessed by those who have not undergone the operation to put it in place. We do not, in other words, help suffering clients attain a level of self-understanding that they would otherwise have had had their lives been different; we help them put a new mental process of self-understanding in place that accomplishes the same work as healthy mental processes, but in a different way and with different means. Healthy persons with an ideal or near-ideal childhood (in the common sense of these expressions) have a benevolent and adequate object world that allows them to take care of themselves and to flourish, but they are not necessarily capable of any insight into the structure and composition of this same object world. Psychoanalysis, if successful, provides the ability to have insight into one's own object world and so to take over personal responsibility for its functioning and, in so doing, compensate for its deficiencies. I think we can say that those who have undergone a genuine psychoanalytic process may not always be as healthy as those who have had a satisfactory childhood, but they understand the true meaning of freedom and of responsibility in ways that the latter group cannot and perhaps do not wish to understand (more on this in Chapter 17).

To this end, in analysis artificial conditions are created within which clients' past relationships are given more opportunity to shape the relationship than they are normally given in everyday social interaction. This is accomplished by the analyst's getting out of the client's way as much as possible. For this reason there are special parameters of analysis that invite the client to rely on fantasy rather than fact in order to decide who the analyst really is and what the analyst is really like as a person. The client's basic assumptions about the other come into view. These parameters range from the relatively trivial – analysts' studied reticence, the tendency to avoid giving advice, encouragement, or criticism – to the relatively significant, e.g. the use of the couch and the positioning of the analyst out of the client's field of vision. In the classical conceptualization of analysis their common aim is understood to be "non-gratification" or at best "optimal frustration" (Kohut, 1977), although in my opinion this is wide of the mark. It is true that "gratification" in the analytic situation is generally a bad idea, but for two reasons: 1) you can't make up for the child's frustrations by gratifying the adult; and 2) any attempt to do so immediately and necessarily narrows down the available freedom to speak, i.e. the analytic space (Viderman, 1982). In fact, the entire purpose of the analytic situation is to create space for the client's fantasies to come to the fore so that they can become topics of conversation rather than unconscious prototypes of the client's relationships. This takes the form of an invitation, not of a refusal, on the part of the analyst. It is important for us to understand that the analyst should be *offering* space to the client, not deliberately inflicting frustration, which – however one chooses to package it – essentially boils down to a sadistic attack upon the client that will *narrow down* the available space, and will also be perceived by the client as what it really is. That the correct offering of space should be so important is a strong indication that space is precisely what has been lacking in the prior relationships of those who suffer from mental conflict. I only wish to add that there are times when frank disclosure is appropriate, but all such situations have to be handled with great skill and care.[1]

The dramatic increase in mental space or mental freedom that the analytic situation entails has to be counterbalanced by strict boundaries intended to contain what is introduced into that space. By "contain" I mean that the fantasies brought forth by the client need to be subjected to reflection, contemplation, and understanding; they should not impel to action on the part of either the client or the analyst. Thus, for example, the prone position on the couch, in addition to providing space for fantasies to emerge, also provides space for reflection rather than attempted discharge through action, keeps the fantasies from immediately triggering responses as they would in everyday life or in a face-to-face situation. For this to occur the client would practically have to jump off the couch (which occasionally does still happen). Similar considerations are true for the positioning of the analyst out of the direct line of sight of the client. This keeps enactments of fantasies largely confined to the purely verbal interaction between client and analyst where they can be studied in a relatively safe manner. It is, so to speak, rather like disengaging the engine from the drive train and feathering the gas pedal so you can listen to the engine sounds without having to take the car out on the road.

The official explanation for the use of the couch is that it is a historical artefact of the beginnings of psychoanalysis in hypnotism, and that since the arrangement has been found to work, there is no reason to change it. There is a further official explanation in Freud's technical paper on beginning psychoanalytic treatment to the effect that he found the use of the couch necessary because he couldn't stand being stared at for eight hours a day (Freud, 1913/1997, p. 193). This explanation is both odd and unconvincing; what would he have done as a regular physician? What was he doing as a university professor?

I believe that there are two real reasons for the use of the couch and the positioning of the analyst out of the client's field of vision: first, the lack of visual information about what the analyst is thinking and feeling invites the use of fantasy to fill the gap, so that it becomes possible to learn something about the client's fundamental (unconscious) assumptions about other people. This is in essence a milder form of the hallucinations that are experienced after longer periods spent in a sensory deprivation tank. Second, the prone dialogue with a disembodied voice blurs the distinction between the inner and outer worlds, so that the voice of the analyst is felt to originate from inside the client rather than from the external world, much like the voice of the conscience or "super-ego" (or, in my terminology, the voice of the object world). Thus the experiences of the super-ego and the analyst become merged. Ideally this would permit clients to test their perceptions of the other against the reality of that other, leading to modifications of clients' basic assumptions about other people and so ultimately to health – *since it is our basic assumptions about other people that are responsible for psychogenic mental illness in the first place.*

One may well wonder, however, whether the analytic situation is not deliberately crafted with artful intent to invite deliberate confusion between the super-ego and the analyst so that in the client's experience the analyst is endowed not only with all the qualities of the super-ego but also with its prestige and, by extension, its power over the client's mind. From this point of view analysis would simply be another form of indoctrination, and one could well ask whether the cure be not worse than the disease. There is no doubt in my mind that historically speaking very many early analyses were conducted in precisely this spirit and that many continue to be performed in this way at the present time. Here I can only address the issue of whether the technical arrangements of psychoanalytic treatment necessarily *must* take the form of indoctrination. In reply two points must be considered:

1. Any professional consultant has some limited power over you, even an accountant or a lawyer; insofar as they are consultants, just by simply evaluating possible courses of action they are in effect exercising a sort of "control" over your power of decision. So the "control" exercised over the client in psychoanalysis – and control is exercised by the mere act of making an interpretation, which opens up some interpretative possibilities to the exclusion of others – is definitely present, but not necessarily all that different from that exercised by any other professional consultant, and that we usually find tolerable and even appropriate.
2. Some clients have the opposite reaction, namely that far from endowing the analyst with prestige and power, the analyst is experienced as an incompetent and useless bozo, because that is the quality defining the important figures in their own object world. So the structural arrangement of analytic treatment does invite clients to mingle their object worlds with their experiences of the analyst, but ideally at least nothing is prescribed regarding the exact form, positive or negative, that this mingling should take.

The analytic situation does not force or demand submission from the client when it is managed correctly; it should be an invitation to experience the analyst in the light of the client's object world so that that object world can be known and studied. A conscientious analyst will always interpret in a tentative and cautious manner, so that the option of rejection is always possible. Another type of analyst will interpret differently, since the aim in this case is forced introjection of the analyst's personal point of view. So the correct way of looking at the matter is that the features of the consulting room are designed to provide better access to the object world; this access *is* easily abused, but it is not *inherently* abusive.

Finally, I want to remark that I have encountered the viewpoint that the use of the couch is essential to the psychoanalytic process and that a genuine psychoanalytic process is impossible without it. Subsequent experience has convinced me that this is entirely false. The most important parameter in my opinion is frequency; the practical layout of the consulting room is an entirely secondary consideration that can and should be entirely subordinate to the individual client's needs.

The question of the analyst's *authenticity* in the analytic situation puzzled me for a long time. The problem is easy to formulate. It is common knowledge that analysts are as a rule "better behaved" in the analytic situation than they are in their own private lives. Say for example that the client happens for whatever reason to be expressing political opinions diametrically opposed to the analyst's; the analyst reacts with an uprush of irritation and anger, immediately "suppresses" these feelings, and goes on listening for analytically relevant content to the greatest extent possible. In a similar situation in the analyst's private life, however, the analyst may well react with open hostility and get into an argument with the offending party. Is it then not the case that analysts in the analytic situation are pretending to be someone they really are not? And is this not essentially deceptive? How then is lying to clients about who you are supposed to be helpful?

The solution to the problem is, however, simpler than expected. The part of you, the analyst, that is able to put aside your immediate hostile reaction for the sake of listening *is* the real you. This is because (as we shall later see in Chapter 16) the fundamental openness to *all* experience, whether pleasant or painful, comes *before* any reaction that would shut it down; it precedes the capacity for judgement, approval, and condemnation. You are not struggling to suppress your real reaction to the client but struggling to regain it. It is the pathological, rejecting part of you that is the unhealthy, inauthentic, and therefore "unreal" part. We confuse this part with our "real" selves because it tends to predominate in everyday life; but this cannot alter the fact that analysts are not "better behaved" in the analytic situation than they are in their everyday lives; insofar as they are really functioning as analysts they are in fact *more themselves* than they can be in everyday life. Thus the apparent problem of inauthenticity posed by the "suppression of counter-transference" is not a substantial problem at all; it is merely a problem of confused perspective.

Of course the real bugbear in any discussion of transference and counter-transference phenomena is the emergence of love and sexual feelings in the analytic situation. The classical way of dealing with this rather sticky issue is perhaps best illustrated with the remark that a prominent psychoanalyst's paper on "Love in the Analytic Setting" begins with the sentence: "The analytic setting is the clinical laboratory that has permitted us to study the nature of love in its myriad forms" (Kernberg, 1994). I can only say that this particular analyst's choice of words strikes me as odd, and I am led in turn to wonder if this is the contemporary equivalent of the 19th-century reticence that led Krafft-Ebing to put all the naughty bits in Latin in his *Psychopathia Sexualis*.

As I have attempted to make entirely clear, in my opinion the analytic relationship is, and must remain, the relationship between a client and a professional consultant. It most certainly should not be the relationship between a scientist and a lab rat. The analytic relationship is, furthermore, defined by certain essential boundaries, but I must, however, object strongly when implausible justifications are given for this necessary restriction of the analytic relationship. In my opinion the analytic relationship is a real human relationship like any other (though necessarily and essentially professional in nature), with the cardinal difference that in analysis the development of the relationship must be subordinated to the best interests of the client. This can be put differently: in everyday life, a certain degree of untruthfulness predominates, because everyday relationships are largely about using each other for our own personal ends. In analysis, however, truthfulness must predominate, because the relationship is about clients using the analyst for their own personal benefit. This is one important reason why analysts need to be paid for their work; letting oneself be used – in the Winnicottian sense of the word (1971b/2002) – is not easy. More on this subject later on in this chapter.

Understanding the role of sexual feelings in the analytic situation requires a certain degree of courage and ingenuity, partly because these feelings are, as a rule, inconvenient and unsettling for both parties, and partly because, as a rule, the official psychoanalytic position on these matters tends to be unhelpful, relying as it does on roughly equal parts of moralizing and of denial. The core of the problem is, I think, inherent in the manner in which "sexual feelings" and "love" are conceptualized in psychoanalysis.

In his technical writings on transference (1915a/1997) Freud approaches the subject from an angle that only further confuses the issue. He makes a distinction between real and unreal love and then attempts to determine whether transference love belongs to the former or to the latter category. The enterprise is not entirely successful and raises more questions than it answers. The problematic aspect of this distinction consists of the mistaken assumption that there is something called "real love" that is, so to speak, conceptually opaque: an irreducible, inexplicable phenomenon that is somehow unquestionably genuine and can be distinguished from "transference love," which is a mere repetition of the past in the analytic situation and therefore illusory or unreal. I think that this is based on a vast misunderstanding of the nature of love. In point of fact, falling in love, whether inside or outside of the analytic situation, always has a job to do: in other words, it is always an attempt to solve some sort of problem. Thus the question to ask in the analytic situation is not, "Is this real?" but "What particular problem is this supposed to solve, and how is it supposed to solve it?" And this is true whether the love is on the client's side or on the analyst's. The difference between love in psychoanalysis and love in everyday life is that the latter emerges in a natural social setting and as a rule no questions are asked, while the former happens in a highly artificial professional setting and questions must be asked. This of course gives rise to a qualitative difference between the two that I will discuss under point (3) on p. 47 below.

It is common knowledge that Freud felt that he had to widen the concept of sexuality to include phenomena that had little in common with mainstream adult sexuality, the ostensible justification being that doing so enabled the study of perversions and in turn of infantile sexuality, or the manifestations of erotic life among children. We can, however, hardly overlook the contradiction inherent in this position: insisting that children experience feelings that are unmistakably sexual but that can only be accommodated within an artificially expanded concept of sexuality because the organs involved are different is quite obviously a form of begging the question. It is in fact both truer and more accurate to say that children have passionate and affectionate lives, and that they are both intimately interwoven with intense physical sensations; but it seems to me that much is lost if we designate these with the conceptual *fourre-tout* "sexual." There is the additional semantic objection that if you have to redefine a word to the point that it no longer means anything much like it originally did and you continually have to remind yourself not to rely on the original meaning, then you had better choose another word; and this, I think, is eminently true of Freud's use of the term "sexual." Freud's expanded sense of the term widens the concept to the point when finer distinctions became impossible, and the general effect is to obscure, rather than reveal, the distinguishing features of children's experiences of bodies and relationships and the specific forms of their erotic attachment to both. I think that Freud must have persisted in this course of action because his ultimate aim was ideological and reductionistic: whatever was observed ultimately had to be explained in terms of the operation of a biological drive, preferably the sex drive. Observations had to be sacrificed for the sake of theory.

I do not wish this very important point to be misunderstood in any way, so allow me to state that there is no doubt that Freud brought to light much that was unacknowledged about children's essentially passionate experiences of their own bodies as well as many aspects of their feelings and conduct towards their parents that had previously been hidden, and that it is a very great achievement to have done so. Freud could quite justly have claimed to have discovered some hitherto overlooked infantile antecedents of adult sexuality, but this is not what he claims: he claims that the infantile activities in question are themselves "sexual," and fails to give any clear idea of what this is supposed to mean. If it simply means "pertaining to bodily pleasure" and nothing more, then why not say so? And if it means something more than this, then what is it? It is almost as if Freud had some unspoken fixation upon the word, as if he needed to insist that children had sexual lives in the same way as adults do, as would perhaps have been the case if it had indeed been easier for him to talk about children's putative "sexuality" than about their feelings. In this regard it is indeed instructive to compare the importance of the practices of children compared with the relative importance given to their feelings in Freud's *Three Essays on the Theory of Sexuality* (1905/1994). As well, this same text seems to me to be guided by a deep-rooted conviction that there is no essential qualitative difference between the sexual feelings of adults and the erotic feelings of children. This seems to me to be false for two reasons: first, that with children, owing to their embeddedness in the family situation, the importance of *attachment* is always a main theme of their passionate feelings and pleasure *as such* is normally a secondary and derivative concern, whereas it seems to me that in adult sexuality pleasure and attachment can often be quite distinct aims; and second, that adult sexuality has a cataclysmic, catastrophic quality (the orgasm) that I think has no true correspondent in infantile experience of the body (this latter point is conceded by Freud). These are fine but not unimportant distinctions that are easily lost if one simply chooses to designate the whole of infantile bodily experience with the catch-all term "sexual."

I think furthermore that in Freud there is an unacknowledged and unspoken assumption that because adults infuse oral, anal, and other bodily sensations with a certain significance for their own mature genital sexuality, children must themselves behave in a similar "sexual" way, i.e. bodily sensations must have a similar significance for the child as they later do for the adult. This seems to me, however, to amount to little more than a *sexualization of the child.* This may well have been a habit common to the adults of Freud's time, which would set up the following sort of vicious circle: adults interpret the behaviour of children according to their own adult conceptions of sexuality and what it involves; they punish and threaten the children in an effort to wipe out the offending behaviour; the children internalize the sexualized and distorted image they are shown of themselves, protecting themselves in the process with a healthy dose of infantile amnesia; and the adults they become in turn perpetuate the same injustices towards their own children. Small wonder, then, that Freud should find his assumptions about the "sexual" nature of children apparently confirmed by actual psychoanalytic investigation. Whose sexuality is it in the end: that of the children themselves, or of the adults who surround them (Ferenczi, 1930/2014)?[2]

To return to our main topic in the light of these investigations: in my opinion there are four basic situations in which "sexual" feelings may arise in the analytic situation in either analyst or client:

1. Dawning feelings of *attachment* (affection and need) may bring with them physical sensations and sexual feelings in the everyday sense. In this case it may simply be that individuals are initially unable to make finer distinctions regarding their actual feelings, since affection and need are, in healthy adults, closely linked with physical excitement and sexual feelings, to which they easily give rise. But to say that attachment is a form of sexuality is a mistake of the same type as saying the affection parents feel for their children is a type of aim-inhibited sexuality, or as saying that same-sex friendships are an aim-inhibited form of homosexuality. It would be unreasonable to deny the passionate and affectionate nature of these relationships, just as it would be unreasonable to deny that both these relationships occasionally involve physical sensations and even fleeting sexual feelings. It would, however, be equally unreasonable to say, purely on the basis of the existence of a passionate and affectionate attachment, that parents and children really want to have sex with each other and that so do friends.
2. At the other extreme, physical sensations and sexual feelings may be used to suppress knowledge of the relationship that is developing in the analytic situation because for either party, or both, it is easier to talk about sex than about relationships. It can be stated with a fair degree of certainty (as Ian Suttie [1935/1999] was the first to point out) that this is a tendency that is virtually inherent in classical Freudian terminology and that afflicts the entire Freudian world-view. The classical term for this type of defence is "reduction to a part-object."

3. Somewhere in the middle, we have the case where falling in love is an attempt, on the part of either party, to solve some sort of problem. And here the question to ask is: "What particular problem is this supposed to solve, and how is it supposed to solve it?" Arguing that the love is "real" and therefore unanalyzable is disingenuous on either party's part, as is arguing that it is "unreal" and therefore will disappear when it is analyzed. Both are tactics that are meant to evade or at least limit the asking of the fundamental question. It can, however, be mentioned in passing that anyone who knows the analytic situation from firsthand experience knows that it is a great way of learning to understand someone's unconscious but a terrible way of getting to know someone socially, and that any extra-analytic relationship that began with getting to know someone in analysis is likely to suffer the fate of the vast majority of the seeds in Matthew 13: 1–9. For this reason there is a certain justification for being quite skeptical about the long-term viability of feelings of love in analysis, but this does not necessarily mean that they are "unreal." They are what they are: a specific attempt to resolve a certain problem at a certain time in a certain situation.
4. Again in the middle, we have the revival of the quality of a past relationship, or "transference" proper. This is the only type recognized by classical psychoanalysis, and, though important, tends to be less troublesome for both parties than the other types described above, and is relatively transitory as a rule. I strongly suspect, though cannot prove, that in many cases where sexual feelings of this sort persist in the psychoanalytic situation for any great length of time, it is because of collusion on the part of the analyst.

Managing all of these situations is of course the analyst's responsibility, and anyone who has ever felt the burden of this responsibility knows how taxing it is. One of the important functions of payment is to act as a reminder of the professional and consultative nature of the analytic relationship. It is also a reminder to analysts that it is *their* responsibility to manage analytic interactions in a safe and curative fashion. Maintaining this responsibility requires, and deserves, financial compensation. Analysts are expected to give without getting in return; to hold themselves to a professional standard, not that of an everyday, informal relationship; and they are expected to focus on the client's needs, to allow themselves to be "used" in the Winnicottian sense (1971b/2002). It would be unreasonable and exploitative to expect someone to enter into such a one-sided relationship without some form of compensation. Analytic work is trying, tiring, and exhausting for both parties, though with the potential to be ultimately rewarding for both of them as well. Nonetheless it is a good idea to have a convenient and persistent reminder that analysts and patients get together to work, and not to enjoy each other's company. The professional client–consultant relationship is the fundamental truth of the analytic relationship. It is not the only truth, but it is the one to which we should return at intervals whenever there is confusion or uncertainty, just as a pearl diver returns to the surface at regular intervals for air.

It is important to keep in mind that while the fee-for-service arrangement does set clear limits to what can be *done* within the analytic relationship, relatively few limits are set to what can be *felt*. Genuine feelings of acceptance, sympathy, and compassion on the analyst's part are entirely possible, just as they are within the type of relationship that clients might have, say, with their lawyers or accountants. Exchanging a fee for professional services does not preclude other types of very different and yet simultaneously coexisting relationships. The error in believing that it does consists in the false belief that relationships, like physical things, are mutually exclusive: if one physical thing occupies a particular physical space, it is true that all other physical things are necessarily excluded from that physical space, and vice versa. Relationship space (for lack of a better term) is characterized by eminently different properties than physical space; it can more accurately be compared with musical space, in which many different notes can coexist at the same time, all characterized by different degrees of mutual consonance and dissonance, and not by mutual exclusiveness.

This fact is quite familiar to us from other spheres of life; after all, most people who decide to have children do so in order to satisfy needs that are at best only peripherally connected with genuine concern for an as-yet-to-be-conceived entity, but the satisfaction of these largely egoistic needs does not, as a rule, interfere with proceedings on either side of the relationship. Healthy relationships are generally robust enough to contain many different and even divergent motivational forces. Of course, feelings in any genuinely profound relationship are usually mixed, but one tends to find in practice that if one is sufficiently interested in people and sufficiently curious about them and their life experiences, it is generally quite easy to feel genuine concern for them.

In my view, however, the exchange of money for analysis does not imply that the analyst is some sort of "authority," as some writers on the subject have asserted (Gabbard, 1996, p. 252). It certainly does imply that the analyst has some sort of expertise in mental health, but I think that there is a significant difference between *expertise* and *authority*. "Authority" implies that the analyst has privileged knowledge of the client that the client cannot challenge and therefore must accept. "Expertise" implies that the analyst has an external – perhaps at times even privileged – perspective on the client's inner life that can be challenged, and so fruitfully integrated into clients' experience of themselves in a way that they find helpful. I fail to see how fee-for-service arrangements imply that the only way of reacting to the analyst's contribution is unquestioning acceptance. Why should clients not be able to use the information they receive from analysts as a means towards forming their own judgements and opinions about themselves – or, alternatively, be at liberty to decline to do so – and in this way make themselves into the people *they* want to be? The analyst may well be a paid professional consultant, but certainly is not a Delphic Oracle.

I think that I should state in passing that I also find it extremely disingenuous to invoke the so-called "incest taboo" as a limiting principle of the analytic relationship (Gabbard, 1996, p. 267). Since we can safely assume that in the overwhelming majority of cases the analyst and the client are not in fact blood relatives, in the overwhelming majority of cases there can also be no real incest. There may of course be incest *fantasies* at play on both sides of the transference–counter-transference field, and these fantasies, under certain circumstances, may even be highly damaging to one or both of the involved parties. Nevertheless, the ultimate reason why the analytic relationship is subject to limitations can only be an ethical one: that analyst and client originally met in order to work together for the ultimate benefit of the client, and not for any other purpose. It seems to me that for any responsible professional this should be reason enough, and I furthermore am of the opinion that an analyst's ethical determination can only be undermined, and never reinforced, by the invention of spurious justifications for the necessity of ethical conduct. I fail to see how it is in any way reassuring for professionals to have more respect for a supposed "incest taboo" than for their personal ethical responsibility to the people they are supposed to have devoted their lives to helping.

## Notes

1 The reason why self-disclosure is potentially problematic in psychoanalysis is that every act of self-disclosure makes an implicit demand on the client for understanding. When one has mistimed or otherwise bungled it, the shift in atmosphere is palpable; it feels like you've stolen the client's space and the session is now about you rather than the client. But there are also other times when avoiding self-disclosure would be an obvious mistake, usually because it would amount to lying. I can find no general rule other than the overarching principle that whatever happens in the session is supposed to happen for the sake of the client's ultimate benefit; beyond this one has to decide pragmatically on a case-by-case basis whether self-disclosure is likely to be helpful or harmful.

2 Along similar lines one may well ask who it is that ultimately has the Oedipus complex.

## References


Bion, W. R. (1962/1977). Learning from Experience. In W. R. Bion, *Seven Servants*. New York: Jason Aronson, Inc.

Ellman, S. J. (2002). *Freud's Technique Papers. A Contemporary Perspective*. New York: Other Press.

Ferenczi, S. (1930/2014). Relaxationsprinzip und Neokatharsis. In S. Ferenczi, *Schriften zur Psychoanalyse II* (pp. 257–273). Frankfurt am Main: S. Fischer Verlag GmbH.

Freud, S. (1905/1994). Drei Abhandlungen zur Sexualtheorie. In S. Freud, *Sexualleben* (pp. 43–145). Frankfurt am Main: S. Fischer Verlag.

Freud, S. (1915a/1997). Bemerkungen über die Übertragungsliebe. In S. Freud, *Schriften zur Behandlungstechnik* (pp. 219–230). Frankfurt am Main: S. Fisher Verlag.

Freud, S. (1925/1997). Die Verneinung. In S. Freud, *Psychologie des Unbewußten* (pp. 373–377). Frankfurt am Main: S. Fischer Verlag.

Freud, S. (1913/1997). Zur Einleitung der Behandlung. Weitere Ratschläge zur Technik der Psychoanalyse I. In S. Freud, *Schriften zur Behandlungstechnik* (pp. 183–203). Frankfurt am Main: S. Fischer Verlag.

Gabbard, G. O. (1996). The Analyst's Contribution to the Erotic Transference. *Contemporary Psychoanalysis* 32: 249–273.

Kernberg, O. F. (1994). Love in the Analytic Setting. *Journal of the American Psychoanalytic Association* 42: 1137–1157.

Kohut, H. (1977). *The Restoration of the Self.* New York: International Universities Press.
Laplanche, J. (2008). *Nouveaux fondements pour la psychanalyse.* Paris: Quadrige/Presses Universitaires de France.
McDougall, J. (1989). *Théâtres du corps. Le psychosome en psychanalyse.* Paris: Éditions Gallimard.
Mijolla, A.de (1981/2003). *Les visiteurs du moi. Fantasmes d'identification* (2nd ed.). Paris: Les Belles Lettres.
Suttie, I. D. (1935/1999). *The Origins of Love and Hate.* London: Free Association Books
Viderman, S. (1982). *La construction de l'espace analytique.* Paris: Éditions Gallimard.
Winnicott, D. W. (1971b/2002). The Use of an Object and Relating through Identifications. In D. W. Winnicott, *Playing and Reality* (pp. 86–94). Hove and New York: Brunner-Routledge.

# 5

# WHAT ARE RESISTANCE AND DEFENCE?

The original name for psychoanalysis – a name that is still used often enough today – was "the talking cure" (Breuer, 1895/2004, p. 34). But from the analyst's point of view, it would make more sense to call it "the *listening* cure." Modern psychotherapy began when Breuer and Freud, instead of focussing on the suppression of symptoms, together discovered the curative power of listening with attention. The fundamental fact that a metapsychological system has to explain is that a certain very special type of listening has the power to help people resolve their inner conflicts. The explanation of this fact is, however, surprisingly difficult, for it requires a thorough investigation of many different aspects of human nature. One of the principal tragedies of psychoanalysis, as Bruno Bettelheim (1984) has made clear, is that a premature concern with the scientific status (or lack thereof) of Freud's work led to the suppression of the fundamentally humanistic aspects of Freudian psychology. The dangerous consequences of this reorientation of psychoanalysis were already anticipated by Ian Suttie (1935/1999), who struggled against what he called "the 'taboo' on tenderness" endemic in modern society. It seems that his voice was not heard. Nowhere, perhaps, is the result to be more clearly seen than in the traditional conceptualizations of *resistance* and *defence*.

Now as I have repeatedly emphasized, the experiences and observations upon which the present system of metapsychology is based are only accessible within a very special type of relationship, namely the analytic situation. It might, perhaps, not be out of place to say a few words about this, and about the consequences this has for our own theoretical enterprise.

From a methodological point of view, it is regrettable that the foundations of metapsychology can only be presented as statements of clinical facts. The obvious consequence is that readers with no personal experience of analysis may not be convinced of what I say. I am not sure that there is any way around this; Freud's own writings are peppered with instructions for self-analysis – to me, at least, *The*

*Interpretation of Dreams* reads as if it were partly intended to be an instruction manual for interpreting one's own dreams – but in my opinion the type of experiences one can have through self-analysis are not very likely to induce real conviction. The experiences that are very likely to induce real conviction are only accessible within an analytic relationship, for reasons that will become clearer later on (Chapter 13). It is for this reason that analysts have traditionally emphasized the importance of a personal analysis for everyone who wants to practise analysis – although one may well wonder, in the light of what was said in Chapter 4, whether making a personal analysis a formal training requirement is not actually working at cross-purposes.

It is perhaps not out of place to mention at this point that it is not an argument against the correctness of the results of analytic observation that it requires a special type of experience – one's own personal analysis – to be able to see and to understand analytic facts. Similarly, it is not an argument against the correctness of the results of x-ray crystallography or of ultrasound technology that the untrained layperson typically sees nothing of interest in the resultant images, whose full yield of meaning can only be brought out through interpretation by a trained specialist. It can be enjoyable to debate the epistemological status of observations, just as we could argue that the image seen through a microscope is unreal because no microscopic eye could possibly see the original in the way that we can see it through the microscope. The proper reply is that there is no doubt that some valid information about the microscopic object is being transmitted through the microscopic image, and our success in using the image to accomplish practical tasks is one argument in support of this assertion.

The intent of these observations is simply to make the reader aware that it is very difficult to appreciate the experience of analysis if one is forced to rely on written accounts for information, and I include the original writings of Freud among the accounts that fail to give a real impression of what the experience of analysis is like. Analysis is simply too concrete and personal for general abstract terms to be able to produce real conviction. In any case, nothing is lost by keeping the general abstract terms on which we are forced to rely as clear and as precise as possible.

Returning to our present area of interest, namely the analytic situation and the information it yields regarding the functioning of the human mind, I want to discuss in more detail what I called failures in contextualization in the previous chapter. It will be remembered that I consider the observation of failures in contextualization as the experiential basis for the metapsychological concepts of repression (or defence), resistance, and the unconscious. Let us begin, then, with a more detailed examination of the concept of *resistance*.

The analytic experience corresponding more precisely to this concept is something like the following. The analyst, with the intention of being helpful, points out a particular failure in contextualization in the client's free associations. Perhaps the analyst makes an interpretation; perhaps the analyst simply tries to draw the client's attention to an omission or inconsistency. The client, instead of accepting the information, reacts with anxiety, annoyance, hostility, or some other variation on these themes. If the analyst persists, the relationship soon devolves into open combat between the two parties. Freud, in accordance with his view of the analyst as a paid consultant, understood this phenomenon as *resistance to the analyst*, since it disrupted the analyst's expert contribution to the work they had jointly agreed to undertake.

Resistance to the analyst has the ultimate effect of sabotaging progress towards the client's own avowed goal, which is clearly not in the client's best personal or financial interests. Since Freud expected the analyst to be motivated by nothing more than professional benevolence and a desire to help the client, he concluded that the real target of resistance was not the analyst as such, but something in the client that the analyst was trying to bring to light, something that the client, unconsciously, was not prepared to face. The analyst is only indirectly a target of resistance; what clients are really "resisting" is something in themselves (Freud, 1917/2003).

In the light of these considerations, Freud decided that resistance was the interpersonal manifestation of an intrapsychic process that prevented the client from making use of the analyst's help and whose ultimate aim was to keep the unconscious from becoming conscious. The analyst, as it were, was an innocent bystander who got caught in the middle of clients' internal fistfights. Freud originally attributed these internal fistfights to the process of *repression*; later on, once the more general concept of *defence* had been introduced, "repression" became a name for one specific defence mechanism, namely the unconscious act of fending off or driving away unacceptable mental images so that they do not become conscious. The common feature that all defences have in common is that they help clients conceal unacceptable thoughts, memories, and feelings from themselves. The aim of the defences is to secure clients' psychological safety from parts of themselves that they find threatening. Clients, apparently, are at war with themselves.

If clients are at war with themselves, it then follows that the function of the analyst is to help clients fight the battle. Accordingly, resistance is something that the analyst has to overcome through effort. The analyst brings reinforcements to the correct faction of the intrapsychic battle by fighting an interpersonal war with the client. By overcoming resistance, the intrapsychic defence is also overcome. Gaps in contextualization can be filled; clients can know themselves; by knowing themselves clients can deal with their inner conflicts in more productive ways. The battle has then been won.

Careful and informed readers will have noted that there are several problems with this account. The most obvious problem, perhaps, is Freud's assumption that the basic motivation of the analyst was professional benevolence. There is, unfortunately, such a thing as a punitive interpretation. Given that this is the case, the target of resistance cannot *always* be some threatening intrapsychic thought or feeling; sometimes resistance *is* directed against the real person of the analyst, and sometimes appropriately as well. It follows that resistance cannot categorically be something that always has to be overcome. Sometimes resistance serves a real constructive purpose, e.g. when the analyst proposes a *wrong* interpretation.

Furthermore, as Freud also observed, some clients initially grow worse rather than better in analysis. He discovered that in these cases of resistance there is an unconscious masochistic conviction on the part of the clients that they must not be permitted to get better because they deserve to suffer. In such cases, Freud spoke of a *negative therapeutic reaction* (1923/2001, p. 316). The important consequence for our theoretical reflections is that not all resistance to analysis is a direct manifestation of intrapsychic fear of the repressed. Sometimes the reason clients cannot know themselves is not that they have to acknowledge something terrible about themselves, but that they have to acknowledge something *favourable* about themselves, i.e. that they are persons of intrinsic value who do not deserve to suffer. It is not *only* horrifying thoughts that are fended off.

Yet another possibility presents itself, namely that in manifesting resistance to the analyst clients may be motivated in an entirely different way, namely by *envy*. Some clients unconsciously simply cannot tolerate that the analyst should have anything of value to contribute to the analytic relationship (Klein, 1957/1984, pp. 183–184). In order to prevent themselves from having to acknowledge that the analyst can help them in a significant way, clients find some way of destroying or minimizing anything the analyst says or does, so that it becomes difficult or impossible for the analyst to help the client. In this case, ruining what the analyst has and is willing to give the client is more important than accepting it and making productive use of it.[1]

According to the classical view, a defence is a bulwark against a drive or the representation of a drive that is unconsciously experienced as threatening or terrifying. In the case of so-called "envious" resistance I think it is implausible to say that a defence of this sort is in operation. I think it is clear that the intrapsychic process in this case is not serving a defensive, but a *protective* function. I mean to say that the intrapsychic struggle is not against a terrifying desire that clamours for satisfaction, but rather a painful image of the self as deficient or lacking. The process in question is more adequately compared with the formation of scar tissue to protect a deep wound so that it will not be made any worse by contact with a potentially damaging environment; it is not at all like choking back a socially unacceptable desire through sheer force of will until it becomes literally unthinkable.

While there is absolutely no need to doubt the essential correctness of Freud's account with respect to certain specific situations that arise in the course of analysis, I want to underline that resistance is not one monolithic clinical phenomenon that is incapable of taking on very different forms in different clients. Resistance itself can be understood in a great variety of ways; Bion, for example, understands resistance as a conflict between the unconscious belief that "consciousness is the best approach" and the unconscious despair that it will be possible to attain the required level of consciousness to make the desired changes (1965/1977, p. 149). He also offers a very sophisticated and nuanced explanation of *why* resistance should be overcome that dispenses with Freud's metaphorical orientation towards war and combat:

> There are occasions in the life of everyone when it is felt to be wise, not pathological, to turn a "blind eye". Such situations become pathological when the "cure" achieved by these means is felt to be more painful than the original dis-ease. It is not always a matter of finding the "cure" more painful [...] dis-satisfaction is felt because the result of the exclusion [of unwelcome elements] is to prejudice the usefulness of the train of thought.
>
> *(1965/1977, p. 149)*

Resistance, as we have seen, is an extremely complex topic in itself. It will, however, be found necessary to further complicate the matter by pointing out that resistance is not by any means the only possible reaction of the client to the analyst's interventions. Other issues that need to be considered in any comprehensive metapsychological account of analysis include the following:

1. Clients may react to certain interpretations with immediate relief from anxiety and recognition of the essential rightness of what has been said. In my experience this reaction is not the rule, but it is also not uncommon. Any metapsychological theory has to explain the dynamics of its occurrence. Compare Colby (1951, p. 93): "Correct interpretations often produce a feeling of surprise or startled illumination which the patient expresses in the form of a short laugh and eye-opening." It is striking that this phenomenon is discussed so rarely in the literature, which seems rather to emphasize the opposite reaction to interpretative interventions. In any case it is clear that Freud has neglected to provide an explanation of this possibility in his metapsychology.
2. There are gaps in contextualization that are harmless and seem rather to reflect a simple inability of the mind to think everything at once. There are others that seem to have a relatively weak motivation, so that one has the impression that they have more to do with an epistemic limitation of consciousness as an instrument for self-knowledge than with defence in the traditional sense. Others represent the awkwardness of people who are not accustomed to reflecting on themselves and their own motives. Finally, there are cases where the healing process itself is concealed by gaps in contextualization. For example, I have observed, particularly in short-term analysis, that as termination nears, there are often signs that an unconscious mourning process is taking place. In some cases the reason the process is unconscious is that the thought of termination is difficult for the client to bear, but another reason can also be the fear that the analyst will interfere with the client's move towards freedom.

   Now one can assimilate these phenomena to the traditional model if one is willing to apply the formula "all things one doesn't like get repressed," but then how do we account for the fact that the mourning process *continues* unconsciously, and apparently achieves its aim as well without becoming conscious? Is it not rather the case that gaps in contextualization can have a *protective* function in the sense that they can protect a process from external interference? I am not so sure that this can be assimilated to the traditional model of being forced to renounce a desire through fear of a punitive parental figure. Can one not conceal a positive quality in order to prevent it from being spoiled by someone else, typically an early family member who was not able to tolerate the child's possession of that positive quality? Can a defence not also be a defence *of* desire rather than exclusively a defence *against* desire? Freud acknowledged, of course, that neurotic symptoms were compromise formations, but it seems to me that this possibility is not included in the classical understanding of repression as such, which is only conceptualized as a fear reaction, and therefore only as a defence *against* desire.

3. It is also sometimes the case that failures in contextualization are due to simple ignorance. Clients simply do not have the vocabulary to talk about their inner lives. Presumably this is due to a developmental lack rather than to an active process of socialization such as gives rise to the phenomenon of defence. For example, a client may be unaware that it is just as possible to weep from frustration as from grief. This *may* be because the client was forbidden to cry as a child. It may also be that no one during the client's childhood was particularly interested in the way the child was feeling. I think that there is a significant difference between the two situations, i.e. passive neglect versus active forbidding. Granted, the passively neglected is "unspeakable" in both the literal and figurative senses of the word, and so ultimately an object of shame; but surely there is a difference between a family that does not acknowledge sadness and a family that actively punishes crying? Here too we find a square peg that fits badly in the round hole of the drive–defence model: what is the repressed libidinal drive in such cases supposed to be? Is it not rather more accurate to say that a type of experience is being blotted out rather than a biologically-rooted desire? Compare the detailed study of such cases of failed verbalization in McDougall (1989).
4. There is also an important set of interventions that has traditionally been conceptualized as "strengthening the defences." The traditional view of this set of interventions and of their appropriate use leads to a distinction between "uncovering" and "supportive" therapy. The former is usually identified with psychodynamic therapies whose explicit goal is insight; the latter is identified with expressive therapies, where the accent is on talking for the sake of "covering," i.e. fortifying the defensive processes that are already in operation. I find the distinction between the two questionable. Take for example a client who has a dream of the death of a close relative and reacts to the dream with extreme anxiety. The analyst may choose to offer support by emphasizing the distinction between dreams and reality. Now according to the distinction between uncovering and supportive therapy, we must label this intervention an attempt to strengthen the client's defences because the analyst has assisted the client in avoiding the issue, namely the presumed wish for the death of

the relative in question. In my view, however, the analyst has done no such thing. Rather, the analyst has strengthened the client's sense of reality in order to make the defence superfluous in the long run. Some clients really do need to learn that dreams do not always come true. In what way is this strengthening the client's defences? Is it not rather at the very worst a case of *reculer pour mieux sauter*, helping the client to be able to do without them over time?

5. Finally, there is the case, observed frequently when clients speak of artistic or creative endeavours, where clients are initially unaware of their real motivations and may even be reluctant to discuss them at all, and yet are able to acknowledge them when suggestions are made as to what they might be. Or perhaps the analyst simply thinks it best to let well enough alone, as in the case of a benign dependence on a religious or fraternal organization (Gabbard, 2005, pp. 347, 356). There are also good reasons for *not* intervening when there is no reason to. Imagine the harm that could be done by a wild analyst who interpreted everything indiscriminately. There are clients who are flooded by the contents of their internal worlds because they have never learned that not everything has to be conscious. I would, however, not see this as requiring "strengthening of the defences" any more than I would see a musician who is just learning to play a certain scale as in need of "repression" of the scale rather than a thorough familiarity with it that allows the same musician to forget the rules and just play. There is, in other words, a type of unconsciousness that is benign and even helpful, and that should not be interfered with, and should even be encouraged. This type of unconsciousness should also not be straightforwardly assimilated to the defensive type. *Not* interpreting at the right time is as important as properly timed interpretation.

This concludes our overview of the alternative responses to analytical interventions. Now it is, I think, reasonably clear that Freud only recognized one possible response, at least insofar as his metapsychological conceptualizations are concerned. I have tried to show that this conceptualization is inadequate by listing five other common psychotherapeutic situations that Freud's model cannot explain. Any truly general system of metapsychology that aspires to give a coherent account of the mind as such must be able to explain these situations. The most striking, I think, is (1), since it is virtually impossible to assimilate to a drive–defence model. An adherent of this model could at most argue that a correctly timed interpretation could bring *relief*, since the effort bound up with repressing the forbidden drive representation is no longer necessary, but I fail to see how a positive sense of *pleasure* could be accounted for.

It seems to be the case that Freud unfortunately conceptualized the analytic situation as basically professional or else basically adversarial in nature. I would venture to suggest that this basic attitude was even carried over into his study of dreams (or perhaps even originated there?). For Freud, failures in contextualization happened in order to hide clients' forbidden wishes from their analysts in their roles as father confessors. It is for this reason that Freud saw the essential dream-process as *distortion* of an unacceptable wish rather than as the best attempt of the mind to *formulate* that wish within the limitations imposed by knowledge and by the internal object world. Why didn't Freud instead see his clients as desperately trying to communicate the truth about themselves to him by the best means they had at their disposal? Why wasn't their ambivalence about knowing themselves seen as a fear that even the truth might not be enough to cure them? The answer, I think, lies in a careful understanding of Freud's personality, but this is not a question that can be pursued within the context of the present investigation.

These last remarks will have made it clear that I do not accept Freud's account of the core mental process at work in the analytic situation. As I think my examples have made clear, we are better served by speaking of failures in contextualization rather than the operation of mechanisms of defence. By this I do not mean to suggest that failures in contextualization cannot be defensively motivated. Often enough, of course, their defensive purpose is clear. I simply mean that the core mental process that comes to light in free association is something rather wider in scope and of rather more interest than a merely defensive process, and that the operation of defences is a special case of this wider, more comprehensive mental process. It also has more to teach us about the mind and about human nature.

If, in reviewing examples (1)–(5), we try to grasp the nature of this mental activity in a preliminary way, we find that it consists in a sort of synthesis of the contents of the mind. It appears as the ability to take stock of ideas, thoughts, and feelings along with the consequences they have for each other as well as whether they do or do not belong to the same context, whether they are or are not mutually compatible, and whether they are or are not consciously known. It is the ability to give a coherent account of a personal history and to form preliminary opinions and even coherent theories about why one is the person that one happens to be. For the moment I will refer to this simply as *the core mental process* because it is clear that it has a central role to play in the act of self-understanding as well as in the interaction with the analyst. Finally there is one important point that should be emphasized because it is all too easily lost sight of: the efficient operation of the core mental process is a source of relief, satisfaction, pleasure, and even joy (Aulagnier, 1975/2007, p. 71). This is an interesting and puzzling aspect of the core mental process that will require future investigation and explanation (Chapter 16).

The next few chapters of this book will be devoted to investigating particular aspects of the core mental process in their relationship with the basic phenomena of the analytic situation that we have identified and emphasized. It is as an explanation of this particular range of facts that the conceptualizations of the present system of metapsychology have been formulated. This is the work that it has been designed to do.

## Note

1 Since this paragraph was first written, further experience has led me to become extremely suspicious of the moralistic vocabulary of Klein in general and, in particular, of analysts

who attribute envious motives to their clients when their interpretations are rejected. The important point is that there are some clients who for a variety of reasons simply cannot tolerate being helped.

## References

Aulagnier, P. (1975/2007). *La violence de l'interprétation*. Paris: Presses Universitaires de France.

Bettelheim, B. (1984). *Freud and Man's Soul*. New York: Vintage Books.

Bion, W. R. (1965/1977). Transformations. In W. R. Bion, *Seven Servants*. New York: Jason Aronson, Inc.

Breuer, J. (1895/2004). Fräulein Anna O. In S. Freud, & J. Breuer, *Studies in Hysteria* (N. Luckhurst, Trans., pp. 25–50). London: Penguin Books.

Colby, K. M. (1951). *A Primer for Psychotherapists*. New York: The Ronald Press Company.

Freud, S. (1917/2003). Widerstand und Verdrängung. In S. Freud, *Vorlesungen zur Einführung in die Psychoanalyse Und Neue Folge* (pp. 285–299). Frankfurt am Main: S. Fischer Verlag.

Freud, S. (1923/2001). Das Ich und das Es. In S. Freud, *Psychologie des Unbewußten* (pp. 282–330). Frankfurt am Main: S. Fischer Verlag.

Gabbard, G. O. (2005). *Psychodynamic Psychiatry in Clinical Practice*(4th) ed. Arlington, VA: American Psychiatric Publishing, Inc.

Klein, M. (1957/1984). Envy and Gratitude. In M. Klein, *Envy and Gratitude and Other Works 1946–1963* (pp. 176–235). New York: The Free Press.

McDougall, J. (1989). *Théâtres du corps. Le psychosome en psychanalyse*. Paris: Éditions Gallimard.

Suttie, I. D. (1935/1999). *The Origins of Love and Hate*. London: Free Association Books.

# 6

# THE FUNCTION OF THE CORE MENTAL PROCESS

The core mental process of which we are witnesses when we work with clients in the analytic situation has the following general features. It is a process, occurring in the presence of another, that contextualizes inner experience in order to prepare it for communication to that other person. This preliminary description suggests a number of important aspects of the core mental process that are worthy of further attention. (1) It is a *relational* process, not merely a solitary activity, but one that essentially involves and is essentially directed towards another person. (2) The process accomplishes the task of contextualizing, of ordering, evaluating, and arranging inner experience for the sake of communication. The implication is that when this process does not occur, e.g. when its functioning is defensively impaired, communication is similarly affected, because the original experiences are such that they cannot be communicated without being contextualized. (3) This process has both a verbal and a non-verbal aspect, or if you prefer, a linguistic aspect and a pre-linguistic aspect. Clients can communicate without words, through tone, gestures, mannerisms, and so on. For there to be communication, however, there must first be a prior selection and arrangement of that which is to be communicated, regardless of whether that eventual communication be verbal or non-verbal.

How are we to understand the different aspects of the core mental process? Let us consider the task it accomplishes for the client in more detail, focusing on aspect (2) above for the time being. We will begin at the beginning of the process: with inner experience.

It would probably be wrong to describe the most fundamental level of experience, whether conscious or unconscious, as utterly inchoate. Presumably the core mental process, in the work of contextualization, discovers communicable structures that are already present, selecting the important aspects and leaving out the rest. I do not think that the core mental process can simply impose any arbitrary structure on inner experience. Nevertheless, in their primeval state, the immediate givens of inner experience are not amenable to being communicated to another person. They are quite simply ineffable. They are pristine in their nakedness; nothing can be said or grasped of them other than that they *are*. They are pure suchness. They are just as they are. They are overwhelming in the singularity of their occurrence. They are a simple flood of information that is meaningless because of its sheer volume. Bion has tried to capture this quality of the fundamental units of experience in the concept of beta-elements (1962/1977, pp. 6–9), though it should be mentioned in passing for the sake of completeness that he tends, incorrectly, to assimilate them to the Kantian concept of a thing in itself.

A justification for conceptualizing the fundamental elements of experience in this way can be derived from the study of manic and hypo-manic states. The origin of such states, insofar as there is a psychogenic component at work, is to be sought in auto-destructive attacks on the core mental process that cripple the work of contextualization, leaving only the most basic, most primeval, barely contextualized experience, in which every single thing is cosmic in its significance and yet utterly devoid of content (Bion, 1959; 1962/1977, p. 8, para. 3). What is striking about first person accounts of descent into insanity, at least for me, is how uninformative these states actually are. Despite all the bizarre ideation, there is little or nothing to be learned from them beyond a sense of the mind-bending shallowness of states of madness, at least when they are *merely* recounted. This is a consequence of the crippling of the work of contextualization (whether by a biological or a psychological agent), whose task it is to elaborate experience into a rich and coherent tapestry. In Winnicottian terms, crippled mental play is rigid, robotic, uncreative and therefore uninteresting play. Genius is in fact not at all close to madness.

States of madness become very interesting, however, when they are not merely recounted, but reflected upon, inquired into, and elaborated after the fact, as in the masterful and utterly peerless science fiction of Philip K. Dick (1969/2002). We should take this as a warning not to confuse states of madness with creative mental states. Where they coexist in the same individual, as they did in Descartes or Isaac Newton, it is often the case that the healthy part of the personality desperately mobilizes any resources it can find, including creativity, in order to help contain the disintegrating part. This can appear, from an external point of view, as a stimulus to creativity, but there is a price to be paid for this sort of artificially stimulated creative hypertrophy: it always wears a crippling straitjacket of desperation. We always should ask the question: but what if they hadn't *needed* to create? These remarks are not intended to minimize the contribution of madness to creativity (McDougall, 1972/1978), only as a warning not to idealize madness or to overlook its immense cost to the humanity of the afflicted individual.

Furthermore, our view of the fundamental elements of experience agrees with some theories of early infant experience. Consider the following series of quotations:

> When you think that excitement means an experience for [a baby] rather like what being put in a den of lions would be for us, no wonder he wants to

> make sure you are a reliable milk-giver before he lets himself go for you. If you fail him it must feel to him as if the wild beasts will gobble him up.
>
> *(Winnicott, 1964/1987, p. 23)*

> It is not possible for an adult or even for a child to know exactly what it feels like to be an infant. The feelings of infancy, although no doubt stored up somewhere in every one, are not easily recaptured. The intensity of infant feelings recurs in the intensity of the suffering associated with psychotic symptoms.
>
> *(Winnicott, 1964/1987, p. 50)*

> In this particular matter of seeing the world as it is, what can we say about the toddler? For the toddler, every sensation is tremendously intense. We, as grown-ups, only at special moments reach this wonderful intensity of feeling which belongs to the early years, and anything that helps us to get there without frightening us is welcome. [...] For the little child, and how much more for the infant, life is just a series of terrifically intense experiences.
>
> *(Winnicott, 1964/1987, p. 70)*

It is particularly important, in this context, not to make the mistake of assuming that infants are naturally psychotic (Klein, 1946/1984). While there are some similarities between the psychic functioning of infants and psychotic states, the all-important difference is that a psychotic state is the result of an auto-destructive attack on the process of contextualization, whereas an infant's mental states are characterized, from our point of view, by an as-yet-undeveloped capacity for contextualization. The infant's states are expressions of as-yet-undeveloped potential, whereas the psychotic state amounts to mental auto-mutilation in a desperate defensive effort to obliterate mental conflict. The resulting mental state bears the traces of the auto-mutilating attack upon the core mental process (Bion, 1962/1977, pp. 9, 12, 25). The infant's mental states, on the other hand, are the naturally occurring form of what psychotic auto-destruction strives with desperate futility to regain. In short, there is a difference between lack of contextualization due to unfamiliarity, and the active destruction of the ability to contextualize. Both infant and psychotic mental states, however, can be valuable sources of information, if we consider them from the right point of view. Our present goal is to understand the nature of experience at an extremely low level of contextualization, so that ultimately we can understand what contextualization contributes to experience.

We are, then, viewing experience at the lower end of the core mental process, at a point where minimal contextualization has occurred. The passages from Winnicott quoted above bring to light the following points. Infant experience differs from adult experience through the sheer intensity of the former. The greater intensity of infant experience leads both to greater possibilities for the experience of pleasure and for the experience of terror and anxiety. This is because, as Winnicott emphasizes, for the infant the very intensity of experience is in itself a source of fear. For the infant, even the experience of joy is potentially terrifying, if it becomes too intense. We can infer that something is absent in the infant that will develop later on in life: the ability to mitigate the intensity of emotion, whether that emotion be pleasant or unpleasant.

We can, perhaps, compare the situation of the infant to the situation of someone who sits at the wheel of a car for the very first time. At first, you're overwhelmed by the vast quantity of information with which you're flooded when you take the car out on the road. There are colours, sounds, and shapes, road signs, traffic lights, other cars, pedestrians, bicyclists, the steering wheel, the gas pedal, the brake: every tiny little detail of the landscape seems to be making an equally urgent and persistent demand on you for immediate attention. But in time you learn to ignore what is not important, and to focus on what is important, and you learn to understand the important signals more quickly as well. In time you know how to deal with the controls and with the inrush of information from the landscape around you at the same time. Then driving a car becomes a matter of routine. This means that there is a vastly decreased sense of fear and anxiety, but also a vastly decreased thrill of accomplishment. To return to our previous examples involving the contextualization of experience: the healthy infant is able for the most part to accept the process of mental development from thrilling anxiety to everyday routine; the psychotic defence strategy is to prevent it altogether from occurring and linger in the mind-numbing rush of uncontextualized experience.

One last point needs to be made regarding the peculiarities of uncontextualized infant experience: "The beings who were important to a child since its birth, its mental and physical experiences, even its body, are originally experienced [*vécu*] as belonging to the external world" (McDougall, 1989, p. 74). McDougall is, presumably, working backwards from the observation of defensive projective mechanisms in the adult to their original healthy basis in infant experience. I would perhaps put the same point slightly differently; it seems that low levels of contextualization produce a low level of differentiation between inside and outside, and while this is healthy and even necessary for infants, who need to be able to import features of the external world into their inner mental worlds, traces of this lack of differentiation can also be exploited for defensive purposes by conflicted adults.

Finally, the third important source of information regarding experience at low levels of contextualization that I would like to introduce is the experience of meditation states. The literature on meditation, along with the scriptures of meditation-based religions, is rife with accounts of mental states that resemble states of uncontextualized mental experience. As Winnicott stressed in the previously cited passages, a major challenge facing us as adults is how to recapture the original intensity of infant experience in a relatively safe way. Although the subject is too vast for me to address at length here, my own experience leads me to view meditation as a willed auto-inhibition of the core mental process with the ultimate aim of re-experiencing mental states that resemble those of infancy. I do not see this as necessarily "regressive" or "defensive" in nature; in such cases, as in any form of creative activity, it is a question of the end rather than the means. Narcissistic withdrawal is a precondition of any creative mental state; the issue is whether it be a playful withdrawal from the external world, or a rigid, compulsive flight. Are meditation states used to enrich life in a creative way by recapturing the innocence of the child and its oneness with its primeval infant environment, namely its mother? Or are they used to avoid the complex tasks of adult living? These are the questions we need to ask.

Our immediate task, however, is to understand the primeval state of the mind when contextualization is absent or minimal. Consider the following quotation in the light of our previous examination of the core mental process:

> All the Buddhas and all sentient beings are nothing but the One Mind, beside which nothing exists. This Mind, which is without beginning, is unborn and indestructible. It is not green nor yellow, and has neither form nor appearance. It does not belong to the categories of things which exist or do not exist, nor can it be thought of in terms of new or old. It is neither long nor short, big nor small, for it transcends all limits, measures, names, traces, and comparisons. It is that which you see before you – begin to reason about it and you at once fall into error. It is like the boundless void which cannot be fathomed or measured. The One Mind alone is the Buddha, and there is no distinction between the Buddha and sentient things, but that sentient beings are attached to forms and so seek externally for Buddhahood.
>
> *(Po, 1958)*

Similar passages abound throughout the vast corpus of meditational literature, so that I feel no need to quote extensively from other sources. I think that the resemblance to the other two forms of uncontextualized experience that we have studied, namely manic states and infant mental states, is striking. Although the link has been made before – though in a crudely embarrassing manner from which I would like to explicitly distance myself (Alexander, 1931) – one could perhaps call psychotic states the results of uncontrollable, involuntary meditation. In my view this opens up extremely intriguing vistas for future exploration. It also suggests that the current trend towards the integration of traditional meditation practices with psychotherapy has a hidden potential that has not yet been clearly understood even by the proponents of this integration.

What conclusions are to be drawn from our discussion of contextualization with regard to the function of the core mental process? I want to begin my answer to this question with a clarification of how I use the word "experience." By *experience* I mean any and all direct encounters with anything whatsoever, regardless of whether this encounter be brought about by the body, by the mind, or by any other means, and regardless of whether the things encountered are internal or external, thoughts or things, real or imagined, acknowledged or unacknowledged, conscious or unconscious. Experience is the totality of whatever has any sort of effect on us in any manner whatsoever. For the sake of clarity I want to emphasize that according to this definition, unconscious experience is clearly possible. I do not see experiencing as contingent upon consciousness, but rather largely independent of it.

Experience taken as a whole, the totality of the internal and external environments, is constantly impinging upon us, making a demand on the mind to do work. Just as water is constantly rushing into the amoeba from its surroundings, experience constantly impresses itself upon the mind. Just as the amoeba's water vacuole collects all the water it cannot use for its own internal processes and expels it into the surroundings, the mind too is responsible either for *dismissing* or *elaborating* the information from the environment. I explain dismissing in the following manner. When the demand made by experience upon the mind is relatively minimal (or, if you prefer, when the intensity of the experience is weak), we can simply ignore it until it goes away, or else discharge the tension it produces in relatively trivial ways: "blowing off steam," distracting ourselves, engineering a change of mood, etc. On the other hand, if the experience is relatively significant and the demand it makes upon the mind is correspondingly greater, it cannot simply be dismissed. In this case the experience must be elaborated.

Elaborating involves taking stock of the experience, acknowledging it as the experience it is, reacting to it emotionally, naming it, and understanding it, after which other activities such as decision-making, taking action, doing something else, and deliberate and appropriate forgetting (genuine dismissing) become possible. The difference between dismissing and elaborating can be clarified by means of the following analogy. Consider the difference between sitting in a slightly uncomfortable chair and sitting on a tack. In the former case one can ignore the discomfort or perhaps fidget until some relief is obtained; in the latter case a rather more immediate course of action is indicated. Dismissing is the mental equivalent of ignoring and fidgeting; elaborating is the mental equivalent of taking action to alter the situation. Dismissing is appropriate to relatively trivial environmental demands, while elaborating is appropriate to relatively non-trivial demands. It is rather like a person at the controls of a piece of heavy machinery, say an airplane. You can ignore relatively trivial incidents such as mild turbulence, but if the plane takes a sudden nosedive, you had better figure out what is happening as quickly as you can. And, of course, there is every possible shade between the two extremes I have focussed on here for the sake of clarity.

I call dismissing and elaborating the two major aspects of *the work of contextualization*. The goal of the work of contextualization is to reduce the overwhelming complexity of experience by rearranging and organizing it. Bion sees the work of contextualization, which he calls "alpha-function," as the mental equivalent of the process of digestion (1962/1977, pp. 6–7, 34–37, 42); this metaphor is shared by Piera Aulagnier, who refers to a similar process as "métabolisation" (1975/2007, p. 30). This is an apt metaphor, and perhaps reflects its earliest origin in the feeding experiences of the infant, but as we shall later see (Chapter 14), it is not the only possible way of experiencing the work of contextualization.

We can now briefly discuss the effects that interference with the work of contextualization – i.e. the activity of the core mental process – can have on the mind.

The difference between dismissing and elaborating becomes relevant when we are discussing a very narrow range of mental disorders in which an attempt is made to evacuate thoughts through action instead of working them out through understanding. For example, an attempt can be made to dismiss something that should really be elaborated, i.e. to ignore, obliterate, or evacuate an impression that is simply too strong to be properly dealt with in this way. This may result, among other possibilities, in somatization, uncontrollable twitching, and the like. With more sophisticated clients we observe the phenomenon traditionally referred to as "acting out." Since dismissing cannot properly cope with the thoughts and feelings in question, in time the symptom ultimately recurs, and nothing is ever really changed. This is the inherent weakness of all "cathartic" methods, and it is the reason why they all ultimately and necessarily fail. In another case, the process of elaboration itself can be interfered with, so that something that can be thought and felt nevertheless cannot be put into words. This is "repression" in the classical sense: preventing a fully-formed mental image from becoming conscious.

Note that one of the major advantages of conceptualizing the mind in terms of the core mental process is that it offers a richer framework for understanding the possible ways in which things can go wrong with the mind than the traditional model. In the classical Freudian model one basically only had the strict focus of conscious versus unconscious (i.e. "repression") to work with. In terms of the core mental process, as we shall later see in more detail in Chapters 10–12, we have a variety of different levels of functioning with many subtle aspects that can be interfered with, and so many different ways of conceptualizing subtly different types of defence.

Now because the possible ways of interfering with contextualization, i.e. with dismissing and elaborating, are virtually infinite in number, I find lists and hierarchies of defence mechanisms extremely unenlightening (Gabbard, 2005, pp. 35–37). I suspect that their main appeal can be traced back to the widespread but false belief that to classify is to understand. They also convey impressions about the value of culturally significant processes that, in my view, are quite misleading. In my view, the fundamental task before the mind is making sense of experience. To classify the processes involved in "humour" and "altruism" in a "hierarchy of defences" among mechanisms such as "splitting," "denial," and "dissociation" can, in my opinion, only be explained by an ideological commitment towards a certain unnecessarily bleak and reductionist view of the human condition, according to which there is nothing human that is not ultimately intended to serve as a "bulwark" against "the black tides of mud" (Jung, 1961/1997, p. 155). I would go so far as to say that this world-view is demonstrably false, and I am puzzled by the apparent inclination that many analysts have towards such a perspective. Surely there are other possible meanings of life than the perpetual quest for ways to hold back the onrushing tides of the drives? This is not to be understood as meaning that humour and altruism can *never* be defensive in nature; as far as I am concerned, anything can potentially function as a defence. I only object to the belief that they *have* to be.

With regard to the role that consciousness plays in the work of contextualization, I want to remark briefly that healthy contextualization *always* results in some elements of experience remaining unconscious (in the descriptive sense), either through pre-elaborative dismissing or through post-elaborative forgetting, or through the work of elaboration itself (e.g. ignoring what is irrelevant). I do not consider this necessarily pathological or defensive in any sense of the words. It is a significant criticism of the concept of defence mechanisms that it can *only* account for the failure of experience to become conscious in defensive terms. The aim of the core mental process is indeed to reduce the overwhelming complexity of experience by rearranging and organizing it, but to speak of this as "defence" is to make the same type of error as when we confuse infant with psychotic states of mind. To speak metaphorically, the proponents of the "all is defence" theory are like physiologists who insist that the process of elimination is nothing but a failure of the digestive process. If we fall prey to this error, our metapsychologies tend to devolve into inventories of defence mechanisms, and so fail to perform their designated function, namely understanding the operations of the mind as such and on their own terms.

I think we, and our clients, are better served by our trying to understand every individual client's own particular flavour of defence rather than trying to match them with some prearranged defensive scheme. This is not an argument against the usefulness of detailed accounts of particular defensive strategies. It is a plea for a healthy respect for client individuality and ultimately for human nature as well.

## References

Alexander, F. (1931). Buddhistic Training as an Artificial Catatonia (The Biological Meaning of Psychic Occurrences). *Psychoanalytic Review* 18: 129–145.

Aulagnier, P. (1975/2007). *La violence de l'interprétation*. Paris: Presses Universitaires de France.

Bion, W. R. (1959). Attacks on Linking. *International Journal of Psycho-Analysis* 40: 308–315.

Bion, W. R. (1962/1977). Learning From Experience. In W. R. Bion, *Seven Servants*. New York, NY: Jason Aronson, Inc.

Dick, P. K. (1969/2002). Ubik. In P. K. Dick, *Counterfeit Unrealities* (pp. 337–510). New York: SFBC.

Gabbard, G. O. (2005). *Psychodynamic Psychiatry in Clinical Practice* (4th ed.). Arlington, VA: American Psychiatric Publishing, Inc.

Jung, C. G. (1961/1997). *Erinnerungen, Träume, Gedanken*. Zürich and Düsseldorf: Walter-Verlag AG.

Klein, M. (1946/1984). Notes on Some Schizoid Mechanisms. In M. Klein, *Envy and Gratitude and Other Works 1946–1963* (pp. 1–24). New York: The Free Press.

McDougall, J. (1972/1978). Plaidoyer pour une certaine anormalité. In J. McDougall, *Plaidoyer pour une certaine anormalité* (pp. 209–222). Paris: Éditions Gallimard.

McDougall, J. (1989). *Théâtres du corps. Le psychosome en psychanalyse*. Paris: Éditions Gallimard.

Po, H. (1958). *The Zen Teaching of Huang Po on the Transmission of Mind*. (J. Blofeld, Trans.) New York: Grove Press.

Winnicott, D. W. (1964/1987). *The Child, the Family, and the Outside World*. Cambridge, MA: Perseus Publishing.

# 7

# THE PLACE OF THE UNCONSCIOUS

Before we carry out any further investigations into the specific details of the work of contextualization, I think that it is important to decide where the core mental process should be placed in relation to the *unconscious*. Doing so is complicated by the various senses in which the word is used throughout the development of Freud's own metapsychology. The main ambiguity we need to resolve is the following: the term "unconscious" has two broad ranges of meaning. In the first sense, the term refers to a particular mental agency – *the* unconscious. When we speak of something being "unconscious" in this sense, we really mean that it is present within a particular mental system with its own characteristic type of functioning. We can also say that this is the "topographical" use of the term (Laplanche & Pontalis, 1973). In the second sense, the term "unconscious" has a purely descriptive meaning. When we refer to something as "unconscious" in this sense, we simply mean that it is not or cannot become conscious, whether momentarily or for longer periods of time. Confusingly, and most inconveniently from a terminological perspective, whatever is descriptively unconscious is not necessarily also unconscious in the topographical sense, as we shall shortly see.

I think that it is fair to say that throughout the vast corpus of Freud's writings the predominant tendency is to use the term "unconscious" in the topographical sense. The clearest statement of this usage – insofar as there *is* any clear statement to be found – is in Freud's paper on the two principles of mental functioning (Freud, 1911/2001). Here Freud draws a line that divides the mind into two broad regions: on the one hand, the unconscious, to which are assigned the "primary" processes governed by the pleasure principle, and on the other, consciousness, to which are assigned the "secondary" processes governed by the reality principle. Freud, I think, makes an unspoken assumption that it is primary process thinking that is actually interesting to analysts, and so for all practical purposes the default meaning of "unconscious" is topographical rather than merely descriptive. Thus the special term "preconscious" is eventually used to refer to the trivially unconscious, that is, to thoughts that are momentarily forgotten or inaccessible, but that do not belong to the system of primary process thinking. This, however, leads to a problem that is both significant and obvious: the preconscious is descriptively *unconscious*, and yet, paradoxically, part of the *conscious* system. The conceptual muddles that such an "unconscious conscious" can engender are all too easy to imagine.

It is possible to see Freud's shift from the earlier "topographical" model to the later "structural" model as directly motivated by the need to resolve terminological ambiguities (de Azevedo, 2000). In the earlier *topographical* model, as we have just seen, "the unconscious" is the name of one of the three mental systems recognized by Freud at this time, namely the unconscious, consciousness, and the preconscious. By contrast, in the later *structural* model (Freud, 1923/2001), as we shall see, Freud attempts to use the term "unconscious" in a purely descriptive sense and to abandon its topographical sense – though not entirely successfully. In any case, Freud introduces his revised model by clarifying the meaning of the phrase "descriptively unconscious." The totality of the descriptively unconscious is divided into two sub-groups. Everything that is descriptively unconscious, but not actively hindered in any way from becoming conscious, is now referred to as *preconscious*. Thoughts that are descriptively unconscious, but also actively hindered in some way from becoming conscious, are now referred to as *unconscious* (or alternatively: unconscious in a "dynamic" sense). According to Freud, the most obvious way of understanding this sense of "unconscious" is by looking to the process of *repression*, since "for us the repressed is the prototype [*Vorbild*] of the unconscious" (1923/2001, p. 284). Thus in the structural model the unconscious is now linked with the operation of defensive mechanisms in general, and with repression in particular, rather than with primary process thinking, as was the case in the topographical model.

Having decided to use the term "unconscious" in a purely descriptive sense, there arises the question of what new names are to be given to the parts of the mind formerly denoted as the unconscious, the preconscious, and consciousness. Freud of course goes on to recognize three different mental systems or agencies, namely the id, the ego, and the super-ego. The primary process activity formerly attributed to the unconscious in the earlier topographical model is now attributed to the id, while the ego becomes the seat of the secondary process activity formerly linked with the systems "conscious" and "preconscious" (Laplanche & Pontalis, 1973). The id, then, is conceived of as the totality of primary process thinking, while the ego is regarded as the totality of secondary process thinking.

More important for our own theoretical enterprise, however, is the following question. What are the consequences of these new structural distinctions for the use of the term "unconscious"? The basic sense of the term is the descriptive sense: something is unconscious when it is not accessible to consciousness. However, we now have two sub-groups of unconscious thoughts. When we speak of the preconscious, of thoughts that are not actively prevented from reaching consciousness, we are speaking of a region of the mind that is present within the structure of the ego and therefore subject to the laws of its functioning. Thus, terminologically speaking, it is now an unconscious part of the ego, and no longer an unconscious part of the conscious system, as it was in the older model. When we speak of the unconscious proper, however, of thoughts that are actively prevented from becoming conscious, we may be speaking of thoughts that are part of the id, and therefore subject to its primary process thinking, but we may *also* be speaking of thoughts that are part of the ego, and therefore governed by secondary process thinking. This boils down to the complete abandonment of the topographical use of the term "unconscious." The id, however, retains a closer association with the term "unconscious" than the ego, since the id is supposed to contain the unknown and unknowable aspects of the individual along with those aspects of the drives that can never become conscious at all.

Why did Freud find it necessary to alter the meaning of the term "unconscious" in this way? Over and above the original terminological difficulties, as we saw in the last paragraph, the shift in meaning is required to accommodate an important clinical observation within the framework of the new theory: large parts of both the ego and the super-ego can be unconscious. Freud explains this as follows.

The task of the ego, according to Freud, is to rein in the passionate id as a confident rider reins in a horse (1923/2001, p. 294). On this view, mounting defences against the drives is conceptualized as an ego function (p. 287). Now it is an everyday clinical observation that clients may be unaware of their own personal defensive strategies, and that part of the work of analysis is to help clients become conscious of the typical and characteristic manners in which they unknowingly hide their own thoughts and feelings from themselves. Therefore, it follows that significant aspects of the rational, secondary process system – the ego – can be unconscious (deliberately and actively kept out of consciousness).

Furthermore, many clients can be observed to suffer from the manifestations of unconscious feelings of guilt, e.g. various forms of self-sabotage, accident-proneness, and so on. Since the super-ego is defined as the internal moral agency, more or less identical with the conscience, and since clients can be unaware of their own guilt feelings and their own need for punishment, it follows that the agency that is responsible for guilt and punishment, the super-ego, must be capable of at least partial unconsciousness (p. 295). The relation of the super-ego to the primary and secondary processes is, in my opinion, rather less clear than in the case of id and ego, but in any event, it is evident that the introduction of this third agency capable of partial consciousness and partial unconsciousness into the model further undermines the earlier use of the term "unconscious" in its topographical sense.

We can summarize all of the preceding explanations by noting that the essential and characteristic features of the structural model consist of the following:

1. The preliminary attempt to restrict the use of the term "unconscious" to the strictly descriptive sense.

2. The division of descriptively unconscious thoughts into thoughts that are actively hindered from becoming conscious, or the unconscious *proper*, and entities that are not so hindered, or the *preconscious*.
3. The tendency to identify the unconscious proper with the totality of the repressed along with the concomitant recognition that some defensive processes other than repression may be at work (p. 287).
4. The division of the mind into two broad regions: the area of primary process thinking, or id, and the area of secondary process thinking, or ego.
5. The attempt to maintain the close association of the ego with consciousness, along with the close association of the id with the unconscious proper, and thus with the repressed.
6. The realization that despite this close association any part of the ego may be conscious, preconscious, or unconscious, and that in theory at least, any part of the id may also be conscious, preconscious, or unconscious (p. 290).

With regard to the last point (6) above, I want to emphasize that most analysts, in everyday discussion, tend to assign consciousness and the preconscious to the ego, while the unconscious is more or less identified with the id, with the caveat added that parts of the ego may at times also be unconscious. In so doing they are adhering to the habit of thought expressed in point (5) above, which is really an artefact of the earlier topographical model. As I hope I have shown in my presentation of the theory, the topographical use of the term "unconscious" is completely undermined by the realization that parts of the ego, or the secondary process system, can also be unconscious. There is no longer anything special about the primary processes to link them more strongly with the unconscious than the secondary processes (or if there is, Freud has not identified what it could be). Freud also emphasizes that it is possible for the "deepest" layers of the mind (presumably those most shaped by the primary processes) to become conscious (p. 290), that extremely sophisticated secondary process thinking can be preconscious, (p. 295), and that the repressed unconscious can "communicate" with the ego through the id (pp. 292–293). All of these passages suggest that there is no straightforward way to link the quality of being unconscious with any one system in the mind, at least when the criterion used to distinguish these systems is primary versus secondary process thinking.

One problem that puzzled Freud in *The Ego and the Id* is the question how parts of the ego could be kept unconscious by a process other than repression. To make a long story short: the problem arose because Freud defined repression in such a narrow way that it could only mean a process that (1) originated in the ego and (2) was directed towards a drive. If, therefore, the analyst discovered unconscious defences – implying unconscious parts of the ego – it seemed that "repression" in this narrow sense could not be the cause of this unconsciousness since it was supposed to originate in the ego and be exclusively directed towards drives. The unconscious parts of the ego therefore had to constitute a "third, not repressed *Ucs*" (p. 287) – the other two "unconsciousnesses" being the preconscious and the totality of the repressed, i.e. the unconscious proper. Ultimately the important point in all these confusions is that even Freud's later structural model is not an adequate description of everything that was known to him to occur in the mind. Repression, in the narrow sense in which it is understood by Freud, is not the sole defensive process that is involved in the formation of unconscious systems. But if this is the case, then what else *is* involved?

Bion's investigations in *Learning from Experience* attempt to address this issue by inquiring more deeply into the nature of repression (however defined) and its importance to the constitution of the unconscious. His work suggests that even the part of the unconscious that is supposed to be resident in the id (i.e. subject to primary process thinking), can be created and maintained by processes other than repression, a conclusion very different from Freud's. A further important consequence to be drawn from Bion's work is that *some regions of the unconscious appear to be governed by processes entirely different from both the primary and secondary processes recognized and described by Freud in the structural model.*

For Bion, repression, and with it the establishment of a particular area within the mind for thoughts that are blocked from consciousness, is only possible once the mind has reached a certain relatively advanced level of structural sophistication (1962/1977, pp. 17–18). Bion calls the mental activity that is responsible for processing mental contents to the level where a distinction between consciousness and the unconscious becomes possible "alpha-function" (p. 27). Alpha-function performs a role similar to that of the "censor" in Freud's theory of dreams (p. 15); it establishes a barrier that only lets certain elements through to consciousness, usually in disguise, and banishes the rest to "the unconscious." According to Bion, this is precisely what prevents the average healthy person from becoming psychotic. It is, therefore, a mental process that is not *only* operative in dreams, but throughout waking life as well.

According to Bion, the "contact-barrier" between consciousness and the repressed unconscious consists of "alpha-elements," i.e. mental contents that have been processed with enough sophistication for them to become conscious, remain preconscious, or be repressed. For mental contents that are *not* processed to this level of sophistication, Bion reserved the name "beta-elements." Beta-elements are thoughts that are so primitive that they are simply ungraspable, "things in themselves" devoid of any possible relation to, and thus significance for, the thinker. To employ the terminology I introduced in Chapter 6, beta-elements are aspects of experience that are so minimally elaborated that the mind cannot get any hold on them; they are so vague and indeterminate that the mind can only make an attempt to dismiss them (or "evacuate" them, in Bion's terminology); and this strategy can only fail, because they are too powerful to be gotten rid of in this way. Why did Bion feel the need to introduce this concept? In his clinical work Bion encountered "borderline psychotic" clients who were so damaged – or, if you prefer, undertook such massive auto-destructive attacks upon their own mental functioning – that repression, in the sense of the formulation of a drive representation followed by its active exclusion from consciousness, by and large could not take place. They were not healthy enough to even begin to repress their conflicts; they were simply torn apart by them.

In Bion's opinion, classical models fail to describe with any real degree of accuracy the sufferings of clients who resort to this type of large-scale defensive campaign. They are best described as people who "cannot dream and therefore cannot sleep" and thus also "cannot wake up" (p. 7). They therefore also cannot "be either conscious or unconscious" (p. 21). Their capacity for making sense of their own internal experiences is so damaged that nothing about them can be taken at face value: "A smile or a verbal statement must be interpreted as an evacuatory muscular movement and not as a communication of feeling" (p. 14). This is because their own auto-destructive mental attacks are so massively devastating to their internal landscape that they cannot even *have* feelings in any real everyday sense of the word. They suffer from chronic mental indigestion that alienates them from every conceivable aspect of themselves.

I have noticed a similar position – to wit, that the distinction between consciousness and the repressed unconscious can only take place at a relatively advanced level of mental functioning – in other authors as well, though this theoretical position accomplishes a slightly different task in each separate context. All of them, however, seem to share the conviction that there is a deeper – or if we prefer to avoid the use of spatial metaphor, more fundamental – level of mental functioning than can be accounted for in terms of a strictly classical Freudian model. My own reading suggests the following lineage for the development of this position. In *Instincts and their Vicissitudes*, Freud identified several possible ways in which libidinal energies could be contained: transformation into the opposite, turning against one's own person, repression, and sublimation (1915d/2001, pp. 89–90). This suggests, given Freud's reliance on spatial metaphor, that there is an area "below" the repressed unconscious in which other drive defences can operate alongside, or instead of, repression. The existence of other means of coping with the demands of the drives led Freud to declare in *Repression* that "repression is not an originally present defence mechanism, that it cannot come into being before a sharp distinction between conscious and unconscious mental activity has been made, and that *its essence only consists in turning away* [Abweisung] *and keeping at a distance* [Fernhaltung] *from the conscious*" (1915c/2001, p. 108). This further led Freud to introduce a distinction between "primeval repression" [*Urverdrängung*] and "repression proper" [*die eigentliche Verdrängung*] (1915c/2001, p. 109). Primeval repression is conceived of as one defence among many, and is presumably located in the same area "below" the repressed unconscious in which the other defence mechanisms are active. Repression proper, on the other hand, is the actual prevention of derivative mental images that are associatively linked with the content of primeval repression from reaching consciousness. It is the dynamic activity that is constitutive of the repressed unconscious as such. It creates and maintains the superstructure of the repressed unconscious, whereas primeval repression lays its foundation.

From the first glimmerings of Freud's acknowledgement of defensive processes that are more fundamental than (or at least coeval with) repression, two lines of development branch off. The first leads through Ian Suttie, who traced the origins of repression back to the pre-Oedipal relationship with the mother (1935/1999, p. 100–101), to Bion's doctrine of alpha-function and its disorders, which we have discussed in the preceding paragraphs. The second line of development branches off from Freud to Serge Viderman and his reading of Freud's distinction between primeval repression and repression proper. For Viderman, primeval repression creates a "primitive unconscious core" that was, by definition, never conscious to begin with. It was created by experiences at such an early stage of development (presumably in the pre-Oedipal relationship with the mother?) that the contextualization required to retain any sort of memory of the experience simply could not take place. The processes involved in repression proper are inaugurated by primeval repression. They operate at later stages of development where it *is* possible to retain memories of the relevant experiences, and in their case a reversal of the "infantile amnesia" preventing the memories in question from becoming conscious is possible. In the case of the unconscious core created by primeval repression, however, no such recovery is possible. Here only more or less reliable *constructions* are possible, since there are no memories to work with (1982, pp. 15–19).

Perhaps the clearest and most elaborate treatment of the subject is to be found in Piera Aulagnier's *La violence de l'interprétation*. As a result of the aforementioned considerations, along with her own clinical work with severely damaged clients, Aulagnier felt it necessary to introduce a *third* type of mental functioning that was both chronologically earlier and more primitive than both the primary and secondary processes. She called this the *processus originaire*. Aulagnier conceives this as a process of representation, like primary and secondary process thinking, with its own characteristic set of rules. Original process thinking results in a special type of mental image Aulagnier calls the "pictogram." For the sake of comprehensibility I will relate Aulagnier's theories using a slightly more accessible vocabulary than we find in the original presentation.

The pictogram is a mental image that is a fusion of a part-object representation, a body representation corresponding to the nature of the part-object [*un objet-zone complémentaire*] (1975/2007, p. 62), and the emotion linking the two. The emotion is characteristically experienced either as a modality of love/swallowing or of hatred/annihilation (p. 77). The mental image as a whole is characterized by a narcissistic-oral style of thinking that Aulagnier believes is dominant during the stage of breastfeeding. The most prominent feature of this style of thinking is a lack of differentiation between self and other along with a belief in the omnipotent power of the self to create the experience of that other. Interestingly, ambivalence towards the object is expressed by this style of thinking as auto-destructive attacks on the activity of representation itself (p. 51). Aulagnier accommodates this auto-destructive activity within the traditional death-drive theory by seeing it as an expression of the "desire for non-desire." Like Bion's beta-elements, pictograms are particularly resistant to becoming conscious, they play a major role in the sufferings of psychotic and borderline psychotic clients, and they are particularly suited to forms of expulsive discharge that include acting out (pp. 78–79). Aulagnier further stresses that she sees the original process and its result, the pictogram, as distinct from the primary process and the unconscious, by which she presumably means the repressed unconscious (p. 77). Finally, Aulagnier sees the original process not as something to be replaced by more sophisticated forms of thinking, but as a vital force that is active throughout life. It is from pictograms, for example, that we derive everyday expressions such as "feeling good in one's skin," "being in shape," "being uneasy," "carrying the world on one's shoulders," "feeling shattered," and so on (p. 78).

What are the consequences of these various points of view for our present metapsychological theory? Freud in *The Ego and the Id* acknowledged the existence of the preconscious, the repressed unconscious in the id, and a further unconscious aspect of the ego whose origin he felt unable to explain. The post-Freudian developments that we have discussed all converge in the recognition of still another unconscious area of the mind, namely a descriptively unconscious area in the id that is hindered from becoming conscious, but through processes other than repression. All together, we now have to account for the existence of at least four varieties of the descriptively unconscious in the mind, and for their apparently haphazard distribution across the mental agencies recognized in classical Freudian theory. All this is ultimately the result of conceptualizing the geography of the mind in terms of primary versus secondary process thinking, i.e. in terms of rationality versus irrationality. Is there any satisfactory way of resolving all of these issues other than by attempting to rationalize the awkwardness of our theoretical results (Freud, 1916; 1933/2007, p. 510)?

## References

Aulagnier, P. (1975/2007). *La violence de l'interprétation*. Paris: Presses Universitaires de France.

Azevedo, A. M.de (2000). Substantive Unconscious and Adjective Unconscious: The Contribution of Wilfred Bion. *Journal of Analytical Psychology* 45: 75–91.

Bion, W. R. (1962/1977). Learning from Experience. In W. R. Bion, *Seven Servants*. New York: Jason Aronson, Inc.

Freud, S. (1911/2001). Formulierungen über die zwei Prinzipien des psychischen Geschehens. In S. Freud, *Psychologie des Unbewußten* (pp. 17–24). Frankfurt am Main: S. Fischer Verlag.

Freud, S. (1915c/2001). Die Verdrängung. In S. Freud, *Psychologie des Unbewußten* (pp. 107–118). Frankfurt am Main: S. Fischer Verlag.

Freud, S. (1915d/2001). Triebe und Triebschicksale. In S. Freud, *Psychologie des Unbewußten* (pp. 81–102). Frankfurt am Main: S. Fischer Verlag.

Freud, S. (1916; 1933/2007). *Vorlesungen zur Einführung in die Psychoanalyse Und Neue Folge*. Frankfurt am Main: S. Fischer Verlag.

Freud, S. (1923/2001). Das Ich und das Es. In S. Freud, *Psychologie des Unbewußten* (pp. 282–330). Frankfurt am Main: S. Fischer Verlag.

Laplanche, J., & Pontalis, J.-B. (1973). *The Language of Psycho-Analysis*. (D. Nicholson-Smith, Trans.) New York and London: W. W. Norton & Company.

Suttie, I. D. (1935/1999). *The Origins of Love and Hate*. London: Free Association Books.

Viderman, S. (1982). *La construction de l'espace analytique*. Paris: Éditions Gallimard.

# 8

# THE REVISED STRUCTURAL MODEL

I think that every thinking analyst must intuitively feel that there is something wrong with a metapsychological model that results in such an extreme dissonance between the agencies it describes and the parameter of consciousness versus the unconscious, if for no other reason than the obvious significance of consciousness and insight to the process of healing. Given the importance of the topographical unconscious to the discipline of psychoanalysis, and given that we agree that this importance should be preserved, might it not be that Freud chose the *wrong* criterion to use as a basis for identifying the different systems at work in the mind?

As we saw in Chapter 4, the experiential basis of the division of the mind into distinct regions is the observation of a definite characteristic structure in free association. It cannot be emphasized strongly enough that the experiential bedrock of our metapsychological formulations is, and must be, our observation of what happens in the analytic situation. We noted that our own experience of the analytic situation suggested that three broad regions could be distinguished within the actual process of free association, regions that unfold before our very eyes as we sit and watch and listen. These three regions, it will be recalled, were the manifest content, the latent content, and the work of association. On what observable basis did we make this distinction? *On the basis of our estimate of the degree to which the content of free association has been contextualized within the framework of what the client consciously intends to communicate to us.* In other words: *the primary phenomenon to be captured within our system of metapsychology is not the distinction between primary and secondary process thinking, but the degree to which mental contents are or are not neatly woven into the tapestry of the client's conscious thinking.*

Accordingly, the criterion we must use to distinguish the various systems in the mind is the *degree of contextualization*, which is equivalent to the suitability of the contents of the systems for conscious thinking. From Freud's iteration of the structural model we have learned the lesson that the contents of the mind are surprisingly mobile. Accordingly, we will suggest that contextualization makes something clearer and therefore more likely to be experienced in consciousness, but it is still possible to experience something consciously that is relatively uncontextualized, though with a reduced degree of clarity. Following this criterion I define the *id* as the relatively uncontextualized (unstructured) region of the mind, as the totality of mental images, thoughts, and feelings that are relatively unprepared for conscious experiencing. Insofar as they are consciously perceived, they are perceived with a relatively low degree of clarity. By contrast, I define the *ego* as the relatively contextualized (structured) region of the mind, as the totality of images, thoughts, and feelings that are relatively well prepared for conscious experiencing. Insofar as they are consciously perceived, they are perceived with a relatively high degree of clarity. By introducing this distinction between ego and id we are in essence classifying the agencies in the mind according to the relative degree of order or disorder that characterizes the systematic integrity of the agency in question. One important result is that consciousness and the ego, along with the unconscious and the id, now largely coincide. We can speak of ego versus id when we wish to emphasize the relative abundance or lack of contextualization. When we want to emphasize the relative abundance or lack of clarity, we can use the terms consciousness and the unconscious. By and large, however, these definitions make both parameters coincide, which is in accordance both with common sense, clinical observation, and the actual linguistic practice of analysts.

In Freud's structural model, the meaning of the term "ego" was vague, so that at times it meant "the part of the id that is modified by experience," and at other times it meant "the part of the mind that attempts to exercise control over the drives," while at yet other times it meant "the willing, perceiving, and deliberating subject." It is hardly clear what, if anything, these three meanings of the term are supposed to have in common. In the present revised structural model, the term "ego" has one determinate meaning: the relatively more contextualized part of the mind. This means that the parameters of the old definition – learning, controlling, willing, perceiving, and deliberating – are only considered part of the ego insofar as they are highly contextualized and therefore more closely woven into the continuity of conscious life, and to the extent that they are not, they are considered as part of the id. In other words, in the revised structural model, "ego" and "subject" are not synonymous.

Another important result of our revisions is that the notion of "depth" in "depth psychology" now ceases to be a mere spatial metaphor and can be assigned a definite meaning in line with the degree of contextualization of the contents of the mind. The meaning of "deeper" in the older pseudo-spatial sense was essentially unclear, since it could mean any one of a number of different things: "more defended against," "more inaccessible," "more unspeakable," "more ineffable," "chronologically older," "more archaic," "more primitive," "more difficult," "simpler," and so on. In the present system of metapsychology the adjective "deeper" has one unequivocal meaning: more uncontextualized, therefore more unconscious or more likely to remain so, therefore more id-like.

It is to be noted that the distinction between ego and id is to be understood as a continuum of contextualization; the healthy adult has a well-established difference between the two systems with a constant flow of exchange between them, like two well-governed neighbouring countries with a shared open border. Other more or less pathological configurations are of course also possible. The difference, however, will make itself felt in the manner in which free association is structured within the analytic situation. "Irruptions" of less contextualized material can also take place in exceptional circumstances: dreams, hallucinations, drug episodes, psychosis, and the like. The common element that all these share in common is the *undermining of the process of contextualization.*

*All these theoretical structures are conceptualizations of observable patterns in free association.* This is the experiential basis from which they derive any meaning they can possibly have. Similarly, the concept of *clarity* has to be defined with reference to the presentation of mental contents in free association. The assessment of clarity is based on the clients' reports of what they are consciously thinking in formulating the manifest content of free association along with the contributions of the work of association as well as the analyst's best attempt to identify the latent content.

For all practical purposes, we can consider that there are two aspects to experience: the *content* of that experience along with its *significance.* I call an experience *adequate* to the degree that its content is accessible, i.e. when it is recognizable as that experience that it really is. An adequate experience can be remembered, reproduced, and recognized. I also call an experience *distinct* to the degree that its significance is accessible, i.e. when it has an emotional meaning that is accompanied by appropriate feelings. In short: an experience that can be remembered is *adequate* to the degree that it can be remembered. An experience that can be felt is *distinct* to the degree that it can be felt.[1]

I call an experience *clear* when it is both adequate and distinct, i.e. when it can be both remembered and felt. An *adequate but indistinct* experience can be remembered, reproduced, and recognized, but its emotional significance is unappreciated or wrongly apprehended because it is not in context with the rest of the individual's life experiences. We know what it is, but not how it feels. By contrast, a *distinct but inadequate* experience is characterized by a definite feeling-tone and by emotions that ultimately are seen to be appropriate to the experience in question, but the nature of that experience is shrouded in mystery. We know how it feels, but not what it is. Finally, an *inadequate and indistinct* experience is a formless mass with no apparent structure, a nameless unrecognizable something of which there is no memory and for which there is no feeling. We know neither what it is nor whence it hails. We are lucky if we can even make out that it is there at all.

A convenient metaphor may be found useful at this point. Compare experiences in the mind to books in a library. Adequacy is then represented by the apparatus that makes it easier to find the books within the library, for example, the arrangement of the books on the library shelves, the cataloguing of the books according to author, subject, keyword, and year, the layout of the floors according to call numbers, and so on. Distinctness can be compared with the apparatus that makes it easier to appreciate the content of each individual book, for example, indexing, arrangement into sections and subsections, appropriate and accessible literary style, neat typesetting and binding, and the like.

The clarity of an experience must be carefully distinguished from the intensity of experience. Intensity and clarity are quite different. Anxiety, for example, is very intense, but hardly clear. It is a very diffuse or general feeling, and it is precisely this quality that sets it apart from fear, which is both clear (specific) and intense. Euphoria is also intense but obscure, while exuberance is intense and clear, and happiness normally merely clear (at least on my understanding of the meanings of these words). In short, clarity is richness and detail of experience. I do not mean that clear experiences must necessarily be complicated, but rather that they give rise to much and do much for us.

"Clarity" (accessibility to personal firsthand experience) and "degree of contextualization" (integration within a coherent personal life narrative) are two parameters corresponding to closely related, but not quite identical, qualities of experience. Analysts, with their external perspective, are better able to judge the degree of contextualization, while clients, with their internal perspective, are better able to speak of the degree of clarity of their conscious experiences. Analysts must use both sources of information when they attempt to understand the manifest and latent content of free association. It follows that we can speak of ego and id when we want to emphasize the perspective of the analyst, and of consciousness and the unconscious when it is more important to emphasize the client's perspective.

Following these definitions, I further define *the unconscious* as the totality of obscure experiences, i.e. the totality of experiences that, owing to their inadequacy and indistinctness, are wholly or partially inaccessible to conscious experiencing. Since these are more likely to be relatively uncontextualized experiences, the unconscious will be largely co-extensive with the id, as I have previously defined it. Similarly, I define the *preconscious* as the totality of clear, and relatively clear, experiences, i.e. the totality of experiences that are, or can be, experienced with relative adequacy and distinctness. Since these are more likely to be relatively contextualized experiences, the preconscious has been defined in such a way that it is largely co-extensive with the ego. The terms unconscious and preconscious have now taken on a topographical sense as well as a descriptive one. We retain the notion of the preconscious as that which can be made conscious with relative ease, and the notion of the unconscious as that which can be made conscious only with relative difficulty. The use of the term "conscious" is primarily descriptive; it indicates what the client is momentarily aware of in the manifest content of free association. The term preconscious refers to relatively clear aspects of the manifest content that are not explicitly being focussed upon by the client at the moment. By and large, however, the client's consciousness will tend to be filled with experiences with a relatively high degree of contextualization, and so as a rule we can speak of consciousness as if it were co-extensive, or at least potentially co-extensive, with the system of the ego.

From this point of view we can state that *contextualization* is the process that prepares experiences (images, ideas, thoughts, and feelings) for compatibility with conscious thinking, i.e. it is the process that effects increases in the clarity (adequacy and distinctness) of experience. It is the process that "moves" a thought closer to consciousness, makes it more amenable to conscious experiencing, since consciousness is more likely to take stock of what is clear than of what is obscure. It is also the process that prevents experiences from becoming conscious, the process that decides what can and cannot, what does and does not need to become conscious. Remembering that the core mental process is a process that takes place within the analytic situation for the purposes of communicating the client's experiences to the analyst, we can add that contextualization makes an experience *more like something that can be shared with another, more like something that someone else could experience, more communicable in the widest and broadest sense of the word.*

Now to return to the question that we posed at the beginning of Chapter 7: what is the relationship of the core mental process to the unconscious? We shall have to answer: the core mental process is the aspect of mental functioning that is responsible for the distinction between conscious and unconscious in the mind. It permeates both id and ego and is responsible both for establishing and for regulating the two-way traffic between both systems. More than that: it can be compared with a selectively permeable membrane that *alters* the nature of the items it allows to pass across its border, making them more suitable to the environment of the new system in which they will then find themselves. The core mental process is the container of the mind, the original matrix in which the mind qua mind comes to be. I see the primary and secondary processes in the classical sense as different aspects of the core mental process, as different but equally important strategies that the mind can use to come to terms with experience. They are not assigned to different areas of the mind, but should rather be considered as different aspects of the mind's core effort to make use of information.

Now there is a further confusion in Freud that I think it is important to address, namely that Freud understands consciousness far too closely along the lines of a perceptual model. The most important consequence for our own metapsychological project is that Freud sees information as streaming into the mind from two opposed directions: from the external world into consciousness, and from the id into the ego. I think this is a mistake. As we have seen, *all* experience, whether internal or external, must first be contextualized before it is suitable for conscious thinking. The important implication is that *all experiences, whether of the internal or external world, whether of the mind or of the body, whether of the self or of another, are all originally unconscious.* Consciousness must always be the *end* of the process of contextualization, never the beginning of the process. Unlike Freud, then, we understand experience in the normal course of events as streaming into the province of the mind through the endless mist-shrouded valleys of the id, undergoing elaboration in successive stages by the work of contextualization, and finally reaching the sunlit summit of consciousness, from whence the experience, altered by its sojourn, can sink back down into the preconscious. Other less ideal procedures are of course also possible.

This is a point of view whose immediate antecedents are to be found in the philosophy of Immanuel Kant and in the metapsychology of Bion (who borrows major aspects of Kant's epistemology without making it clear that he is doing so), but there are also important steps in this direction to be found in the work of Freud as well. In *Totem and Taboo*, for example, we find the following cryptic passage:

> But projection is not made for defence, it also occurs where there is no conflict. The projection of inner perceptions towards the outside is a primitive mechanism to which e.g. our sense perceptions are also subject, and which thus normally has the greatest part to play in the shaping of our external world.
>
> *(1912–13/2003, p. 354)*

There can be no serious doubt that Freud is here expressing a basic adherence to the Kantian doctrine of perception, according to which the raw material furnished by the senses is elaborated through a succession of unconscious mental processes into ever more sophisticated images, and the results of this long series of elaborative modifications finally presented to consciousness as an apparently immediate given in which the mind apparently plays no part. In practice the significance of this doctrine for us is that the basic distinctions upon which conscious experience is founded, such as the distinction between mind and body, self and other, inside and outside, all actively crystallize out of the primeval flow of experience within the matrix of the core mental process. If this is indeed so, if conscious experience is a *product* and not a simple immediate given, it follows that there can also be *errors* in the production of conscious experience. This conceptualization of conscious experiencing has the advantage of making it easier to understand defensive processes such as projection and repression. Projection is a failure of contextualization that involves the false localization of the contents of the mind in the external world, whereas repression can be seen as an attempt to deal with something in the internal world through flight as if it were something in the external world that really could be fled. In short, our experiences of the body, of the external world, and of everything else are all originally unconscious (uncontextualized). It is only as a result of a long and complex process of contextualization that they become elaborate enough to be suitable for conscious experiencing. In our present system of metapsychology this is the only meaning that can be assigned to Freud's notion that the id is the psychic manifestation of biological drives. Everything that is experienced is at first experienced unconsciously. Consciousness is an ending, not a beginning. It is an extremely complex product of a bewildering array of unconscious mental acts the nature of which it is the task of both the analyst and the philosopher to investigate and ultimately to understand (Thera, 1962/2005, pp. 25–29).

Now there is one important aspect in which I would like to distance myself from the Kantian theory of experiencing, and that is with regard to its doctrine of representation. Kant makes the fundamental assumption that it is the task of the mind to form representations, i.e. mental images that are in some non-trivial sense "copies" of originals that are outside the mind. Of course, in Kant's system it turns out that these originals or "things in themselves" are utterly unknowable. Whether or not they are is a matter of indifference from my point of view; I only wish to point out that Kant's emphasis on representation had a deep effect on Freud's own conceptualization of the functioning of the mind. Significant traces of the doctrine are also to be found in Bion, and I think it is fair to say that Piera Aulagnier's theory of the mind is in essence a theory of different forms of representation. Whether or not the representational theory of the mind is correct is a contentious issue among post-Kantian philosophers; I will mention only one criticism that to me seems well-founded. It is obvious that in speaking, for example, of a tree, we are concerned with the tree, and not with the mental image that allows us to speak about the tree – *if* any such thing is really present in our minds. We would immediately notice a difference in the style of speech if a friend began talking about representations instead of trees, just as it would be obvious if someone began talking about "the image on my retina" or about "the glasses on my face" instead of the tree in the garden. However experience happens to be produced, whether through "representations" or through some other means, it is clear that at the everyday level we are intentionally oriented towards the things themselves, and not towards the contents of our own minds.

I think that further considerations make the point still easier to grasp. If we compare the difference between the experiences of taking a car out on the road for the first time, after several months' practice, and for the nth time after 25 years of driving experience, I think it fairly evident that the difference in the quality of the experiences is not to be explained by the different variety of "representations" that are present in our heads in each case. It seems to me that the difference is to be sought in the ability of the mind to make sense of the experience in question. At first the experience in question is overwhelming; then it is complex yet familiar; then it has become so routine that its complexity fades into the background. The basic issue is the degree to which the *original experience*, not a mental picture or "representation" of it, can be handled, made sense of, made use of, given a meaning, and experienced with richness or poverty of content. Again, consider the example of reading a text in a language that we are familiar with but have not yet mastered. Is it the case that we cannot form accurate *representations* of the meaning of the text? Or is it rather the case that the *experience itself* is obscure because we are unable to extract enough meaning from the original text?

In short, I think that working with an *information processing* model of the mind is theoretically more productive and also far more consonant with actual experience than working with a *representational* model of the mind. Representational models, furthermore, have the inconvenience of introducing an epistemic gap between knowledge and experience: if all our knowledge is mediated through representations, how are we supposed to know whether our representations are accurate representations of the originals? Our minds never have any contact with the originals, so there is nothing to compare our representations with to give us a sense of their accuracy. It seems to me that if this doctrine were true, one implication for clinical practice is that it would be impossible for clients to ever understand and overcome transference distortions of the analyst. Information processing models, on the other hand, assume that our experiences basically are experiences of the "originals," and it is merely a question of how much of the significance of those experiences we can grasp, and how well or how poorly we can do so. On this account transference distortions of the analyst can be worked through when our experiences of the analyst are sufficiently contextualized – when individual experiences are weighed against each other, when the influence of the past is recognized and acknowledged, when we occupy ourselves sufficiently with assuring the internal coherence of the various aspects of the experiences in question, and so on.

Now consciousness, as I have already said, always contains a mingling of relatively clear and relatively obscure elements. This is in line with the distinction between the manifest and the latent content of free association. We expect the client to be able to tell us more about the former, and the analyst to tell us more about the latter. The work of association I understand along similar lines as Freud's concept of the dream work, according to which a censor that is turned against intrapsychic innervations attempts to regulate the degree to which they can intrude into consciousness during sleep. In our system, of course, the core mental process is not exactly a censor (though it can also play this role); rather it is a process that is turned against the undifferentiated mass of experience that contains all the information from which both the internal and external worlds are eventually distinguished and elaboratively differentiated. The analyst and the client have different perspectives on the same mental experiences. Something that is plain as day to the analyst might only be dimly perceived by the client. Think of Andersen's tale "The Princess and the Pea": the core mental process corresponds to the mattress in the story; its aim is to ensure the comfort of the princess who lies above, but at the same time it transmits information, however obscure, about what lies beneath. The *work of analysis*, in short, is to support the activity of the core mental process and its work of contextualization of experience. This fact underlines the importance of the influence of others on the proper working of the mind.

One final concluding remark. I have essentially defined the relationship between consciousness (the preconscious) and the unconscious as that of a continuum of degrees of contextualization, so that we can speak of a particular experience as more or less conscious or unconscious, as "deeper" or "shallower" in the layers of the mind. This should not frighten anyone into thinking that I have done away with the absolute concept of the unconscious. There is of course an absolute unconscious in the sense of something that is completely uncontextualized and therefore completely incomprehensible and unknown to consciousness, though its influence can still make itself very much felt. In the vast majority of cases, however,

I think we tend to work in grey areas. After all, if clients cannot confirm our hypotheses about their unconscious experiences – and the absolute unconscious by definition contains experiences about which clients know absolutely nothing – our hypotheses have to remain hypotheses.

## The revised structural model

*Explanation of the diagram*: On the far left of the diagram is the original undifferentiated stream of experience. Here is where information enters the mind. There is initially no distinction between inside and out, mind and body, self and other, real and unreal. On the far right is the consciously elaborated stream of experience: contextualized, a mix of clear with obscure elements, and the result of successive stages of elaboration. It is the level of everyday conscious thinking. The arrows represent the activity of the core mental process, i.e. the progressive work of contextualization. Of particular interest are the last three bent arrows, which illustrate deliberate failures in contextualization, i.e. modes of *defence*. In the case of *secondary repression*, an experience that would normally be accessible to consciousness is held suspended in a preconscious state. This is the type of defence that is involved in the

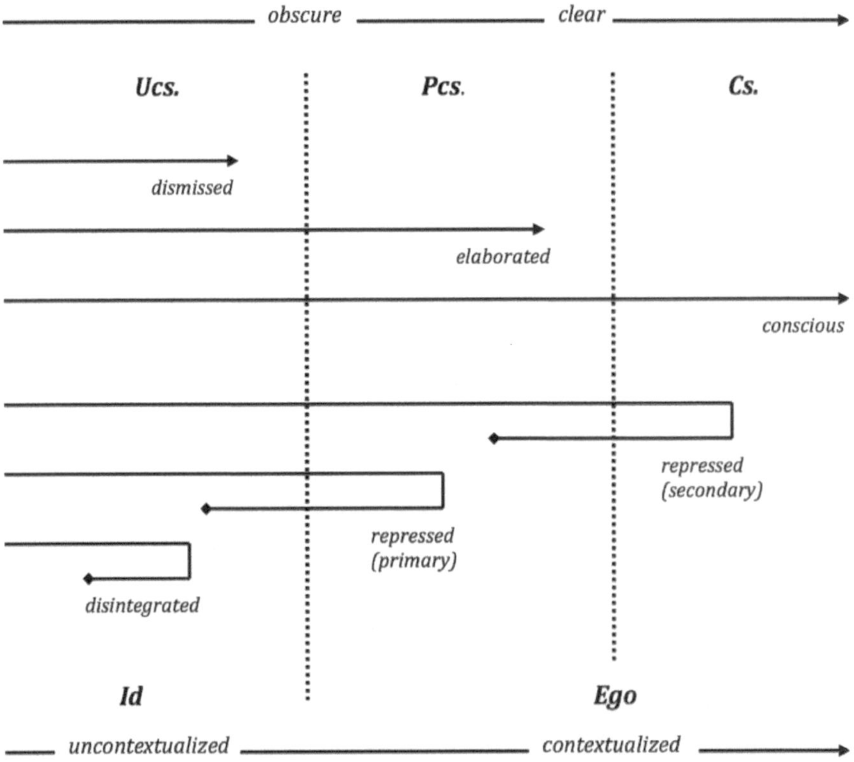


**FIGURE 8.1** The revised structural model

more harmless types of slip that Freud discusses in *The Psychopathology of Everyday Life*. It is relatively transient and relatively easily overcome. In the case of *primary repression*, an experience that has been elaborated to the point where it is potentially suitable for conscious thinking is prevented from appearing in consciousness. It is a relatively sophisticated thought of which one remains unaware, yet it is typically observable by the analyst who witnesses the work of association. It may or may not consist of actual historical events. Primary repression typically involves relatively sophisticated thoughts and so constitutes the level of neurotic suffering. It is not particularly amenable to treatment through self-analysis. In the case of *disintegration* (McDougall's *pulverisation* [1989]), an experience is kept from being elaborated into anything thinkable, and so remains in a primeval, unthought state. Its effects on the mind are crude (e.g. psychosomatic discharge). This is the level of psychotic suffering. All three defensive processes involve the premature interference of dismissal with the process of elaboration. Note that the end point of the arrows is to some extent arbitrary, e.g. in cases of severe dissociation, the dissociated content may lie deep in the unconscious and not in the preconscious. See Chapter 15 for other explanatory details.

## Note

1 These distinctions can fruitfully be compared with similar ones put forth in Locke's *Essay concerning Human Understanding*, II. XXIX.

## References

Freud, S. (1912–13/2003). Totem und Tabu. In S. Freud, *Fragen der Gesellschaft. Ursprünge der Religion* (pp. 291–444). Frankfurt am Main: S. Fischer Verlag.

Locke, J. (1689/2008). *An Essay concerning Human Understanding*. (P. Phemister, Ed.) Oxford: Oxford University Press.

Thera, N. (1962/2005). *The Heart of Buddhist Meditation*. Kandy, Sri Lanka: Buddhist Publication Society.

# 9

# PRIMARY AND SECONDARY EXPERIENCE

I find this an appropriate point to return to an issue that I raised in the previous chapter, namely the repositioning of the primary and secondary processes in our revision of the structural model. As I have already explained, I prefer not to see the primary and secondary processes as convenient means of distinguishing between different regions of the mind. Insofar as it is a question of actual processes, I prefer to see them rather as different strategies that the mind can use to contextualize experience, and so as different aspects of the core mental process. Over and above this technical point, however, I think that there are some basic issues with the way Freud conceptualized the two processes. Freud introduced the distinction between primary and secondary process thinking on the basis of the distinction between the pleasure principle and the reality principle. The type of thinking whose aim is to maximize pleasure and minimize pain through purely mental strategies constitutes the primary process; the type of thinking involved in the secondary process has the same aim, but acknowledges that purely mental strategies are not enough, and so seeks to accommodate mental strategies to the demands of the external world in order to come up with truly workable strategies to avoid pain and maximize pleasure (1911/2001, p. 22). In keeping with this doctrine, Freud assumed that one of the basic tools employed by the primary process in the pursuit of its aim was the *hallucinatory satisfaction of wishes*. Freud further assumed that this method of wish fulfillment was the basic strategy of the infant, and that an atavistic resurgence of this primitive mode of mental functioning during sleep was the basis of the dream.

When one considers the actual evidence for the belief that hallucinatory gratification is the infant's basic strategy for wish fulfillment, one is surprised to find that in fact it is quite slim. Freud appears to have worked backwards from his theory of dreams as wish fulfillments, having made the additional assumption that in sleep we regress to a state of mind that is largely identical with mental functioning in infancy. I fail to see, however, how this assumption can be justified. It seems reasonable enough to grant that the type of thinking that takes place during dreaming is different from the type of thinking that takes place during waking life, but on what basis do we conclude that it is therefore identical with the thinking of the infant? The only truly justified conclusion is that it is a different form of adult thinking, and I think this is fairly evident from the dreams of children, which are also different forms of their own style of thinking, and not unbroken continuations of their waking mental activity. If this is so, what basis can there be for believing that infants indulge in hallucinatory wish fulfillment any more than adults do?

Taken at face value, Freud's theory implies that in the continually wishfully hallucinating infant there is no difference between the mental activity that occurs during the waking and sleeping states. Since the infant has not yet learned to distinguish between fantasy and reality, its hallucinatory activity is not restricted to dream life, as it is in the adult; therefore, it is continually hallucinating, whether awake or asleep, and the two states make no difference to the infant's hallucinatory mental activity. This is, however, most implausible. In fact, the only time this could ever be true is during the period of intrauterine existence; and during this time the infant's needs are automatically met, so that there is no experience of frustration and so also no experience of satisfaction to hallucinate. From all these considerations I conclude that hallucinatory wish fulfillment in adult dreaming is not the atavistic resurgence of an infantile function, but an aspect of a specialized mental function that is common to both the infant and the adult, and that plays a similar role in their respective mental lives.

It now remains to inquire whether the function officially designated as "hallucinatory wish fulfillment" really deserves this designation. I obviously do not wish to deny the presence of wish fulfillment dreams in both infants and adults; I merely wish to clarify the nature of the process that makes wish fulfillment dreams at all possible. Let us begin with the commonly accepted theory of infant experience: just as the hungry adult dreams of food, the hungry infant hallucinates the breast. I see no reason to doubt that the hungry infant has some sort of mental image (a fantasy, if you will) of the breast, whether present or absent; but on what basis do we assume that this mental imagery uniquely consists of attempts at hallucinatory wish fulfillment? What possible purpose could hallucinatory attempts at wish fulfillment serve in the infant? If the infant feels hungry, for example, it seems peculiar to claim that hallucinating a feeding experience could still the infant's hunger. How can a hallucinated breast provide any satisfaction at all when there is a real physiological demand for a real feeding? And if the hallucination can actually satisfy hunger for a time, why can it not satisfy hunger forever? How would the infant ever be able to make contact with reality? Why would it not just blissfully starve to death? Of course the official reply to these objections would be that hallucinatory gratification can indeed satisfy physiological needs for a time, but then the biological demand gains the upper hand and outweighs the limited satisfaction that the hallucinatory gratification is able to offer; to which the correct reply is that if the gratification offered by the supposed hallucinatory process is so limited to begin with, then it hardly makes any sense to designate gratification as its specific purpose.

Turning again to the dream, is it really so certain that it is the guardian of sleep because it satisfies nocturnal desires? Or is it not, perhaps, the guardian of sleep because it transforms a confused and inchoate mental state into one that is clear and structured, and therefore tolerable even if there is no immediate real satisfaction? I see the fundamental process involved not as an attempt at self-gratification through hallucination, but something rather more along the lines of *an ability to formulate a mental image of the need in question* – i.e. a process of contextualization, and therefore something whose functioning is much more in conformity with the reality principle than with the pleasure principle as Freud understood it (Laplanche, 2008, p. 78). Attempts to invoke hallucinatory wish fulfillment to deal with frustration seem to me to be best understood as defensive exploitations of this fundamental mental process, not as expressions of its basic nature.

This whole line of argument can be vastly simplified if we consider the following everyday example. An individual feels sexually excited and has a sexual fantasy in response to this excitement. Now is the purpose of the fantasy really to satisfy the sexual desire in question? If so, it is a matter of common experience that it accomplishes its task quite badly. Is it not rather far more the case that the purpose of the fantasy is to formulate the desire, to give it shape and form, in order to indicate the general lines along which satisfaction of the desire is to be found?

Of course (to drive the point of my argument home) in contemporary practice no one treats dreams as if they were nothing but nocturnal hallucinatory wish fulfillments. The occurrence of what Fairbairn called "state of affairs" dreams, or dreams that simply take stock of the current layout of the dreamer's internal landscape, is far too common (1944/2008, pp. 98–99). I think it is fair to say that even dreams that are obviously wish fulfillments could be assimilated to the "state of affairs" theory, since a wish fulfillment dream would be the result of the sleeping mind taking stock of a desire for the fulfillment of a wish. Again, I think that the results of Freud's investigations were unnecessarily skewed by his basic assumptions. Why can the dream not be seen as the labour of the mind during sleep to make as much sense as it can out of its experience, to elaborate it according to the best means at its disposal during the sleeping state, both in order to cope with the nocturnal demand on the mind for action and in order to offer the waking conscious mind an opportunity for self-investigation and so ultimately more comfortable waking mental functioning? This same point can also be put in a different way. Since, following Freud, we are apparently seeking the origin of adult mental functioning in the mental life of the child, how do we explain the fact that children do universally and consistently form infantile sexual theories, of all things? What exactly is supposed to be the impulse behind this precocious theoretical activity? Surely it is the child's healthy instinct that its natural urges lose much of their urgency when they can be identified, known, and understood? In other words, surely the child feels that knowledge – what I called elaboration – must take away the greater part of the confusion that is created by originally blind emotional and physiological needs whose nature cannot be formulated, clarified, and put into images or words? Why then do we find no trace of this natural need for self-understanding in Freud's theories of dreams? Why is the dream never presented as the mind's best attempt to get to know itself better during sleep? Granted, writers such as Klein make scattered references to the importance of the so-called "epistemophilic impulse" in the mental life of the child, but I fail to see that this innate thirst for knowledge has ever been integrated into psychoanalytic theory in any truly satisfying way, despite Freud's explicit emphasis on the central role that knowledge plays in overcoming the pleasure principle and therefore, we must conclude, also in child development (1911/2001, p. 22).

Let us, then, begin to make good the omission. For the supposedly antagonistic primary and secondary processes of the old structural model we will, accordingly, substitute different and complementary strategies for the comprehension of experience. These will be similar to the three processes identified by Piera Aulagnier, with the exception that we will not understand them as representational, but as elaborative strategies. Now from my previous remarks I think it will be clear that I conceive of the core mental process – the work of contextualization – as an extremely complex and extremely personal, but fundamentally *creative* activity of the mind. Its essential nature is its spontaneous responsiveness to the demands made by the burden of experience. As such, a significant part of the analyst's task with any given client is to understand the client's own particular bundle of personal strategies for coming to terms with experience. This implies in turn that a truly exhaustive and truly universal account of the work of contextualization is not possible. We can, however, outline some of the common tasks that all individuals have to accomplish in the course of their own individual development, and focus on some likely approaches that the majority of individuals will tend to share.

As I mentioned towards the beginning of this chapter, I do not find it convenient to speak of primary and secondary processes as such. However, I do feel that Freud has captured an essential distinction in the way that the mind deals with information, or, if you prefer, an essential distinction in degrees of elaboration of experience (Lecours & Bouchard, 1997). The characteristic feature of experience in the id, according to our revised structural model, is its lack of differentiation. From a conscious point of view, experience at this level of contextualization is largely obscure. Few of the distinctions that we take for granted at the level of conscious thinking have been established, and so the information that the mind can potentially acquire from its experiences has not been processed to the level where it could become truly useful. To apply a convenient metaphor: the id is like a list of words with no definitions that has not yet even been sorted alphabetically. This, incidentally, is not to be taken as implying that the unconscious consists primarily of anything resembling a language; as I hope I have made clear in the preceding chapter, the id contains *all* the experiences and information that the mind has to work with, including non-verbal information, auditory, tactile, and bodily sensations, and intrapsychic stimuli of every sort. I simply mean that the id is a cornucopia of information that as yet lacks any sort of organization or classification, and so has not yet been made useful, like a library that lacks a catalogue. I will call the totality of information that exists in this state *primary* experience.

By contrast, the characteristic feature of information in the ego is its relatively high degree of organization. I call information that exists in this highly organized state *secondary*, or derivative experience. The adjective "derivative" is pertinent because here we are concerned with experience that has been reorganized and therefore modified through the application of a variety of *themes*. These themes have an essentially social nature and function; they are learned ways of coping with the influx of information into the mind, and their ultimate aim is to organize experience so as to make it, first, tolerable, and second, useful, both to the individual and to the social group of which that individual is a member. This is in line with Freud's conception of the ego as the part of the id that has been modified by its relationship with the external world. Again I feel that I must warn against a possible misunderstanding. I do not mean to say that the application of social themes to experience *creates* information where there is none, nor do I mean to put forth any sort of perspectivist theory of truth. I only mean to underline – and this is surely an indubitable point – that different societies do different things with the information that they derive from shared human experience, that they have different ways of coping and coming to terms with the reality that we all share in common.

For all practical purposes, the difference between primary and secondary experience dovetails with the distinction between uncontextualized and contextualized experience. In the latter distinction we mean to emphasize the difference between disorder and order, or the degree of organization that has been effected; in the former distinction we emphasize the difference between immediate and mediated (derivative) ways of knowing: primary experience is naïve, atheoretical, and unsystematic; secondary experience is worldly, theoretical, and systematic. Secondary experience, as I said earlier, arises through the reorganization of primary experience through the application of what I call "themes." I define a *theme* as a rule or principle employed by the core mental process in the act of contextualization. Themes are the interpretative instruments employed by the core mental process in the act of establishing secondary experience on the basis of primary experience. The application of a theme to experience results in a distinct change in the nature of experience that permits it to be recognized as belonging to a certain type or class (this is a preliminary definition; it will turn out later that a theme is actually a fantasy of someone else's judgement of or anticipated reaction to the thing in question). For those familiar with Kant's philosophy, I want to emphasize the difference between my themes and Kant's "categories"; for Kant, a *category* is a representation of a representation, a mental image that structures other mental images, and therefore ultimately representations of external entities as well. It is like a universal mental filter or lens that everyone has and that no one can remove, and that changes experience beyond all possible recognition, making any and all knowledge of the original thing in itself impossible. A theme, as I employ the term, is better compared with a social recipe for the preparation of experience for shared consumption (Berger & Luckmann, 1967). Just as different chefs with different backgrounds could make different dishes from the same ingredients, the themes involved in the work of contextualization allow the core mental process to make sense of experience in a way that anchors individuals with all their individuality in a particular shared social context, and the original ingredients can and should very well be recognizable in the final products.

That the themes involved in the contextualization of experience are acquired and therefore social in nature is obvious to anyone who has, for example, heard a young girl ask her father, "Daddy, when is tomorrow?" or attempted to make sense of the French Republican Calendar. The experience of *time* as such is not created by social themes, but the subjective manner in which we make sense of the experience of objective time takes place within a social framework and has an ultimately social function. Imagine the temporal environment of the ancient Greeks, where the time of day was measured by the length of a shadow, and the difference in the subjective experience of time that this entailed when compared with our modern digital timepieces. The experience of entities within the flow of time also changes along with the differing temporal frameworks that are available in any given social setting. Music that was progressive and revolutionary in the Sixties of the 20th century sometimes sounds dated in the early decades of the 21st century. Classical music can only be heard as "classical" retroactively, not at the time of its creation, when it can only be heard as "contemporary."

On a more personal level, it would seem that for us the primary adult experience of time is *episodic* in nature. It is organized into meaningful units or scenes: eating breakfast, going to the movies, reading a book. The passage of this primary time is variable. It is slower in the dentist's chair than at the ice cream parlour. It does not consist of equal temporal units. By contrast, the secondary experience of time is sequential. It is an inference based upon the use of timepieces: I went into the dentist's office at 3 pm; the watch now shows 3:45 pm; therefore I remained in the dentist's office for 45 equal temporal units. The passage of secondary time is constant: one second per second. It is infinitely divisible into an infinite number of infinitely small temporal units in which the meaningful episodic units of primary time are not present.

The experience of *space* is a social, shared experience as well, from the simple fact of family togetherness all the way to sophisticated conceptualizations of existent and non-existent spaces, i.e. Euclidean and the various non-Euclidian geometries. The infant can as yet have no clear notion of the creative possibilities of working with space. "For the infant, therefore, people will not 'come and go', they will 'appear and disappear' as for us they still do in dreams and in supernatural fantasies" (Suttie, 1935/1999, p. 25). The ability to conceive of an external space filled with others who exist and persist outside of the internal space of the self is a considerable creative achievement.

At a more personal level, it seems that for us the primary adult experience of space consists in the experience of *proximity*. Environmental features are present as near and far. These features cluster together in meaningful units. They form places or areas in which different relations of proximity are present: in the secondary space of the classroom, the teacher's desk is nearer to the blackboard and farther from the students. In primary space, the experience of proximity is extremely elastic. The glasses on my face are farther from me (less proximal) than the students across the room whom I am addressing and upon whom my attention is focussed. Primary space does not consist of equal spatial units of a fixed size. By contrast, the secondary experience of space consists in the experience of extension. Every object has a determinate quantifiable size and is at some determinate quantifiable distance from every other object. Quantification occurs by means of the act of measurement: my glasses are 1 cm from my face, the students are 3 metres from me, therefore my glasses are closer to me than the students. For all practical purposes, the size of secondary space is constant, 1 cm per cm. It is infinitely divisible into an infinite number of infinitely small spatial units in which the meaningful proximal units of primary space are not present.[1]

The image on our retinas is flat, yet we see a world with depth. Consider the existence of dreams with their peculiar simulated worlds. A flat painting of the *trompe l'œil* genre carries all the information from which we can extrapolate a third dimension and perceive the objects in the painting as characterized by depth. No one has ever actually seen the inside of a brick. We infer depth, width, and height from colour and shading, and we infer solidity from primary experiences of perceptions and tactile sensations. There can be no doubt that the mind plays an *active* role in the constitution of our everyday (secondary) experience of ourselves, the world, and others. This is no less true of the experience of the body. When I wish to move my arm, I am not usually aware of the material properties of the arm. I am unaware that it is a solid mass with a certain weight, unaware of its solidity, resilience, the strain placed upon its joints by gravity, of the inner ear fluid which helps me to orient myself in space. Instead, at the level of primary experience there is an image of the limb, of how it looks, functions, and moves. There is a somatic image of each part of the body, all of which collectively make up the lived body. The material body, which is only presented in secondary experience, is by contrast a construction derived from the lived body that is presented in primary experience.

The boundary between the body and the world, between the self and not-self, is also an active achievement of the core mental process. By this I mean to say that the distinction between self and not-self is not simply passively given to the mind; rather it is actively created and maintained. Here again the social nature of the act of construction is clear. Consider the following example:

> How very intimate (propriate) the bodily sense is can be seen by performing a little experiment in your imagination. Think first of swallowing the saliva in your mouth, or do so. Then imagine expectorating it into a tumbler and drinking it! What seemed natural and "mine" suddenly becomes disgusting and alien. Or picture yourself sucking blood from a prick in your finger; then imagine sucking blood from a bandage around your finger! What I perceive as belonging intimately to my body is warm and welcome; what I perceive as separate from my body becomes, in the twinkling of an eye, cold and foreign.
> *(Allport, 1955/1961, p. 43)*

If we view these examples with a psychoanalytic eye, we can hardly fail to see the pervasive role that toilet training, along with its associated themes, plays in the experience of the distinction between self and not-self, between things that are part of the body and therefore "warm and welcome," and things that become "cold and foreign" due to their sojourn outside of the body. It therefore seems natural to conclude, as Freud did, that the first ego is a body-ego, i.e. that the word "self" originally means "body." Yet even if this is true at a primary level of experience, the progressive work of contextualization generates a vast multiplicity of secondary experiences of the self:

> When asked, some people will say that they *feel* the self in their right hands, or in the viscera. Most, however, seem to agree [...] that a center midway between the eyes, slightly behind them within the head, is the focus. It is from this cyclopean eye that we estimate what lies before and behind ourselves, to the right or left, and above and below. Here, phenomenologically speaking, is the locus of the ego.
>
> *(Allport, 1955/1961, p. 42)*

This is, however, still a commonsensical notion of the self, one that is based on a relatively high level of contextualization, and therefore one that is highly rooted in social themes. Some authors in the meditative tradition have been able to use willed auto-inhibition of the core mental process to generate glimpses of an entirely different experience of self, one that is perhaps closer to the primeval infant experience, though the results clearly bear traces of an attempt to tear free from adult thinking:

> Somehow or other I had thought of myself as inhabiting this house which is my body, and looking out through its two little round windows at the world. Now I find it isn't like that at all. As I gaze into the distance, what is there at this moment to tell me how many eyes I have here – two, or three, or hundreds, or none? In fact, only one window appears on this side of my façade, and that one is wide open and frameless and immense, with nobody looking out of it. It is always the other fellow who has eyes and a face to frame them; never this one.
>
> There exist, then, two sorts – two widely different species – of human being. The first, of which I note countless specimens, evidently carries a head on its shoulders (and by "head" I mean an opaque and coloured and hairy eight-inch ball with various holes in it) while the second, of which I note only one specimen, evidently carries no such thing on its shoulders.
>
> *(Harding, 1986/2004, pp. 29–30)*

It is clear, I think, from these examples that a very wide range of differing experiences of the self and the body is still possible within the domain of the "average and ordinary." That there are contextualizations of self and body experiences that are highly problematic cannot be doubted; we need only consider the significance of distorted self-images in the occurrence of body dysmorphic disorder, gender identity disorder, and the various eating disorders to prove the point. As well, important links have been made between the distortions of the experiences of space and time and the psychogenesis of borderline personality disorder and psychotic states (Rey, 1996). Other writers have traced the themes that shape the fundamental experience of the body back to the mother's handling of the child's body during routine care and during play (Bollas, 2000/2006). For the psychoanalytically minded, all of these factors underline the importance of the social element in the work of contextualization that begins within the family milieu and continues within the individual mind. In traditional Freudian terms, the analysis of childhood is vital to an understanding of the mode of being of the adult.

Despite the importance of this field of study and its relative neglect by psychoanalytic investigation, I will not attempt to make good this omission here; the possible lines of inquiry are simply too numerous, and the area to explore simply too vast. We will not follow Kant in making the investigation of the themes and the limits of their application to experience the main object of our undertaking.

I will end, instead, with a concise statement of the facts as I see them in the form of a paraphrase of a citation from the work of Philip K. Dick. The fundamental building block of the universe is information; ultimately there are neither temporal nor spatial phenomena, but only experiences to which we attribute independent substantial existence and that we reinterpret as spatial and temporal phenomena (Dick, 1991, p. 230). We will return to this idea in Chapter 18.

## Note

1 Note that what I called primary space and time in the above examples are only relatively so; they too arise through the application of the relatively unsophisticated themes "episode" and "proximity," and thus already represent an elaboration of the absolutely ineffable character of time and space insofar as they are primeval raw givens. My aim is simply to illustrate the deep involvement of creative mental activity in the contextualization of everyday experience.

## References

Allport, G. W. (1955/1961). *Becoming. Basic Considerations for a Psychology of Personality.* New Haven: Yale University Press.

Berger, P. L., & Luckmann, T. (1967). *The Social Construction of Reality. A Treatise in the Sociology of Knowledge.* New York: Anchor Books.

Bollas, C. (2000/2006). *Hysteria.* London and New York: Routledge.

Dick, P. K. (1991). *VALIS.* New York: Vintage Books.

Fairbairn, W. R. (1944/2008). Endopsychic Structure Considered in Terms of Object-Relationships. In W. R. Fairbairn, *Psychoanalytic Studies of the Personality* (pp. 82–136). London and New York: Routledge.

Freud, S. (1911/2001). Formulierungen über die zwei Prinzipien des psychischen Geschehens. In S. Freud, *Psychologie des Unbewußten* (pp. 17–24). Frankfurt am Main: S. Fischer Verlag.

Harding, D. E. (1986/2004). *On Having no Head. Zen and the Rediscovery of the Obvious.* Carlsbad, CA: Inner Directions Publishing.

Laplanche, J. (2008). *Nouveaux fondements pour la psychanalyse.* Paris: Quadrige/Presses Universitaires de France.

Lecours, S., & Bouchard, M.-A. (1997). Dimensions of Mentalisation: Outlining Levels of Psychic Transformation. *International Journal of Psycho-Analysis* 78: 855–875.

Rey, H. (1996). *Universals of Psychoanalysis in the Treatment of Psychotic and Borderline States. Factors of Space-Time and Language.* London: Free Association Books.

Suttie, I. D. (1935/1999). *The Origins of Love and Hate.* London: Free Association Books.

# 10

# THE WORK OF OBJECTIFICATION

I have found it convenient to divide the work of contextualization into three major aspects: the *work of objectification*, the *work of imagination*, and the *work of symbolization*. I see these as three complementary ways of making sense of experience. One can, if one wants, set these within the framework of a rough hierarchy, but I see no real need to do so. It is true that one has to feel comfortable with the fundamentals of making music before one goes on to play complex pieces, but the fundamentals are never replaced by the complexities whose basis they are; and not everyone has to be a virtuoso.

In selecting precisely these three aspects of the work of contextualization I have made use of Freud's original distinction between primary and secondary processes as well as Piera Aulagnier's rationale for adding a third level of functioning that is in some sense more fundamental than both. I have replaced the activity of the primary process by the work of imagination and that of the secondary process by the work of symbolization because I feel that these two, fantasy and language, are the essence of Freud's conceptualizations of the two processes. I will try to demonstrate the truth of this assertion in the chapters that explicitly address the work of imagination and contextualization. For Aulagnier's *processus originaire* I have substituted what I call the work of objectification, feeling that most of what Aulagnier has to say about the *pictogramme* can be assimilated to the work of imagination. I also feel that Aulagnier's distinction between the three processes retains too much of the "stagist" thinking that marred early psychoanalytic metapsychology. This type of thinking divides human development into neat stages, the successful completion of each of which is a prerequisite for progress to the next stage. The metapsychological result is a conceptualization of mental agencies in terms of a hierarchy that is simultaneously a chronology. Thus for Aulagnier, the *processus originaire* is chronologically the first and mentally the most primitive stage of functioning; it is followed by primary process thinking, and succeeded by secondary process thinking. In fact what we observe even in severely damaged clients is rather a greater or lesser degree of confusion between mental systems and styles of thinking, and sometimes a predominance of one type of process over another; the rigid logical-chronological sequence is never observed. Against the predictions of stagist models, there is no straightforward one-to-one correlation between deficiencies in more basic and in more advanced psychic structures. Someone with psychotic personality traits can very well also be a tremendously accomplished, sensitive, and creative individual. The history of the arts and sciences is replete with such figures, including Vincent van Gogh, Virginia Woolf, Isaac Newton, Kurt Gödel, and many others.

In this chapter I will focus on the fundamental process that Freud called *reality-testing*. Although I have argued against the thesis that the infant's basic strategy for dealing with frustration is hallucinatory satisfaction, it does seem quite plausible to me that infants initially have some difficulty telling the difference between fantasy and reality, and that the ability to make this distinction develops over time. In our model too, as we have seen, there is initially an undifferentiated stream of experiencing from which content is spontaneously elaborated by the activity of the core mental process. In other words, one important aspect of the work of contextualization is the decision regarding what type or class a given experience belongs to, namely fantasy or reality, intrapsychic or extrapsychic, mind or body, self or other, and so on. Although I have tried to preserve the use of traditional psychoanalytic terminology as much as possible, in the case of "reality-testing" I have made an exception. In the first place, I find the term too narrow: the mental work I have in mind is responsible not only for establishing the distinction of real versus unreal, but also for elaborating our experience of time, space, causality, objectivity, and so on. As well, I find that Freud's use of the term tends to imply that the basic fundamental distinction between real versus unreal happens definitively, once and for all, somewhere in the unconscious, whereas I see the involved processes as beginning deep in the unconscious, but remaining inconclusive for vast stretches of elaboration as they continue to extend into the highest reaches of consciousness, where they appear as the deliberate pursuit of careful and methodical, and yet open-minded, investigation – ideally, at any rate. (On the subject of reality-testing also compare note 1 of Chapter 13.)

I do not believe, in other words, that the distinction between real and unreal is established firmly and definitively prior to all subsequent experiencing. To borrow a concept from Winnicott, I believe that the vast majority of our conscious experiencing takes place in a "transitional space." I do not, however, see this as a "third" space that is distinguished from an "objective" and a "subjective" space by our refusal to make up our minds which it is. Rather, I see our everyday experience as a complex commingling of given and actively contributed elements (i.e. of primary and secondary experience), a spontaneous creative achievement of the human mind from which the "objective" and "subjective" spaces can be further distilled by means of another spontaneous creative achievement. *Everyday experience is itself the result of a creative act.* Everyday experience is a product, not a brute given; it is a "transitional space," but in this respect it is not the result of an uneasy compromise between the inflexible demands of external objective reality and the internal subjective omnipotence of the infant. The transitional (undifferentiated) space is given first, as the basis of all subsequent experiencing; it is not a blending of "hard" external and "soft" internal reality brought about by the refusal to enforce the distinction. Rather, it is within the transitional space itself that the distinction between "objective" and "subjective" can first be established and subsequently maintained. To borrow a metaphor from Joyce McDougall, everyday experience is the theatre in which we stage the play of our lives, the play of ourselves. The terms "objective" and "subjective" only have meaning within the unfolding action of the play, not outside of it; and if they do have a meaning outside the play, it is an entirely different meaning.

For all these reasons I have chosen to call the totality of processes involved in the initial classification of experience the *work of objectification*. This is a term inspired by the philosophy of Schopenhauer (1818/1988), the further details of which do not concern us here. The important point is that the work of objectification, in my sense of the term, has a dual meaning. It is, first, the process by which the existence of an objective, independent world is opposed to the existence of a subjective, internal world. Second, it is by extension also the process by which the existence of "objects" is established, in the technical psychoanalytic sense of the word "object." In short, the work of objectification is the reorganization of experience according to multiple external perspectives that differ from the initial, purely internal perspective of the self. It is the application of the theme "Reality" to primary experience.

There is almost certainly a biological basis of the work of objectification, as we know from the possibility of interfering with its functioning through the administration of hallucinogens, psychedelics, and the vast spectrum of psychoactive drugs. As analysts, however, as I have previously underlined, we are properly concerned not with psychophysiology or with psychopharmacology, but exclusively with the mental analogues of the corresponding biological processes. We are not concerned with the physiology of perception as such, but with clients' experiences of perception, with the fantasies and feelings that they link with the act of perception. It is accordingly upon these that the following investigations will be focussed. For what follows, the biological aspect of the work of objectification is certainly interesting, but at the same time not directly pertinent.

To anticipate a later point for the sake of clarity: objectification begins when the infant is able to question enough of its primary experience to realize at the level of secondary experience that there are indeed others like itself that are outside itself. I think ultimately this must mean something like the recognition that there are needs in the surrounding environment that the infant does not itself experience as needs, but that some other does. The official doctrine is of course that the recognition of other people begins when the infant realizes that it has experiences that it does not *control*, but this seems to me to be a deficient argument. As we know, it is quite clear that there are very many aspects of the mind and the body that we do not control in the least, and yet we still experience them as *our* mind and *our* body. Furthermore, the folk psychology upon which this psychoanalytic viewpoint is based would have us believe that the sense of control comes from the exercise of the will followed by the obedience of the mind or body; but as Schopenhauer has pointed out (1818/1988, § 18), there is no such thing as an act of will prior to and distinct from the supposedly ensuing willed act. Both occur together or not at all. Furthermore, there is no such act as *willing harder* if your body or mind doesn't respond. If this is the case, one can hardly assert that the sense of self arises by empirically testing which events do and do not respond to energetic acts of willing. The sense of self ultimately must be something entirely different than a sense of control and its lack, something far more plastic that has, perhaps, far more to do with the capacity for empathy than with a need to outline the world with lines of control. In any case, although the ultimate origin of the sense of self remains obscure for the moment, we can content ourselves with the definition of objectification as *the recognition of a personally binding not-me*, i.e. the acknowledgement of an external reality. The precise concrete forms that this recognition takes will ultimately differ from environment to environment, and so from society to society, family to family, and individual to individual.

What, then, is the origin of the theme of Reality? Let us consider this question in a little more detail. The main accomplishment of the work of objectification, as we have seen, is the establishment of a perspective that permits the recognition of an independently existing and persisting outside world. It is the fundamental act of contextualization that makes the experience of a separate surrounding environment possible. A rather more technical way of putting the same point is the following: the work of contextualization is the mental act that allows the individual to move from primary undifferentiated experience to a set of commonly agreed on, socially acknowledged (but not necessarily socially constructed) rules for construing this experience within a shared frame of reference. It is the act that allows us to create and maintain the distinction between "inside" and "outside," between a "subjective" and "objective" world in the everyday sense of these terms. But what exactly does this act of contextualization involve? What are its presuppositions, and what are the specific operations it performs on primary experience in order to transform it into the secondary experience of a shared external world?

I propose to answer these questions in the following way. Consider again, for a moment, the distinction between primary and secondary experience. Secondary experience is dependent upon primary experience, from which it is derived by the work of contextualization. Now what must the criterion of Reality be when we move along the continuum of experience towards the level of minimal contextualization? The less elaboration has taken place, the more we are dependent on the immediate givens of our senses. When we are currently involved in the experience of something, it is clear that that something exists; and when the experience of that something ceases, it can be said not to exist, at least for all practical purposes. We have already alluded to this criterion of Reality in our previous discussion of the experience of space: it is likely that for the infant, who can as yet have no concept of independent existence, people seem to pop into and out of existence, rather than continuing to persist independently of the infant's experience of them, or lack thereof (Suttie, 1935/1999, p. 25). The classical rational elaboration of this point of view is to be found in the works of Berkeley, and it is concisely expressed by his famous slogan "*esse* is *percipi*," "to be is to be perceived" (1988, p. 54). We can render the same idea in somewhat more colloquial English by quoting the old saying: "Out of sight is out of mind," and if we add to this the sentiment expressed by the phrase "seeing is believing," we arrive at a position something like the following: "Reality equals experience, and what is not experienced is not Real."

This criterion leads, of course, to a number of difficulties that philosophers especially have taken great pleasure in investigating. We normally believe that solid objects have an inside that we cannot see or feel; that whatever has a front must have a back, notwithstanding its momentary inaccessibility; and that despite Sylvia Plath's profoundly startling poetic assertions to the contrary, the world does not actually drop dead when we shut our eyes, and is not actually born again when we lift our lids (1981, p. 207). According to the basic criterion for Reality that we have just formulated, however, none of these statements is true. When I close the door of my closet, the inside of the closet must in fact cease to exist, since there is no one present in the closet to experience it from the inside. It is clear, then, that the notion of the continuing existence of the inside of the closet in the absence of anyone to experience it is a type of inference from or modification of primary experience, and according to the strict criterion of Reality that we have laid down, no contextualization of this experience is permitted. Only what is immediately given in experience, without inference or addition, is truly Real.

Philosophers of the Idealist persuasion have made much of this apparent paradox, and I will only say that from a philosophical perspective one particular error of Idealism consists in holding too strongly to a criterion of Reality that confuses *non-verifiable* states with *non-existent* states. Our immediate interest, however, is to understand what must happen within the mind for the transition from a primary to a secondary experience of Reality to occur. Interestingly enough, Berkeley's works contain a hint of the solution to this problem. We find that Berkeley, unwilling to surrender the point of view that "existing is being perceived," and equally unwilling to surrender the concept of the independent existence of entities outside of the immediate sphere of experience, introduces the notion of a *universal observer* that he calls by the name of "God":

> HYLAS: [...] Ask the fellow, whether that tree has an existence out of his mind: what answer think you he would make?
>
> PHILONOUS: The same that I should myself, that is, that it does exist out of his mind. But then to a Christian it cannot surely be shocking to say, the real tree existing without his mind is truly known and comprehended by (that is, *exists in*) the infinite mind of God.
>
> *(1988, p. 182)*

The analyst familiar with the theories of Winnicott and his school of thought will of course immediately think of what Bollas calls "God the mother" (2000/2006, p. 16; Winnicott, 1988, pp. 114–115); but before we further explore this line of thought it is worth considering the implications in a little more detail. The ability to recognize the independent existence of a persistent external world is a direct function of the ability to acknowledge that what I cannot experience may indeed be experienced by someone else. This amounts to the recognition that I am not the sole locus of experience; rather, there is another who is equally well an experiencer, and whose experience differs in at least some respects from my own, and who therefore constitutes an independent and equally valid locus of experience. There is another who is also the world's vortex (Peake, c. 1939/2008, pp. 44–45), another who has stolen the world from me (Sartre, 1943, p. 301).

There is, then, no secondary experience of Reality without the fantasized other. *The experience of Reality is at bottom the experience, within one's own self, of a fantasy of another's point of view.* It is clear that the notions of "persistence," "independent existence," "continuity of experience," and so on, are all linked with the notion of an observer, separate from the self, with a different perspective on the same experience. I call this the fantasy of the universal observer. The fundamental characteristic of the universal observer is its ability to see and know beyond the limits of the individual. It allows us to conclude that even though we ourselves can only see the front of the box, someone else with a different perspective could see the back of the box, and therefore the back of the box exists along with the front, even though the front is all we can see at the moment. The fantasy of the universal observer, it should be noted, does not prevent us from making mistakes at times. It may well be that we occasionally mistake a *trompe l'œil* painting for the real thing. The value of the fantasy of the universal observer does not lie in certainty, but in possibility. The ability to imagine alternate perspectives does not make us incapable of error, but it does allow us to imagine a world that exists above and beyond the narrow range of experiences disclosed in the immediacy of the senses. The universal observer allows us to transcend ourselves and reach out to the others who exist in the world along with us. In this act of contextualization – the disclosure of the possibility of otherness, and so also the possibility of a reliably persisting environment, i.e. one that does not pop into and out of existence according to the fluctuations of primary uncontextualized experience – individuals can also discover themselves. This is so because ultimately where there is no witness, there is also no self. The fantasy of the universal observer is an essential concomitant of the intrapsychic function that permits the mind to establish its own stable and persisting environment, both externally and internally. Where this function is damaged, one's sense of the real is undermined, and so one's relationships both with others and with one's own self are disturbed.

How are we to understand the fantasy of the universal observer in psychoanalytic terms? Following Berkeley's lead, it is easy to begin by making a link between the universal observer and the fantasy of God. Many children are told that God is an omniscient being who always sees and knows what everyone is doing and thinking. From here it is a small step to the concept of the super-ego. Now it is clear that the super-ego is a complex mental structure whose function is obviously not limited to accomplishing the work of objectification. Nevertheless, I see the work of objectification as central to the super-ego structure, for without the concept of an outside other, none of the more elaborate super-ego functions can be accomplished, including praise and censure, guilt and reconciliation, the assumption of responsibility, and self-judgement according to a shared moral standard (Bouchard & Lecours, 2004). All of these concepts are essentially relational in the sense that they necessarily imply a relationship with others. It goes without saying that this is an extremely complex topic that cannot be comprehensively addressed within the limited space at my disposal. My fundamental concern is merely to grasp the essence of the fundamentally relational character of super-ego activity and to trace it back to its original source.

As we have seen, the recognition of Reality requires the ability to imagine how one's own experience would appear from someone else's perspective. This ability makes the progression from primary to secondary experience possible. It will be recalled that the low level of contextualization of primary experience precludes any clear distinction between self and other. This mode of experiencing is the basis of what Freud conceptualized as primary narcissism. Secondary experience requires contextualization on the basis of the recognition of the other, or, to speak plainly, an abandonment of the self as the only conceivable nexus of the universe. Secondary experience is only possible when primary experience is contextualized according to external criteria. Secondary experience can therefore be understood as *the result of the effect of the recognition of the other upon the mind.* From here it is but a short step to the realization that the totality of the activity of the core mental process – the work of contextualization as such, not merely the work of objectification – is an artefact of the early experience of the other.

The demonstration of this point does not require any observations beyond those available within the framework of classical analysis and its view of the super-ego. It is, I think, reasonably clear that in the adult experience of the super-ego important aspects of the infant's experience of both its parents are preserved. There is, for example, the experience of the parents as the arbitrators of what it is and is not permissible to think, i.e. the function of the parents as the originators of repression. As well, the super-ego dictates *how* the individual should think about experience, and in this respect it can be seen as the repository of culture and tradition. It is also highly likely that any form of self-observation can ultimately be seen as a derivative of super-ego functioning, since self-observation requires the capacity to see the self from another external point of view, and the super-ego is the internal carrier of external perspective *par excellence*. More contemporary inquiries (Bion, 1962/1977; Winnicott, 1967/1999) have drawn attention to the fact that children apparently do not know their own thoughts except insofar as their parents, and most especially their mothers, are able to think them on their behalf and re-introduce them into their minds in a thinkable form. This suggests that children often experience their parents as (apparently) knowing their children better than they, the children, know themselves. From this point of view, the super-ego – or the "internal object," to use a wider and more modern concept – is the agent of cognition as well, to be identified with the thinking part of the mind (Loewald, 2000, pp. 539–540). This dovetails nicely with our view that the core mental process is an artefact of the influence of the other upon the self.

The narcissistic gratification that can be derived from basic super-ego functioning is well understood. One can enjoy being the saintliest of saints or the chief of sinners (or, more commonly, both). But there is another source of narcissistic gratification associated with the super-ego that is, perhaps, less familiar. The super-ego gives the infant a sense of familiarity with itself. It imposes form upon originally formless chaos. As well, the super-ego allows us to identify things that we can experience at first hand, such as our own thoughts and bodily sensations, that another could *not* experience in this way. Thus the infant is enabled, for increasingly long periods of time, to be its own other. The infant can think its own thoughts without outside help. It can make and keep its own self-made laws. The function of the super-ego is not just to limit thought (repression), but ideally at least, to encourage creative individual thinking as well. The recognition of Reality – taking others' points of view into account and reacting to them with a profoundly individual creative response – can be a moral and ethical imperative. This all implies that potentially at least, the recognition of Reality can in itself be a major source of personal satisfaction. Knowledge is an acceptable substitute for power. It is here that we find one major origin of the otherwise so mysterious "epistemophilic impulse." Of course, this is obviously also one of the aspects of super-ego functioning that we hope to influence for the better in the course of analysis. Insight can be experienced as rewarding in itself independently of the obvious benefits it confers – though it is also a major task of analysis to familiarize ourselves with the latter.

The intellectual elaboration within philosophy of the primary ("narcissistic") experience of the world gives rise to the doctrine of Idealism: the position that the world has no true existence independent of the perceiving mind, and that all true existence is ultimately mental in nature. In our terms, all such reflections boil down to the following: there is no coherent secondary experience of Reality without the internal fantasized experience of an internal fantasized other that gives form and structure, and therefore the capacity for continuity and coherence, to the mind, the world, and the self. In my own language I prefer to call this internal experience of an internal other the fantasy of the universal observer; in traditional Freudian terms, it can be more or less identified with the core functioning of the super-ego. This should not be construed as an attempt at a psychoanalytical refutation of Idealism, which, it will be recalled, is something that I would consider an oxymoron (Chapter 2). In this place I intend only to point out the experiential wellspring from which Idealism has drawn.

Taking all of the preceding into consideration, it is both surprising and disappointing that Freud himself (in the fifth last paragraph of section VIII of "Group Psychology and the Analysis of the Ego") at one time attributed the function of reality-testing to the "ego ideal" (1921/1997, p. 107), only to change his mind and later attribute it to the ego. Perhaps this error was due to his tendency to neglect the role of the mother in the formation of the super-ego and his extremely strong inclination to see in both the ego ideal and the super-ego only a crystallization of the child's relationship with its father. I find it more plausible to see the super-ego as the most fundamental image of otherness, and as such its psychological origin is to be sought in the infant's primeval experience of the other, in its experience of its first primary caretaker, to whom it is usually most convenient to refer as the infant's mother. The core of the super-ego is the recognition of something with desires that need to be satisfied but that are not the infant's own. This is why, at higher levels of contextualization, it is the recognition of the real external world, of necessities to which one has to conform but that are not of one's own choosing; this is also why, in a different sphere, it can be linked with the concept of God. It is here in this primeval and foundational relationship that we must seek the origin of the intrapsychic interplay with the universal observer.

## References

Berkeley, G. (1988). *Principles of Human Knowledge/Three Dialogues*. London: Penguin Books.

Bion, W. R. (1962/1977). Learning from Experience. In W. R. Bion, *Seven Servants*. New York: Jason Aronson, Inc.

Bollas, C. (2000/2006). *Hysteria*. London and New York: Routledge.

Bouchard, M.-A., & Lecours, S. (2004). Analyzing Forms of Superego Functioning as Mentalizations. *International Journal of Psycho-Analysis* 85: 879–896.

Freud, S. (1921/1997). Massenpsychologie und Ich-Analyse. In S. Freud, *Fragen der Gesellschaft. Ursprünge der Religion* (pp. 65–134). Frankfurt am Main: S. Fischer Verlag.

Loewald, H. W. (2000). Psychoanalysis and the History of the Individual. In H. W. Loewald, *The Essential Loewald* (pp. 529–579). Hagerstown, MD: University Publishing Group.

Peake, M. (c. 1939/2008). *Collected Poems*. Manchester: FyfieldBooks/Carcanet.

Plath, S. (1981). *The Bell Jar*. New York: Bantam Books.

Sartre, J.-P. (1943). *L'être et le néant. Essai d'ontologie phénoménologique*. Paris: Éditions Gallimard.

Schopenhauer, A. (1818/1988). *Die Welt als Wille und Vorstellung. Erster Band*. (L. Lütkehaus, Ed.) Zurich: Haffmans Verlag.

Suttie, I. D. (1935/1999). *The Origins of Love and Hate*. London: Free Association Books.

Winnicott, D. W. (1967/1999). Mirror-role of Mother and Family in Child Development. In D. W. Winnicott, *Playing and Reality* (pp. 111–118). Hove and New York: Brunner-Routledge.

Winnicott, D. W. (1988). *Human Nature*. New York and London: Routledge.

# 11

# THE WORK OF IMAGINATION

The main conclusions that I would like to draw from the preceding chapter (Chapter 10) are the following. It is well known that the ability to see cannot develop if no light is permitted to enter the eye. If children born blind have their sight restored later on in life, they may develop some limited capacity for seeing, but as a rule they never attain the degree of visual acuity that is possessed by a person with the usual developmental background. While it is unnecessary to be quite so pessimistic in the case of analysis, this much is clear: the ability to make sense of the elements of experience cannot develop without a social environment that confers an initial structure to individual experience. There is, if you like, a need for the shared social "illumination" of experience in order for an individual to have experiences at all; and this is ultimately true even of private experiences. We can express this interesting state of affairs in the following way: *individuals cannot contextualize any experience for themselves that is not first contextualized on their behalf by another person* (Freud, 1895/1950, p. 331). With regard to entirely novel, entirely individual experiences, we can say that at least the basis of the contextualization of these experiences must have been given to the individuals in question by another person. They must have had a good-enough basis to start from in order to go on to have their own experiences. Without this core of validation of experience by another human being there ultimately can be no contextualization and therefore no mind.

I have found it necessary to underline this point repeatedly throughout the course of my ongoing exposition, perhaps more dogmatically than I would have preferred, for I think it is a point that requires some rather extensive demonstration. Nevertheless, here as elsewhere we run up against the inherent and unavoidable difficulties of communicating the nature of analytic experience to third parties. In order to illustrate the point I want to make regarding the origin of the mind, I find it necessary to resort to a type of storytelling, for the simple reason that I do not wish to give an account of any particular person's mind, but of the mind as such, the mind qua mind (Chapter 1). In order to do this I obviously cannot provide biographical detail; what is required is a type of "just so" story, a narrative that is flexible enough to explain the usual state of affairs without pretending that it can account for every possible variation. It is, if you like, a deliberate myth with possible heuristic and explanatory value, but one that cannot be wholly applied to any particular person without appropriate modification. In short, I need to resort to an *analytic construction*.

I know that in speaking of the relationship between the infant and its primary caregiver and of the influence of this relationship on the formation of the mind I am going to be taking a path through well-travelled territory that has been covered by many authors, including, but of course not limited to, the following: (Benjamin, 1990; Chodorow, 2010; Kohut, 1971/2009; Mahler, Pine, & Bergman, 1975/2000; Ogden, 1983). In reviewing the literature on the subject I came to the conclusion that my readers are best served if I put forth a modest yet transparent account that eschews detailed criticism of these other writers. Sometimes the best approach to a tangled thicket is not to try to disentangle all the individual branches but just to go around it and avoid it altogether. I apologize to any proponents of these theories who may feel that in so doing I am reinventing the wheel; my only reply is that if any one of these existing theories were as simple and straightforward a device as the wheel, there would have been no need for me to write this book in the first place. In any case my goals are not ambitious; I do not wish to put forth a complete theory of infant psychological development, but to highlight several specific features of that development that are important to understanding the development and functioning of the mind.

I have already explained and defended the use of constructions in analysis in an earlier chapter (Chapter 3). I will take a few moments to expand upon this justification. The process of analysis is a type of human relationship that is intended to support the activity of the core mental process. It is a sort of shared work that has as its aim the furthering of the work of contextualization. In traditional terminology, the goal of analysis was expressed as the undoing of repression; within the framework of the present system, we can make much the same point by saying that analysis offers an opportunity to re-process and so retell the greater part of one's own life story. Everyone who has had a successful experience of analysis knows how, over time, the pieces of the puzzle slowly begin to fall into place, how one's past experiences slowly begin to make sense where before they seemed incomprehensible or unfathomable. In the course of this process, constructions – well-founded and well-timed educated guesses as to what might or might not have been a significant past experience, or what might be a significant present experience in the unconscious – play a significant role. In practice, the validity of constructions is confirmed in any of three ways: *pragmatically*, by the obvious healing effect they have; *historically*, by the memories that clients recall over the course of analysis and by accounts provided by other family members; and *hermeneutically*, by the increasing sense they make of clients' personal life stories.

I find that analysts are all too inclined, when speaking of truth in analysis, to gravitate to one of two extremes: either to maintain that analysis does not occupy itself with the truth, but exclusively with fantasy (this is the more modern tendency); or alternatively to conceive of analysis as a type of archaeological work and to maintain that its task is to reconstruct the whole of clients' infantile histories with the greatest literal accuracy possible (this is the more classical tendency). While we must not underestimate client individuality – there may indeed be individual analyses in which an extreme attitude towards the truth is just what is needed – as a general rule, I find that analysis is most comfortable in a position somewhere between the two extremes. It is not correct to say that analysis occupies itself exclusively with fantasy, for in the contextualization of their fantasies clients gain greater access to, and a greater appreciation for, the factual events in their own personal life histories. And it is not correct to say that analysis is focussed on the quasi-archaeological reconstruction of the past, for reconstruction cannot occur without an appreciation of the fantastic element that necessitates the act of reconstruction, and it is often a reconstruction not of actual events, but of the history of the inner fantasy life of the client that has the desired curative effect.

It is much more accurate, in my view, to say that the work of analysis is centred on increased contextualization of experience, and whether the work of analysis takes us more in the direction of literal history or more in the direction of fantasy is really a function of the individual needs of the client in question at any given time. It is not a decision that analysts have to take. There is, I think, no truer statement that can be made about the work of analysis than that it is precisely in aiming directly at the truth that we are most likely to miss the truth.

The following construction, then, is in essence a synthesis of many different observations during analysis, a summary of many different constructions that have been more or less successful in a variety of situations and with a variety of clients. It is not meant as an authoritative scientific statement about infant experience or about the origin of the mind. It is meant rather as a pragmatic tool by the use of which the field of meaning in the analytic exchange can be expanded and enriched. This is not to say that I believe it to have no truth value whatsoever. The fact that constructions about events that can eventually be recalled and verified are often more accurate than not leads us to suspect, in turn, that constructions about events that cannot be recalled and verified are also often more accurate than not. But in any case, in analysis, as in so many fields of life, the proof of the pudding is in the eating.

I believe that we must – for now at least – conceive of the infant as originally *mindless*. By this I mean that there is at first no core mental process and therefore also no process of contextualization. (Where these processes do take place, I will, for the moment, speak of a mind being present in contrast to the infant's original mindlessness.) The infant has no internal means of making sense of its experience, at least as far as we can tell. This means that in the infant there is no process of contextualization, and thus nothing resembling a core mental process as we have described it in previous paragraphs. In consequence the infant has no means of its own for coming to terms with experience and is entirely dependent on its primary caretaker's work of mothering to respond to the demands experience makes upon the infant.

Parenthetically I would like to note that I prefer the term "primary caretaker" to "mother" in this context. While I am reasonably sure that being breastfed by a nursemaid or nursed by a man with a bottle must make some sort of difference to the developing infant's mind, I am not now concerned with these differences, but with the uniformities that are common to infants that are nursed by their natural mothers and those that are nursed by someone else, whether through natural or artificial means. I am concerned with identifying the central task to be accomplished, not with identifying all its possible variants or all the possible ways in which the task in question can fail to be accomplished.

The work of mothering is a complex process in which the mind of the primary caretaker serves as an auxiliary core mental process for the as yet mindless infant. The infant, being mindless, can as yet have no true conception of self or other, inside or outside, mind or world. The stream of experience is an undifferentiated torrent of happenings without reference to personal agents of whatever sort. Demands are made upon the infant by the body without any recognition of the fact that it is the infant's own body making the demand; the environment challenges the infant to respond, and yet there is no recognition of the challenge as originating from outside. Since there is as yet no process of contextualization active within the infant, there can be no organized experience, and therefore no ego as we have defined the term. It would therefore not be incorrect to say that the infant is all id, i.e. the life of the infant is one of complete or near-complete unconsciousness.

It seems reasonable to assume that the infant would also remain this way if not for the intervention of the work of mothering. Originally, of course, the work of mothering centres around the bodily needs of the infant, to which it is the task of the work of mothering to respond on the infant's behalf. Foremost among these needs is the need for food and the various associated bodily comforts and discomforts (i.e. digestion and elimination). In the beginning, therefore, we can see the infant's experience as composed of bodily sensations with no wider established context; it is this that Freud captures in his conception of the id as the unknowable repository of the biological drives. In responding to the infant's needs in a more or less adequate fashion, the work of mothering does not, however, provide the mere experience of satiation, as the classical drive-discharge model would have it. This is because satisfactory mothering can only occur when the primary caretaker has adequately *understood* the infant's moment-to-moment needs.

In a typically adequate response to the infant's demands there is, therefore, not merely satisfaction, but also a tacit communication of a tacit understanding of the infant's experience. Of course the infant cannot as yet put this experience into words, but from our point of view the experience of an adequate mothering response must involve something along the lines of: "That horrible painful emptiness was a need for food, it can be stilled by sucking on the breast, which cures the pain and replaces it with warm, blissful fullness, and I know by the way I am held and touched and fed that I am understood and loved." Every adequate response to the infant's needs is a tacit contextualization of the infant's experience. The work of mothering in this case does not consist in the mere satisfaction of a physical need. It also teaches the infant what hunger is, how it should be responded to, what pleasure is for, and what love is. In this way the work of mothering begins to lend structure to the infant's inchoate flood of experience. A tiny core of independent mental activity patterned after the work of mothering begins to form. The caretaker's external work of contextualization becomes the infant's internal work of contextualization. The caretaker's mind becomes the child's mind (Loewald, 2000, pp. 539–540).

It would be entirely appropriate to say that by thus becoming the official advocate of the infant's needs, the role of the primary caretaker is to create the infant's experiences of mind, world, and self and then to hand them over to the growing child as a gift. We can easily imagine the consequences if this gift is not willingly given. We then understand how deficiencies in the work of mothering can result in gross distortions of the infant's experience, distortions that cannot fail to make themselves felt when the infant becomes an adult:

> in addition to the obvious penalties that follow from an inability to learn from experience there is a need for awareness of an emotional experience, similar to the need for an awareness of concrete objects that is achieved through the sense impressions, because lack of such awareness implies a deprivation of truth and truth seems to be essential for psychic health. The effect on the personality of such deprivation is analogous to the effect of physical starvation on the physique.
>
> *(Bion, 1962/1977, p. 56)*

The core of the mind thus consists of the infant's earliest experiences of the contextualization of its physical needs by the work of mothering. Since these needs centre around the experiences of feeding, digestion, and elimination, it is unsurprising that in later life mental activity, or thinking in the widest sense of the word, is often experienced in similar terms (Bion, 1962/1977, p. 57). We can speak of having to "digest" some new fact, of having "bitten off more than we can chew," or of our brains being "full," of having mental "indigestion" or having a "brain fart." It is striking that in English at least there seem to be relatively few metaphors for the pleasure that can be derived from thinking. It is nevertheless conceivable that the infant's pleasure (or lack thereof) in feeding is likely to echo on in the adult's pleasure (or lack thereof) in learning. This means that the primary caretaker's pleasure in knowing and meeting the baby's needs becomes the baby's pleasure in knowing and meeting them as well. From this point of view, Rousseau's enthusiasm for breastfeeding is perhaps not as misplaced as is commonly supposed: "But let mothers deign to breastfeed [*nourrir*] their children, and morals will reform themselves, feelings for nature will awaken in all hearts; the state will repopulate itself: this first point, this point alone, will gather everything together" (Rousseau, 2009, p. 58).

Just as the infant's body is fed by milk, the infant's mind is fed by truth; and these two, milk and truth, have a common source, namely the work of mothering. It would, however, be a mistake to assume that the infant experiences the work of mothering in a purely passive way. Just as the offer of the breast (or bottle) solicits an active response on the part of the infant, namely suckling, the offer of truth solicits a similar active response on the infant's part, namely thinking. The type of thinking that is most readily available to the infant at its own level of development differs in significant respects from other types of thinking that are readily available to the adult, for which reason I have chosen to refer to it by a special terminological phrase, namely the *work of imagination* (this should not, however, be taken to imply that imagination is the sole prerogative of the infant, or is in any way necessarily "infantile," or that it necessarily ends in adulthood).

The work of imagination constitutes the infant's attempt to contextualize its various experiences of its primary caretaker. It is originally set in motion by the work of mothering and then, in the ideal case, works in tandem with it to produce still more elaborate and satisfactory contextualizations. In this way the primary caretaker's external regulation of the infant's emotional states becomes, over time, the infant's own internal self-regulation by means of internal images of satisfaction. In plain English: the primary caretaker's work of mothering teaches the infant how to formulate its own needs and then to communicate them, first to itself, and then to its primary caretaker, so that they may ultimately be satisfied. This ability is what Freud misunderstood as hallucinatory wish fulfillment, when in fact it should be understood as the first stirrings of mental self-understanding. No wish can be satisfied that has not first been understood qua wish, as that wish that it is, and for which the appropriate fulfillment can then be sought. Something like hallucinatory wish fulfillment only appears when, for pathological reasons, an internal mental attack is directed towards the existence of the other, i.e. the work of objectification is purposefully undermined. This is best characterized as an attempt to substitute self-created images of satisfaction for real satisfaction; its motive is the denial of the dependence of real satisfaction on the willing co-operation of the other.

As we have seen, the result of the work of objectification is the establishment of a distinction between the self and the not-self, between an internal world and an external world, between a subject and an object. We must now devote some attention to this latter term "object." We can hardly abandon the term, as both tradition and convenience speak in its favour; however, examination of the psychoanalytic literature suggests that it is burdened with at least five distinct meanings:

1. At times it has the everyday meaning of "physical object" or "thing."
2. At other times it has the original psychoanalytical sense of "object" as opposed to "aim," i.e. the sexually attractive person, conceived of solely as the target of a drive, as opposed to the desired sex act (Freud, 1905/1994). This meaning has been largely preserved in the later term "part-object."
3. At times it is used to designate an internal representation of another person in contrast to the actual other person as he or she actually is. This is the meaning that is predominant in the "object relations" school of psychoanalytical thinking.

4. It can mean an actual other person taken as a whole and as such, in which case its meaning is incompatible with (2) and also the precise opposite of (3).
5. It can mean any general fixture of the internal landscape whatsoever insofar as it is the recipient of "action upon the self by the self." Thus the "ego," "super-ego," and "mind" can all be referred to as "internal objects" (Levin, 2010).

One not insignificant consequence of all these equivocations is that the adjectival use of the term "objective" to mean "based on fact" as opposed to "subjective," meaning "based on personal opinion," is also spoiled. One is never sure which "object" one is referring to. By this point it should, I think, be all too evident that without adequate terminological precautions, the main contribution of these ambiguities to psychoanalysis is likely to be a most unholy confusion (Perlow, 2004).

Let us take some preliminary steps towards clarification. I find it convenient to restrict the use of the term "object" to a meaning that is similar to (3) above, but with one important difference. The term "object," for me, never has the sense of a "representation" (as noted in Chapter 8); an object is a *mental paradigm*, i.e. a sort of mental recipe for combining the ingredients of primary experience into the secondary experience of otherness. An object in this specific technical sense is a sort of mental tool that we use for relating to others, a bundle of observations, rules, expectations, hypotheses, and conjectures that we use to contextualize our experiences of others. Its mode of functioning is closer to that of a catalyst than that of a lens or filter. An object is always a mix of real experiences and educated guesses because no one individual has direct first-person access to the experiences of another. Our experience of someone else's actions and of the mental states which underlie them is always a secondary experience derived from primary experience by means of the object. Thus an object is an "artefact" in two important senses of the word: it is both a historical remnant of the past and a product of creative invention.

It should be noted as well that I will also at times use the term "object" in the everyday sense of "physical object" or "thing," as this can hardly be avoided without extremely clumsy linguistic maneuvering; however, I will always ensure that the context makes the currently intended meaning entirely clear.

Now in my terminology, the ability to acknowledge the existence of points of view other than one's own is an achievement of the work of objectification. The ability to make educated guesses concerning the actual *content* of these other points of view (or: the ability to relate to objects) is the achievement of a different process that I call the *work of imagination*. The work of imagination has the function of bridging the epistemic gap between distinct individuals; because we do not know the experiences of others with certainty, we have to make educated guesses based on our own experiences of them. This is the process that has its origin in the relationship between the infant and its primary caregiver, where the epistemic gap between the two is in some respects even greater than that between two adult individuals. The infant has fewer experiences and more primeval ones to use to bridge the epistemic gap, to understand what its primary caretaker is on and about. This means that the mental images it forms of its caretaker will always be fashioned in its own image. In traditional terminology, the object is always a rich blend of actual and projective experiences.

It would, however, be a mistake to conclude from this that the infant's objects consist purely of projective material and in no way reflect the actual conduct of its actual primary caretaker. As we have seen, the infant's response, whatever that response may be, is always solicited by the primary caretaker. Of course, the opposite is also true, so that in this tightly-knit dyadic relationship it is never really clear, within the relationship at least, who is doing what to whom. True objectivity is impossible within a dyad; for this reason the presence of a father, who makes a third-person and thus truly objective perspective possible, is indispensable for the infant.

As a result of the essentially fusional nature of the dyad, the viewpoint characteristic of this stage is: "They are bad (or good) to whom bad (or good) things happen." In other words, every experience of the other is also inherently and necessarily an experience of the self. Because of the unique blend of preverbal fact and preverbal conjecture that characterizes the images the infant forms of this relationship, I have chosen to assign them the technical term of *fantasies*. This term is to be understood in an entirely descriptive and non-pejorative sense. I define a fantasy as a primeval image of self and other. I mean by this that it is a mental image, typically existing at a low level of contextualization, of a relationship with another person along with the concomitant view of the self emerging from that particular kind of relationship. An "object," then, is really just the part of any given fantasy that refers to the other, whereas a "self-image" is the part of any given fantasy that refers to the self.

It needs to be stated that not every element of a fantasy may be clear at a given time. For example, in Chapters 2 and 14 I refer to Freud's fantasy that the mind is a nation at war with itself. In this case the self-image is clear, the relationship is unclear, and the object for whom this self-image is necessary is obscure. Nevertheless, we can be sure that all three elements are ultimately present in each and every fantasy, even when one or more of them is initially unconscious and unknown.

To return to Joyce McDougall's metaphor of the theatre (1989), we can say that a fantasy is like a script for the part that we expect one sort of other person to play in the theatre of our lives, and for the role that we expect ourselves to play within that particular kind of scene. Whereas the work of objectification produces realities, the work of imagination makes relationships possible. Nevertheless, both of these, realities and relationships, are to be understood as differentiations within the original, primevally undifferentiated flow of uncontextualized experience. In other words, realities and relationships crystallize out of the unconscious by means of the intervention of the infant's primary caretaker and the infant's own spontaneous creative response to this intervention. This is the origin of the experience of an external world.

It seems to be a distinguishing (and most regrettable) feature of the present state of psychoanalytic writing that terminological digressions are constantly necessary, at least for the writer for whom being understood is of paramount importance. It would be interesting to consider the possible origins of this peculiarity, but for the moment we will unfortunately have to content ourselves with the task at hand. It needs to be explicitly stated that I reject the convention, introduced by some post-Kleinian writers, of spelling "fantasy" with a "ph." Supposedly, this is meant to distinguish unconscious fantasies from mere conscious fancies or daydreams. As far as I can tell, the only real basis for this distinction is a brief remark on orthography by Strachey (Freud, 1966, p. xxiv) which is based in turn on a passage in the Oxford English Dictionary that, if it was ever true, in my view certainly no longer is. Furthermore, I see no point to an orthographical convention that cannot be communicated in speech; I see no reason to suppose any significant difference between the structure of a conscious fantasy and an unconscious fantasy; and I do not believe that all really important fantasies must be unconscious. While the "ph" spelling may indeed be more correct from the point of view of ancient Greek etymology, I would venture to suggest that nothing else speaks in its favour, and therefore see no reason to continue its use.

There is of course a sense in which discussion of the role that fantasies play in the shaping of the mind can degenerate into mere quibbles about terminology, but I want to make a case for taking fantasy as the source of the fundamental building blocks of the mind. In order to do so I will first introduce a critical passage from Fairbairn:

> [...] as it seems to me, Melanie Klein has never satisfactorily explained how phantasies of incorporating objects orally can give rise to the establishment of internal objects as endopsychic structures – and, unless they are such structures, they cannot be properly spoken of as internal objects at all, since otherwise they will remain mere figments of phantasy.
>
> *(1949/2008, p. 154)*

It is clear enough from the locution "mere figments of phantasy" that Fairbairn is using the term "phantasy" in opposition to the term "reality" in some wider sense, and this is underlined by his dogmatic statement to the effect that "phantasies" are incapable of producing psychic realities, i.e. "endopsychic structures." in the first place, however, it runs contrary to the earliest findings of psychoanalysis to treat fantasies as *mere* fantasies, since psychoanalysis has from the very beginning underlined the role that fantasies play in causing very real mental suffering. It is a psychoanalytic truism to say that in the unconscious there is no clear distinction between fantasy and reality and that therefore the psychic efficacy of the former is in no way compromised by its putative lack of "reality." In the second place, Fairbairn has given no indication in what the supposed reality of the "endopsychic structures" is supposed to consist. It is clear at least that endopsychic structures are not physical objects and do not belong to the external world; we must therefore conclude that the reality of which they partake is psychic reality; but does Fairbairn really intend to make a distinction within one and the same mind between psychic reality ("endopsychic structures") and psychic unreality ("mere phantasies"), between a real and unreal part of the same mind? It seems to me that this would lead to considerable philosophical difficulties. Furthermore, Fairbairn takes it for granted that a structure is a type of mental "thing" with more substantiality than a "phantasy," but he does not pause to explain in what this putative substantiality is supposed to consist. It is presumably supposed to be more "solid" than a mere "phantasy," but what possible sense can this "solidity" have in the mental sphere of existence? It clearly cannot be solidity in a physical sense; is it then permanence or persistence? But "phantasies" too can be permanent or persistent, and so it seems rather that there is no obvious way of distinguishing a structure from a "phantasy." What Fairbairn really intends is a difference between the effects that different mental images can have on the functioning of the mind as such, between images that are not acted upon ("mere phantasies") and images that are acted upon ("endopsychic structures"); and this clearly does not dovetail with the distinction between unreality and reality; for nothing prevents unrealities (and this too is a truism of psychoanalysis) from being acted upon.

I find it convenient to reply to Fairbairn's question of how fantasies can produce endopsychic structures with the following parable.

Imagine that we give an eager child a sealed box and say that it contains a fragile, priceless treasure. How will the child behave? One possibility is that the box will be taken with awe and thankfulness; others without a box will be denigrated; possession of the box will give rise to arrogance. The child will hide the box from prying eyes, perceive anyone as an enemy who seems to threaten his possession of the box, and fight to the last to keep it. Now suppose it finally occurs to the child to open the box and find out what precisely this fragile, priceless treasure really is; and the box turns out to be completely empty. How will the child behave now? The child will throw the box away, wonder at its effect on the child's own character, and finally go about some other, more pertinent business. Is it fair to say that the unreality of the contents of the box, regardless of whether this unreality is supposed to consist in its fantasized fullness or its actual emptiness of physical contents, cannot have any permanent and lasting effect on the child? Then with what right do we conclude that fantasies are incapable of doing the work supposedly attributed to structures alone?

To be fair, Fairbairn's confusion is not entirely his own. It has respectable roots in Freud's structural model, which relied heavily on biological and physical metaphors, and in so doing, invited confusion between mental structures and physical objects. Of course this was not entirely incompatible with the aims of the later Freud, namely to ground psychoanalysis in the biological sciences; but it is no less misguided and misplaced for that.

## References

Benjamin, J. (1990). An Outline of Intersubjectivity: The Development of Recognition. *Psychoanalytic Psychology* 75: 33–46.

Bion, W. R. (1962/1977). Learning from Experience. In W. R. Bion, *Seven Servants*. New York: Jason Aronson, Inc.

Chodorow, N. J. (2010). Beyond the Dyad: Individual Psychology, Social World. *Journal of the American Psychoanalytic Association* 58: 207–230.

Fairbairn, W. R. (1949/2008). Steps in the Development of an Object-Relations Theory of the Personality. In W. R. Fairbairn, *Psychoanalytic Studies of the Personality* (pp. 152–161). London and New York: Routledge.

Freud, S. (1895/1950). Project for a Scientific Psychology. In S. Freud, *The Standard Edition of the Complete Psychological Works of Sigmund Freud, Volume I (1886–1899): Pre-Psycho-Analytic Publications and Unpublished Drafts* (J. Strachey, Trans., pp. 281–391). London: The Hogarth Press and the Institute of Psycho-Analysis.

Freud, S. (1905/1994). Drei Abhandlungen zur Sexualtheorie. In S. Freud, *Sexualleben* (pp. 43–145). Frankfurt am Main: S. Fischer Verlag.

Freud, S. (1966). *The Standard Edition of the Complete Psychological Works of Sigmund Freud, Volume I (1886–1899): Pre-Psycho-Analytic Publications and Unpublished Drafts*. (J. Strachey, Ed. & Trans.) London: The Hogarth Press and the Institute of Psycho-Analysis.

Kohut, H. (1971/2009). *The Analysis of the Self. A Systematic Approach to the Psychoanalytic Treatment of Narcissistic Personality Disorders*. Chicago and London: University of Chicago Press.

Levin, C. (2010). The Mind as a Complex Internal Object: Inner Estrangement. *The Psychoanalytic Quarterly* 79 (1): 95–127.

Loewald, H. W. (2000). Psychoanalysis and the History of the Individual. In H. W. Loewald, *The Essential Loewald* (pp. 529–579). Hagerstown, MD: University Publishing Group.

McDougall, J. (1989). *Théâtres du corps. Le psychosome en psychanalyse*. Paris: Éditions Gallimard.

Mahler, M. S., Pine, F., & Bergman, A. (1975/2000). *The Psychological Birth of the Human Infant*. New York: Basic Books.

Ogden, T. H. (1983). The Concept of Internal Object Relations. *International Journal of Psycho-Analysis* 64: 227–241.

Perlow, M. (2004). *Understanding Mental Objects*. London and New York: Routledge.

Rousseau, J-J. (2009). *Émile ou de l'éducation*. Paris: Éditions Flammarion.

# 12

# THE WORK OF SYMBOLIZATION

Before going any further into our ongoing investigations I want to pause for a summary of what we have learned so far about the work of the core mental process. We found it convenient to view the activity of the core mental process from three different perspectives, dividing its accomplishments into the work of objectification, the work of imagination, and the work of symbolization. The work of objectification is a type of mental accomplishment that results in the recognition and acknowledgement of perspectives outside the self. It produces a mental image of the other, an object in our technical sense of the term. The work of imagination produces mental images of relationships with these objects. We called these mental images fantasies because they occur at a level before reality testing is firmly established. Fantasies initially make no strict distinction between self and other, between truth and falsehood, or between reality and unreality. Fantasies are what is believed at the deepest level about others, and by extension about the self. It is from the complex web of relationships defined by these fantasies that a comprehensive self-image can slowly crystallize over time. Finally, we turn to the work of symbolization. I define *symbolization* as the aspect of the work of contextualization that prepares experiences for potential communication to others. This task it accomplishes by the light that fantasies shed upon personal experience. The basic question we must therefore ask is: what mental accomplishment makes it possible to reorganize experience so as to make it more like something that can potentially be shared with another? As we shall shortly see, asking this question is equivalent to inquiring into the origin and production of *thoughts*.

The word "symbol" is derived from the ancient Greek word *symbolon*, literally "something thrown together." In actual fact a *symbolon* was a token of recognition: a ring or other similar object that was broken in half and each piece kept so that each of the two possessors of the *symbolon* could identify the other. When we use the term "symbol" in everyday speech, on the other hand, we often mean to indicate something that stands for or represents something else in an arbitrary sort of way. In speaking of the work of symbolization I have something more like the original meaning in mind: the pairing of an experience with a matching mental token whose nature is such that one can begin with the token and trace one's way back to the matching original experience. It is clear that in order to be communicated, an experience has to undergo a peculiar sort of transformation. It is linked with or enshrined in a medium, whether this medium be thoughts, words, gestures, signs, or images. The carrier medium can then be shared with others (the given half of the *symbolon*) who can use it to find their way back to the original experience (the half of the *symbolon* that is kept for oneself). The entire process can only happen within a personal relationship that envelops and yet is distinct from the process as such, much as the original partnership is what lends the *symbolon* its meaning, and yet transcends and is distinct from it. I call the work of symbolization that aspect of contextualization that prepares experience for communication to the other by linking appropriate experiences with appropriate media for transmission in the light of one's relationship with the other (i.e. in the light of the object). Its most sophisticated manifestation is the ability to put feelings into words. The work of symbolization, then, is essentially bound up with the use of *language*.

Much – I am inclined to believe too much – has been written on the topic of language in psychoanalysis, both by Freud and by others; and I am also inclined to believe that what has been written was written in the wrong way. This was, perhaps, in keeping with the general spirit of the times. We find that the ideological tenor of 20th-century philosophy is not dissimilar. In that century many philosophical sects were marked by an excessive and misguided interest in questions of language and linguistics. The so-called "Anglo-American" or "analytic" currents in particular possessed a type of belief in the identity of language and reality that was essentially Pythagorean in its application of mathematical thinking to philosophical issues. I will refer those interested in a systematic criticism of this methodology to Henry Veatch's *Two Logics* (1969), which in my opinion offers the last word on this particular subject. This should incidentally not be construed as an endorsement of the "Continental" current so-called, which was characterized by different yet equally exasperating stylistic excesses. In any case these brief remarks on the subject will have to do; our immediate concern is with other avenues of inquiry that are more relevant to our interests.

For experience to be meaningful at all, the mind must react to it. Experience that has not been engaged by the mind, that has not evoked an active response from the mind, or that the mind has refused an active response, is uncontextualized experience, obscure. If it were possible for an experience to be wholly and completely obscure, to be an experience that makes no demand whatsoever on the mind for work, then that experience would be no experience. Very close to this category are the myriad inconsequential experiences that are part of everyday life but that are so trivial that they are immediately dismissed or not even noticed. I mean by all this that there is a constant, normally unconscious process of contextualization that at every moment of waking and sleeping life is continually preparing experiences for more sophisticated operations, including dismissal (in the case of relatively trivial experiences) and elaboration into conscious thinking (in the case of relatively non-trivial experiences). Without being touched by this process to some degree, however slight, an experience does not exist as an experience for the mind. The essence of this process is the receptivity to possible meaning. How are we to understand its origin and nature?

I think it is reasonable to assume that in the infant, under normal circumstances at least, there must be an inherent capacity to respond to experience. If the infant were ever truly an entirely closed and self-contained system, there would be absolutely no way for it to develop in response to experience, both from internal and from external sources. The mind of the infant, therefore, initially consists in an openness to experience, a readiness to have experiences and to begin making sense of them. Before any other characteristic we can attribute to the infant, including the activity of biological drives, we have to posit the existence of a mind that actively responds to the demands made upon it for work by experience. The need to make sense of experience is itself the fundamental need; the drive to understand experience is itself the fundamental drive that makes the experience of biological drives at all possible. More on this in Chapter 16.

But what about the condition we spoke of in Chapter 11 as the original mindlessness of the infant? It is clear that we need to introduce more careful and more subtle distinctions. In speaking of the mindlessness of the infant, I meant to indicate the relative non-involvement of an object in the process of contextualization at the earliest stages of life. In speaking of an inherent capacity to respond to experience, I mean an essential tendency to form a mind at all. From the very beginning, the infant reacts to experience using whatever means are at its disposal, however limited these may be. In reacting to experiences, the infant alters them in an attempt to make them thinkable. The initial core method for dealing with experiences is to think them. Without some sort of minimal structure, some sort of minimal coherence, the infant cannot respond to experiences by any further means. It is these minimally processed experiences that can then trigger various basic attempts to deal with them through motor discharge and the like. In other words, Freud erred in seeing motor discharge as the primary avenue for the discharge of excessive stimuli. Attempts at motor discharge are only possible when the infant, so to speak, is already in possession of a theory – however embryonic – of experiences and how to disenburden oneself of them; and this implies that the primeval response of the infant to excessive stimuli is to think them. I know that biologically-minded readers will probably deny that any sort of thought or theory is involved, preferring to understand the infant's crying and wriggling as an automatic response of the central nervous system. But in my view the fundamental principle still stands: there is no experience without some sort of understanding of experience. Whether one ascribes this understanding to the "nervous system" or to the mind, as I prefer to do, is ultimately of no significance. The point is that some sort of information processing must occur, for without this no experience, and by extension no reaction to experience, is possible. Thinking is clearly the initial and fundamental response of the infant to accretions of stimuli.

Thinking in the adult, however, is a highly derivative shadow of what it is in the infant. To the infant, thinking is a first attempt to impose soothing order on the formless chaos of its experiences. Thinking is also a cry for help. In the infant, where no strict distinction between inside and outside as yet exists, thoughts are a part of the environment. That is to say, the infant's thoughts are not contained within its head, as an adult's are, but are immediately broadcast throughout its surroundings by means of innumerable subtle (and not so subtle) means, where they have the potential to influence the primary caretaker's moods and actions by a curious process of induction that we have yet to understand fully. This is the process that neo-Kleinians call "projective identification." Originally a type of wordless contextualization of experience that does not distinguish between infant and caretaker, with appropriate encouragement and support this thinking eventually develops into the capacity for the creative use of language.

It is probable that the earliest experiences of the infant, owing to the influence of the sojourn in the womb and the trauma of birth, are organized around the two opposing poles of pleasure and pain (absence and presence of overwhelming stimulus respectively). This is the origin of what Freud called the "pleasure principle." The activity of the pleasure principle, however, is itself dependent on a prior process that contextualizes experience into the two themes "pleasurable" and "painful." since the activity of this process seems to be to group like with like, to classify similar experiences in similar ways, it can be understood as a process of simplification, of leaving everything irrelevant out of a particular experience. It can therefore be seen as acting in such a manner as to "disenburden the mind of excess stimuli." This does not alter the fact that it is prior to the pleasure principle, even if it often appears to act in conformity with it. I will call the result of this process, an experience that has been relieved of everything except what the mind considers to be relevant or pertinent about that experience, a *thought.*

A thought is a mental image in the widest sense, an experience that has been given a structure through progressive simplification in order to eliminate the overwhelming aspects of the experience and to make it manageable, i.e. thinkable. Thinking makes experiences bearable by reducing their complexity, i.e. by giving form and intelligibility to the formless and unintelligible. Thinking is the basic, inherent response of the infant to the demand made by experience for work; it acts to relieve the pressure of experience by making experience understandable and therefore capable of being appropriately responded to. The infant is surrounded by thoughts that it attempts to think because a thought experience is less insistently demanding than an unthought one. There is, then, a type of preverbal thinking present in the infant that structures experiences before any thinking in words has become possible.

There is a tendency in some contemporary schools of thought – I have in mind Heidegger and Lacan – to see in this primeval structuring of experience the activity of language. To some extent, this is merely a terminological quibble that depends on precisely what one cares to designate as "language." To Heidegger, for example, any and all forms of preverbal thinking count as "language" (Sembera, 2007, pp. 91–99). If an abstract argument be made that the foundation of something should count as a form of that something, then we can argue that the most basic form of preverbal contextualization, being the basis for the ultimate development of linguistic contextualization in the infant, should also be termed a form of "language." Nevertheless, I prefer to adhere to simpler and more commonsensical terminology that is based on the generally agreed upon sense of words.

In any case, I think that there is a real empirical basis for making a distinction between verbal and preverbal forms of contextualization. We are familiar with a certain type of client, often very disturbed clients, with a peculiar talent for evoking strong counter-transference responses in the analyst. They are hypersensitive to our moods, have a well-developed ability to get under our skins, and tend to provoke a weird sense of long-forgotten familiarity, as if they made us remember feelings and sentiments we knew long ago but had almost forgotten how to feel. On closer examination, we usually find that these clients have an uncanny ability to communicate non-verbally through such subtle means as body posture, tone of voice, facial expressions, and the like. In many cases the communication is so rarefied that it is very difficult to determine the exact medium of transmission, even though its presence can indubitably be sensed. This seems to be the meaning of Freud's cryptic remark (in the fourth last paragraph of section VI of "The Unconscious"):

> It is quite remarkable that the *Ucs* of one individual can react upon the *Ucs* of another while bypassing the *Cs*. The fact deserves closer investigation, especially in the direction of whether preconscious activity can be excluded in such a case, but from a descriptive point of view it is indisputable.
>
> *(1915b/1997, p. 153)*

It seems that clients of this sort have a diminished capacity for contextualization compared to the run-of-the-mill adult, so that with them the original hyper-attunement of the infant to non-verbal cues and signals is preserved. We can hypothesize that the infant develops this hyperattunement because no other form of communication is yet possible. As we develop the ability to speak, however, we tend to abandon our original non-verbal modes of communication because of their inherent unreliability, inefficiency, uncertainty, and so on. At the same time we tend to lose the immediacy and the sheer power of non-verbal modes of communication. To return to our original point, experience shows us that there is a certain tension between language and preverbal modes of expression, with the former tending to supplant and even suppress the latter. That is to say, the contextualization of preverbal modes of communication into linguistic modes vastly reduces their emotional immediacy and impact. This being the case, there is a good practical reason for making a distinction between the two modes, and not simply grouping them both under the common rubric "language," as some philosophers are inclined to do.

There is a further point that I think is worthy of our attention, namely the fact that we often find it difficult or even impossible to translate preverbal communications into words. When working with the client population described above, the communications are in fact so subtle and even ephemeral that it is often difficult to pin down exactly what is happening, and even when this has been done, it is often extraordinarily difficult to translate the communications into words. One is often just forced to rely on a description of the counter-transference reactions. This suggests that there is a very definite gap between the verbal and preverbal modes of communication, that the former tend to supplant the latter, at least in our culture, and that it is a mistake to see primeval modes of communication as continuous in any straightforward sense with later linguistic modes of communication.

Now we shall turn our attention to the particular characteristics of the use of language as such. Freud in "The Unconscious" evolved a highly complex theory of the relationship between word representations [*Wortvorstellungen*] and thing representations [*Sachvorstellungen*] and of the changes that mental conflict as well as the analyst's intervention were supposed to effect in their mutual relationships. As I have previously mentioned, this theory is clearly marked by the philosophical and linguistic preoccupations of Freud's day. I am, moreover, disinclined to believe that the essence of internal conflict and the nature of psychoanalytic treatment of conflict can be adequately grasped by abstract technical theories of this sort. Surely the matter cannot simply consist in connecting "conscious representations" with "unconscious memory traces" with the help of the analyst's insistence that resistance to the process be overcome. In the first place, as we have seen, there are nonverbal modes of communicating and therefore of thinking, and while these may be less contextualized and therefore more likely to be wholly or partially unconscious, they need be neither, as artists of all persuasions are well aware. It is thus demonstrably not the case that a "thing representation" must necessarily be unconscious when it is not accompanied by a "word representation". It is also not the case that accompanying a "thing representation" by a "word representation" must necessarily lead to the "thing representation" becoming conscious, as Freud himself notes earlier in the essay, when he strives to understand why the mere act of the analyst's naming the client's unconscious thoughts and feelings does not in itself suffice to make them conscious (here as in so many other places he invokes the concept of "resistance" to fill gaps in theory, coming perilously close to blaming the client for the inadequacy of his own theoretical excursions). Further proof of this last assertion is provided by reflecting that if the matter were really so simple, in order to make the unconscious conscious it would suffice to read a dictionary until the proper "word representations" linked up with their corresponding unconscious "thing representations," which is patently absurd, even if we choose to factor in the urgings of the analyst to overcome any "resistance" that may or may not be present.

What is it that is really enshrined in the word? What is it that the ability to name and describe an experience confers on that experience that makes it different, more contextualized? As we have seen (and as is obvious in any case), the original act of naming is not accomplished by the infant, but by the infant's primary caretaker on the infant's behalf. What is important about words and naming is not the intricacies that they produce among various sorts of "representations" – and there would be no point in denying that such intricacies do indeed arise from a certain theoretical point of view – but rather that they are a relic of the recognition of the infant's experiences by the other. This recognition first occurs at a purely non-verbal level in the primary caretaker's responses to the infant's non-verbal communication of its needs, developing a sort of mutual "body language" that, over time, becomes sophisticated enough to function as a basis for the development of a verbal language. The non-verbal dialogue between infant and caretaker has to become sophisticated enough for the infant to begin to appreciate the significance of the caretaker's voice and to attribute importance to the caretaker's words qua words. It is in the original need of the infant to phrase its needs in terms understandable to its caretaker that one important motive for the displacement of communication from non-verbal to verbal means is found. The infant is, so to speak, drawn to words by the need to get inside the other's mind. But in order to satisfy this need for effective communication, the infant first has to get inside its own mind in order to name and to express what it finds there. This succeeds when the caretaker has succeeded well enough in getting inside the infant's mind for the infant to have a basic reserve of understanding to work from.

As previously discussed, it seems that over time the verbal level of communication tends to suppress the original preverbal vocabulary of the infant; this is an inference, on the one hand, from the analyst's difficulty in understanding the preverbal level of communication employed by a certain range of client (as discussed earlier), and on the other hand, from the general difficulty in putting subtle non-verbal artistic and aesthetic experiences into words. We can hypothesize that the original non-verbal mode of communication eventually gives rise to anxiety in the infant owing to its perceived ambiguity and relative ineffectiveness (non-verbal communication is notoriously unreliable, as anyone who has ever been in love knows from firsthand experience). Too many mistakes are made, leaving the infant helpless to induce the caretaker to assuage its own needs. It is likely the need to escape this anxiety that drives the infant into language along with the caretaker's gradual loss of interest in the maturing infant's bodily functions, which are carriers of so many of the non-verbal signals that are part of preverbal modes of expression. Of course we also have to factor in the infant's own pride and happiness at the mastery of language and at the achievement this implies, as well as the caretaker's pride and happiness at the infant's accomplishments.

*En passant*, it is possible, later on, for the relatively unstructured and ineffable nature of preverbal communication to be retroactively identified with the feminine (the mother with whom this form of communication was established) and for the relatively structured and intelligible nature of verbal communication to be retroactively identified with the masculine (the father with whom a relationship at a distance, mediated through words, was established). This is, perhaps, the primeval experience that leads to some later perceptions of language and literary achievement as "masculine" achievements, while more non-verbal modes of expression, such as the visual arts and music, are seen as more "feminine." We are of course familiar with the later tendency to equate the female with the formless and unstructured genital "abyss," while the male is often equated with the structure- and form-imposing phallic *logos* (word) of the demiurge. I am of the opinion that whether or not the media of communication are verbal or non-verbal, the essential underlying content is the same: fantasies that express relationships between self and other. I think that the main difference is in the mode of communication, though of course different modes of communication tend to be suitable for different types of content. However, I would not seek anything other than fantasies behind non-verbal communications, regardless of any observable difference in manifest content. Granted, the fantasies involved in non-verbal communication may be of a more primeval, less contextualized sort, and when put into words they may as a result appear truly bizarre, as the work of Melanie Klein tends to suggest, but they are fantasies nonetheless.

With this we have now completed our description of the three main aspects of the work of contextualization. In conclusion, I would like to take a few moments to summarize the entire process of contextualization and its relationship to the mind as a whole. I find that this is best done by means of a simple metaphor. The vast inventory of experience can be compared to the holdings of a library. Imagine that there is a set of orderly, well-catalogued shelves containing more recent and well-used volumes. These volumes are in good shape and their pages are all where they are supposed to be. This corresponds to the ego. Now imagine that there is also an ill-ordered, erratically catalogued library annex that holds older, infrequently consulted volumes. These volumes are shabby; pages and entire sections have been torn out, wrongly replaced, and lost. This corresponds to the id. Just as volumes in the first section will be consulted and checked out more frequently than volumes in the annex for the simple reason that they are easier to find, the experiences that constitute the ego will have a greater tendency to become conscious than those in the id. The unconscious/conscious dichotomy, however, is not straightforwardly equivalent to the id/ego dichotomy: you still can take books from the annex, but as a rule they will be much harder to find and make sense of than those on the regular shelves, at least if you're looking for something in particular. Of course, the ego will be largely coextensive with conscious and preconscious experiences, and the id largely coextensive with unconscious experiences, but there is no need for them to overlap precisely. The process of contextualization can be compared with the process of creating a library catalogue and organizing the books on the shelves so that the catalogue becomes useful. Just as a library catalogue is ordered by author, subject, keyword, publication date, and so on, experiences in the mind are contextualized according to the themes of time, space, pleasure, pain, social acceptability, and all the rest.

Although the precise nature of consciousness is still unclear from both a psychoanalytical and a philosophical viewpoint, I think that becoming conscious can be understood as a form of contextualization. Using our metaphor, making something conscious corresponds to tucking the books under your arm, checking them out at the front desk, and reading them. It is clear that finding the books you want is going to be easier in a library with a well-ordered catalogue and an extensive collection. It is also clear that this specific form of contextualization, namely becoming conscious, is greatly facilitated by other prior forms of contextualization (cataloguing and arranging the books on the shelves makes it much easier to find them in the library). So to sum up: the distinction between ego and id is based on *degree* of contextualization; with increased contextualization (higher levels of organization), the possibility of a certain specific *subtype* of contextualization, namely becoming conscious, is greatly increased.

With this, I believe that we can say that we have completely resolved the difficulties regarding the descriptive and the structural unconscious that Freud introduced when he replaced the topographical with the structural model (refer to the original discussion in Chapters 7–8).

One final aspect of Freud's structural model needs to be accounted for, namely the *super-ego*. It almost goes without saying that we have replaced the classical concept of the super-ego with the much richer concept of the *object world*. For our own practical purposes we can treat the two expressions as more or less equivalent, though the expression "super-ego" has the disadvantage that it suggests the existence of one sole object of monolithic simplicity, whereas the mind invariably contains many complex and multifaceted objects, even if it is true that only a few of them are of cardinal significance (de Mijolla, 1981/2003). To be fair, we also tend to speak, not absolutely correctly, of "the" object when we really mean "the particular object of this particular fantasy," but I have found alternative turns of speech too clumsy for regular use. In any case, it is evident that in speaking of the super-ego, Freud himself tended to focus on a small subgroup of object properties of an autoreferential nature, i.e. self-observation and self-judgement. It is easy to see that both of these are dependent on the ability to elaborate a fantasy of the self as it might be seen from an external perspective. They can therefore be straightforwardly assimilated to the work of objectification and the work of imagination, which are also capable of accounting for the many other object properties that Freud tended to overlook or simply mention in passing. With this final translation of the classical structural model into our new idiom, our model becomes complete in all essentials.

## References

Freud, S. (1915b/1997). Das Unbewußte. In S. Freud, *Psychologie des Unbewußten* (pp. 125–164). Frankfurt am Main: S. Fisher Verlag.

Mijolla, A. de (1981/2003). *Les visiteurs du moi. Fantasmes d'identification* (2nd ed.). Paris: Les Belles Lettres.

Sembera, R. (2007). *Rephrasing Heidegger. A Companion to "Being and Time"*. Ottawa: University of Ottawa Press.

Veatch, H. B. (1969). *Two Logics. The Conflict between Classical and Neo-Analytic Philosophy*. Evanston, IL: Northwestern University Press.

# 13

# THE DIALECTICAL STRUCTURE OF THE SELF

In working out the three main aspects of the core mental process we have identified a unique sort of movement that appears to be characteristic of selfhood as such. This movement is the result of the concerted activity of the three major aspects of the work of contextualization that we have just described in detail. We will now proceed to consider their activity as a unified whole. The fundamental task of the mind is to respond to the demands of primary experience by elaborating it into secondary experience. This it does in a first movement of ascent towards the object (objectification). In this ascent the world is disclosed concomitantly with the object. Having established the object, the mind then descends back towards the self-image that it infers in the light of the object (imagination). In so doing the mind can take stock of its own personal experiences and begin to articulate them with the help of language (symbolization). Since language has a fundamentally communicative purpose, it necessitates a reorientation of the mind towards the object in order to induce a response. Thus a new ascent towards the object is begun, and the process repeats itself. The mind is thus seen to exist in a continual process of exchange with the environment in the course of which it is continually changing as a result of its interactions with objects and its reactions to them. In short, the mind, the world, and the self – the totality of experience – are not merely passively given to a mind that is forced to abandon its internal fantasy world and accommodate itself to their demands. In fact, the totality of experience, including the experiences of self and of others, are *active* achievements of the mind's own inherent creative potential.[1]

Nevertheless, our investigations suggest that there is a certain priority of objects over the self that, perhaps rather poetically, can be described in the following terms: the real external world, along with the real external people it contains, and the concomitant view of self they disclose, all spread out from the object like a corona around the sun. To continue the metaphor, it is as if the object were indeed a type of sun, the light of the world, without whose illumination all would be in darkness. If we keep this in mind, we can turn to the myth of the cave in Book VII of Plato's *Republic* and see rather more in it than a mere birth fantasy. When we consider the role that the sun plays in the myth and compare this role with what we have learned about the activity of the core mental process, we recognize that the raw experiential material that Plato draws on is the role played by the object in the life of the mind.

There is a further nuance to be gleaned from Plato's myth, namely the notion that we spend most of our lives in darkness and that our immediate surroundings are largely obscure to us. This corresponds to another interesting consequence of our analysis of the work of contextualization, to wit that on the whole, objects seem to be far more familiar and cohesive than the self, while the self is in relative obscurity. It is almost as if all the experiences we have are streaming in towards us from the outside, and that the whole notion of an inside itself comes from the outside. In other words, the self is a type of precipitate of the object. This stands in an interesting contrast to the worldview of Plato's *Timaeus* and of Western common sense so-called, according to which an encapsulated, pre-existent, and eternal self-substance reaches out to a contingent world that it remakes in its own image (this is perhaps more appropriate as a description of the projective aspects of the work of contextualization). In contrast to this, the truth seems to be that we *infer* what we are *hither from* the object, that based on our interactions with objects we conclude what sort of persons we must be in order to have had that specific type of interaction. Or, to paraphrase Schopenhauer, our intelligible and essential characters are beyond all comprehension, forever unknown and unknowable by any direct route. We learn who and what we are on a roundabout path, by means of a detour through the world of experience, and it is through experience and through experience alone that the outlines of the self slowly fade into view as a gradual emergent pattern, contained in that experience and implied by it, and never as something immediately given (Schopenhauer, 1851/1988).

In the psychoanalytic literature this aspect of the creation of selfhood has been addressed largely under the rubric of "mirroring." The classical paper on the subject in the English-speaking world is probably Winnicott's "Mirror-role of Mother and Family in Child Development" (1967/1999), which was in turn based on the classical paper on the subject in the French-speaking world, Lacan's "Le stade du miroir comme formateur de la fonction du Je" (1949/1999). What strikes the contemporary reader who approaches these papers is their excessive literalness; Winnicott emphasizes, "I refer only to infants who have sight. The wider application of the idea to cover infants with poor sight or no sight must be left over till the main theme is stated" (p. 111), while Lacan seems uniquely preoccupied with understanding the infant's reactions to its own real image in a real mirror. Second, it is also striking, given the imagery, that neither paper includes an explicit mention of the myth of Narcissus. Finally, it is striking that neither author makes an explicit connection with Freud's technical injunction that the analyst be "opaque" for the client, "showing nothing other than what is shown him by the client," like a "mirror plate" (1912b/1997, p. 178). This is enough to stimulate our curiosity and to justify more detailed investigation. Untangling the tangled threads of the mirror metaphor in psychoanalysis is a difficult task that cannot be exhaustively accomplished in the limited space at our disposal. I mean only to identify primary themes of which a brief discussion is adequate to our immediate purpose.

Freud's own comments in the aforementioned paper are in fact not as puritan in content as they are usually made out to be. If one looks closely at the context, Freud is merely underlining the difference between psychoanalytic and suggestive treatment modalities; the injunction to be a "mirror plate" is not meant to frustrate the client, but to ensure that analysts respect professional boundaries and do not misuse the analytic situation either to exert an undue influence on the client or to satisfy their own need for social interaction. It is meant to keep the analyst's own social exhibitionism and lust for power in check. In short, it is not primarily clients that Freud intends to frustrate, but analysts. Given the rather peculiar development of the discussion of this topic in the secondary literature over time, one is inclined to suspect that generations of analysts have either missed the point (Lipton, 1988) or were unable to tolerate this demand with grace. Incidentally, despite repeated searching, I can find no passage where Freud recommended that the analyst be a "blank screen" or even compared the analyst with anything of the sort. One paper that is often cited to support the claim that this was Freud's technical ideal, "The Dynamics of the Transference" (1912c/1997), does not refer to screens or mirrors, though he compares the individual's characteristic relationship patterns to "a cliché (or even several) that is regularly repeated, newly printed off in the course of life" [*ein Klischee (oder auch mehrere), welches im Laufe des Lebens regelmäßig wiederholt, neu abgedruckt wird*; Strachey translates this inconsistently, first more etymologically as "a stereotype plate," and then more functionally as a "prototype"] (p. 159). I do not see that there are any technical recommendations in this paper for analysts to conduct themselves as screens or mirrors in any sense of the words. For Freud, then, the mirror is a purely limitative concept that helps rather more to define what analysts should not do rather than to explain the specific nature of their specific contribution to the analytic process.

Insofar as I understand it, Lacan's main purpose seems to be to demonstrate that there is a core of the infant's self-image that is not constituted in and by its relationship to its primary caretaker, but uniquely in its experience of its own body and limbs, the unity of which is not a primeval given, but something that has to be established by the infant's own independent cognitive efforts (1949/1999, p. 93). Lacan is more interested in identifying inherent limitations of the infant's epistemic situation (the fact that the self is not an immediate given, but a construction) and in drawing philosophical conclusions regarding the supposedly necessarily fragmentary nature of the self. It is almost suspicious that Lacan barely mentions the existence of a primary caretaker at all; it is as if the infant existed on its own – or as if the lifeless, unfeeling mirror were all that Lacan's infant had to work with to create a self. The mirror itself creates an enticing illusion [*leurre*] that seduces the infant into seeing itself as a spatial unity (p. 96), tempting the infant to quit the Edenic wholeness of its inner world for the sake of fractured spatial body-images derived from the environment that by nature can never be glued together into a coherent self-image. Worse is yet to come, for this "mirror stage" merely creates a desperate need for the infant to repair its damaged self-image by means of an identification with parental figures; and this in turn leads to the full horror of the Oedipal situation, namely frustrated jealousy and frustrated desire. Lacan's investigations focus almost exclusively on themes of helplessness and dependence, so much so that it would almost seem more appropriate to speak of a "flypaper stage" rather than a "mirror stage." Small wonder, then, that Lacan's conclusions are what they are. Lacan concludes his peculiar paper with a reference to the *Chandogya Upanishad*, "*Tu es cela*," the famous "*Tat twam asi*," "Thou art that," implying, one supposes, that an insight into and acceptance of the supposedly necessarily fragmentary nature of the ego is a hallmark of a successful analysis, though it is doubtful whether either clinical observation or the *Upanishads* would ultimately sanction this view.

Winnicott, on the other hand, describes a situation in which there is an active caretaker who partners with the infant. Unlike Lacan's shadowy caretaker, who does little more than to abandon the infant before the reflection in the mirror, Winnicott's caretaker is one who shows the infant the infant's own self: "What does the baby see when he or she looks at the mother's face? I am suggesting that, ordinarily, what the baby sees is himself or herself. In other words the mother is looking at the baby and *what she looks like is related to what she sees there*" (1967/1999, p. 112). It is when the caretaker fails to do this that problems arise. When the infant looks at its caretaker's face and sees the caretaker, or the caretaker's defences, the caretaker ceases to be a mirror: "So perception takes the place of apperception, perception takes the place of that which might have been the beginning of a significant exchange with the world, a two-way process in which self-enrichment alternates with the discovery of meaning in the world of seen things."

Lacan's infant is faced with an inanimate object, Winnicott's with a real live caretaker. Lacan sees the mirror as a sort of trap, lure, or illusion. It produces a necessary but ultimately unsatisfactory and false synthesis of the self. Winnicott has in mind a two-way exchange between two living beings. Over and above this they seem to agree on what is required of the mirror in both cases: that it reflect the infant's self. For Winnicott it is when this does not happen, and when the mirror fails to reflect, that pathology develops. For Lacan, on the other hand, it seems to be the mirror itself that creates the germ of psychopathology by inducing the infant to strive for an impossible synthesis that can never be achieved.

It is strangely curious that the metaphor of the mirror should have arisen at all within the framework of analytic discourse. One wonders if perhaps it was introduced to make some sort of sense of Freud's original metaphor, or if perhaps at bottom the real question concerns the appropriate behaviour of the analyst towards the client. If we return to Lacan's description of the situation, I think that one thing at least is certain: the pathological element arises because the infant looks into the mirror and sees nothing but itself. There *is* no true other, or to put it differently, the other withdraws from the scene, leaving only the infant where another person should be. The phenomenon described by Lacan as "mirroring" occurs only where there is a calculated *absence* of the other. Where another person is really and truly present, some process of exchange takes place that is not best described as "mirroring," but as something else. This is, I think, clear from Winnicott's description of the process. Surely when the infant–caretaker relationship succeeds, what results is not mere reflection of the infant, but a fantasy (to use the terminology we introduced in Chapter 11) of a relationship that involves both parties, not one party alone. This is why Winnicott backtracks, first claiming that the infant sees itself in the caretaker's reflected gaze, and then claiming that what in fact occurs is a "two-way process." Every infant–caretaker interaction that is truly adequate results in a fantasy that includes both parties to the interaction. As Lacan's description makes clear, what causes damage is not when the caretaker fails to "reflect," but when the caretaker is so absent from the situation that the infant has nothing but itself to see, when the caretaker does nothing but reflect the infant back to itself, as coldly and impersonally and as objectively as a pane of silvered glass.

As both Winnicott and Kohut (1977) have pointed out, what the infant really needs at this stage is a sort of merger experience in which both the infant and caretaker are present, both as differentiated and as undifferentiated, and where neither of these images is challenged by the caretaker. It is when this living symbiosis cannot be tolerated by the caretaker that the relationship devolves into *mere* mirroring, and it is this stripped-down relationship of which the mirror metaphor is the most suitable description. This conclusion is also in line with the actual content of the myth of Narcissus. Many commentators have concluded that it was because of Narcissus's self-love that he perished by his own reflection, but experience suggests a deeper interpretation: *it was because nothing was shown him but his own reflection that he fell in love with himself, and because he had no one to love but himself that he perished.*

Our aim in this chapter, it will be recalled, is to understand the role of the other in the constitution of the self. In order to do so I think that it is important to return to a point made by Lacan in his paper on the "mirror stage." It will be recalled that Lacan believed that an inherent limitation of the epistemic constitution of the human individual necessarily gave rise to a limitation in the formation of a coherent image of the self. As this idea is also to be found elsewhere – my earlier paraphrase of the philosophy of Schopenhauer regarding the empirically given nature of selfhood (1851/1988) is similar enough – I think it important to formulate this notion in as much detail as possible. On this view, the mind can be compared with an eye. Just as the eye is the organ that is receptive to waves of light, the mind is the organ of experience. Now it is clear that all organs are characterized by a certain "directionality," that is to say, no organ is able to sense itself as such; rather, organs transmit information about entities external to the organ in question that impinge upon that organ. Thus, to continue the metaphor, the mind itself is "outwards looking." It is in the first instance built to transmit information about entities that are outside itself, and not to transmit information about its own states and properties.

To continue the metaphor of the eye, just as the eye is not contained in its own field of vision, the mind as such is not, properly speaking, the subject matter of its own experiences. We find an extreme form of this view promulgated in Ludwig Wittgenstein's *Tractatus Logico-Philosophicus*. In sections 5.63–5.641, Wittgenstein claims that the metaphysical subject (which, for our purposes, can be equated with the self) is not contained anywhere within the field of experience; this, incidentally, is a point that was made long before by David Hume (*A Treatise of Human Nature*, Book I, Part IV, Section VI). For Wittgenstein, the subject or self is a purely limitative concept. That is to say, it serves to create a boundary between the intelligible and the unintelligible, or, still better, it is the name of the boundary itself. For Wittgenstein, intelligible discourse is confined to logically well-formed empirical propositions. Since the organ of experience is not itself given in experience, it is therefore something about which nothing intelligible can be said. To quote Wittgenstein himself,

> Where in the world can a metaphysical subject be observed?
>
> You say it is just like it is with the eye and the field of vision. But you really do *not* see the eye.
>
> And there is nothing *in the field of vision* that permits the inference that it is seen by an eye.
>
> *(1922/1990, section 5.633)*

It should be noted in passing that the obvious objection, namely that one can use a mirror to see the eye, is not a particularly strong objection; rather, it tends to prove Wittgenstein's point: that the only possible source of knowledge concerning the self is the field of experience, and that there is no unmediated or transcendental route by which anything like a self could be known. Let us now turn to the conclusion that Wittgenstein draws:

> Here we see that solipsism, when all its conclusions are strictly drawn, coincides with pure realism. The ego [*das Ich*] of solipsism collapses into a dimensionless point, and the corresponding reality is left over.
>
> *(section 5.64)*

Wittgenstein simply means to express, in his typically cryptic fashion, the idea that we have no direct experience of anything like a "self," that the only material we have to build a self from is derived from the external world. Thus to claim that only the self is real is functionally equivalent to affirming that only the external world is real. Furthermore, the existence of a metaphysical subject is, so to speak, an implication of the existence of limiting perspective in experience. Returning to the eye metaphor, the eye cannot see all things from all angles, but is limited to a definite point of view. The existence of something like an eye can therefore be inferred from this point of view even though the eye itself and as such can never be directly and immediately contained in the field of vision. The situation is similar with the self: the fact that the particular world we experience is qualified by a limited perspective that not everyone shares – for example, not everyone is an analyst, teacher, or author – is the sole experiential content that defines a "self." In short, the fact that I have these particular experiences and not others is what makes me me. This is what Wittgenstein means by saying: "The ego enters into philosophy through the fact that the 'world is my world'" (section 5.641). Again, to express Wittgenstein's conclusions in ordinary language: the self is an inference, a construction, that is derived from experience, but not itself a content of experience.

Despite their respective exaggerations, I am inclined to believe that Lacan and Wittgenstein are correct in their belief that there is an inherent limitation in the human epistemic constitution that compromises our ability to obtain direct self-knowledge. The difficulty, then, is in deciding how best to understand this limitation. As we saw in Chapter 9, there is a real sense in which experience is given along a continuum from least contextualized and least knowable to most contextualized and therefore most knowable. We divided this continuum into two broad regions, the area of primary experience and the area of secondary experience. In primary experience, it is true that there is no experience of the self as such, since there is no distinction between inside and outside, between self and other. To continue with the mirror metaphor:

> So underprivileged, indeed, is my head in the mirror, that I don't necessarily take it to be mine: as a very young child I didn't recognize myself in the glass, and neither do I now, when for a moment I regain my lost innocence. In my saner moments I see the man over there, the too-familiar fellow who lives in that other bathroom behind the looking-glass and seemingly spends all his time staring into this bathroom – that small, dull, circumscribed, particularized, aging, and oh-so-vulnerable gazer – as the opposite in every way of my real Self here. I have never been anything but this ageless, measureless, lucid and altogether immaculate Void: it is unthinkable that I could ever have confused that staring wraith over there with what I plainly perceive myself to be here and now and always!
>
> *(Harding, 1986/2004, pp. 36–37)*

Despite their obvious perspicacity, Harding's observations, like those of most classics of the genre, are tinged with a clearly schizoid colour; they contrast a narcissistically immaculate idealized inner reality with an ugly image of the self originating from the outside. Harding's conception of the role of the mirror can, however, fruitfully be compared with those of Lacan and Winnicott. The immediate point to be made is that it is possible for the self to be experienced as an object at low levels of contextualization. Or perhaps more accurately: at low levels of contextualization, the self *is* an object, the self originating in the experience of the other from whom the self-image is only gradually distinguished and differentiated. I think that from all this we can draw the conclusion that there is indeed some sort of epistemic limitation in some non-trivial sense that results in a certain emotional emphasis being placed on the experience of the object. Clinical observations also seem to suggest that for most people objects are experienced with more distinct outlines than the self. It is, after all, obvious that the infant is dependent on its primary caretaker in almost every way, including for the thinking of its own thoughts. It is also the case that the infant is forced to rely on its primary caretaker to put order into its mind, and yet the caretaker is epistemically isolated from the infant, so that the caretaker's knowledge of the infant's inner states always has the nature of an empathetic inference. We may expect that there is never really a complete correspondence between the understanding the caretaker communicates to the infant and the infant's actual experiences, so that even in near-ideal cases the infant's knowledge of its own mental states always bears the stamp of something that comes from outside itself. Put differently, it is the object that allows the infant to think, but the object is indelibly marked by its origin in the other, so that self-knowledge inevitably always has the form of knowledge-from-outside. Self-knowledge always has the form of a detour through the other. The self is always an inference of the form: "in order to have had that particular experience with that particular person, I must have been such-and-such a person myself." This explains the metaphor I introduced at the beginning of this chapter, where I called the object the sun of the inner world.

The cyclical process through which the mind ascends towards the object and then re-descends towards itself and in the course of which the world and the self are concomitantly disclosed in the light of the disclosure of the object bears a striking resemblance to the primeval phenomenon that Heidegger calls "transcendence" (1929/1976). From a purely psychoanalytical point of view, Heidegger's writings as a whole become much more intelligible and, I think, more interesting if one substitutes the term "object" (in the psychoanalytical sense, of course) for each occurrence of the term "Being" [*das Sein*] (Sembera, 2007, pp. 38–45). I find the adjective "transcendent" unsuitable for our purposes, however, as it is burdened with quasi-religious and quasi-existential connotations that I find misleading in the present specific context. I have elected instead to use a term from an older philosophical tradition and so to speak of the *dialectical*, rather than of the transcendent, structure of the self. The term "dialectical," as it will be used in the present context, is a borrowing from the technical vocabulary of G. W. F. Hegel. It may be helpful to include some history of the term.

The word "dialectic" is derived from the ancient Greek verb *dialegô*, literally "to talk through," its usual meaning being "to have a conversation." It first achieved prominence in philosophy through Plato's introduction of the Socratic dialogue as a written form of exposition. The Neoplatonists of the third century CE, under the influence of Aristotle, conceived of the conversational approach of Plato's Socrates as a particular formal method that they called "dialectic," the further details of which do not concern us here. Finally, in the 19th century, Hegel appropriated the term for his own use. Struck by the oscillation between opposing points of view that is exhibited by the Platonic dialogues, Hegel referred to the conceptual unification of opposites through the recognition of their mutual conceptual interdependence as the *dialectical* movement of thought. Only one specific form of this dialectical movement is of interest to us within the current context. In section IV of the *Phenomenology of Mind*, entitled "The Truth of the Certainty of Oneself," Hegel discusses the struggle of the individual mind for recognition and acknowledgement by the other. (I am aware that Lacan has his own take on this issue in Hegel, but it does not concern me here.) This struggle occurs in three broad stages according to Hegel:

1. The first immediate object of self-consciousness is "pure undifferentiated ego [*Ich*]."
2. Paradoxically, maintaining this initial undifferentiated (narcissistic) state characterized by absence-of-otherness can only be maintained by means of a relationship with the other. That is to say, self-consciousness is necessarily limited and therefore dependent on the other for assistance in satisfying its needs. Self-consciousness is now at pains to secure its own self-sufficiency by securing the co-operation of the other, willingly or unwillingly. Hegel calls this state "desire" because its main feature is the struggle with the other for absolute control and therefore absolute satisfaction of need.
3. Finally, through this struggle for control, self-consciousness realizes that, first, subjugation of the other does not produce independence from the other, because it prevents self-consciousness from developing its own capacity for satisfying its own needs. Subjugation of the other is thus seen to be the extreme of dependence upon the other. And second, self-consciousness learns, through its experience of the other's eventual resistance to its attempts at omnipotent control, that the other is a self-consciousness with needs just like its own. In short, it finds itself and its own needs reflected in the other. The fulfillment of individuality, therefore, is to be found in the mutual recognition of two self-consciousnesses that recognize each other as self-conscious beings despite all apparent differences: *"Self-consciousness only attains its satisfaction in another self-consciousness.* [...] One self-consciousness exists for another self-consciousness. It is first through this that it really exists; for it is first through this that unity of itself in its otherness exists for it" (Hegel, 1807/1988, pp. 126–127).

Hegel explores the detailed vicissitudes of this relationship in one of the most famous passages of the *Phenomenology of Mind*, the master–slave dialectic (Kojève, 1947). For our purposes, however, the most important contribution that Hegel's thinking can make is in clarifying the notion of developing identity through otherness. This is the conceptual loom we will use to weave together all the disparate philosophical threads we introduced in the present chapter. It is Hegel's specific notion of the definition of the self via a detour through the other that makes the term "dialectical" so suited to our purposes; but more on this subject later.

I find that the concept of mind to which psychoanalytical investigation leads has been glimpsed by a number of philosophers, but that we are best served by working with these glimpses and attempting to synthesize them into a coherent whole rather than by working within one single philosophical tradition. For this reason I have permitted myself to quote rather extensively from a wide variety of philosophers, perhaps a wider variety than I would have preferred. Be that as it may, the nature of the mind is not simple but complex, and it is important to do justice to this complexity, while still keeping one's inventory of basic explanatory units as simple as possible. All this is by way of introduction and apology, as I need to introduce one last philosophical concept in this chapter, one to be found in the classical philosophical works of Leibniz.

In Leibniz' ontology, the fundamentally existent real units are particular individual minds. In alignment with ancient Greek philosophy, Leibniz considers the fundamental characteristic of whatever is genuinely existent to be *unity*. For this reason, Leibniz calls each individual existent mind a "monad," from the ancient Greek *monas*, "unit" or "unity." I find that the term "monad" has been frequently misused in psychoanalytic literature, to the extent that it has acquired an almost pejorative meaning, for which reason I wish to remind my readers that the term is here being used solely in its original, Leibnizian sense. A monad is an individual existent mind. Monads are characterized by two internal processes, one of which is responsible for the introduction of content into the monad, and the other of which is responsible for the alterations in this content (for the monad's changing inner states). The former process Leibniz calls "perception" (*Monadology* § 14), while he refers to the latter as "appetition" (§ 15). In psychoanalytical terms: minds are centres of experiencing and of desiring.

It is important to note that for Leibniz all monads are living entities; the only difference between an animal monad (or "soul") and a human monad is the degree of clarity of its perceptions (§ 14, 19, 26–30). Since monads are the only truly existent entities, nothing exists outside of them. That is to say, the entire inanimate material world exists only as the content of monadic perceptions. Inanimate matter has no separate independent existence in and of itself (it should be noted that this interpretation has been disputed by some Leibniz scholars, but in my view there can be no serious doubt that this is in fact Leibniz' position, although I cannot address matters of textual exegesis within the limited space at my disposal). Even the body does not exist except as a body-representation in the perceptual and appetitive life of the monad whose body it is (§ 62).

The perceptual activity of monads can be further classified into a number of different subgroups. These include self-perceptions or "apperceptions" (§ 14) and the so-called *petites perceptions* (literally "little perceptions") which I will translate here as "microperceptions." Microperceptions are those perceptions that are too obscure to pass into conscious awareness. In our own terminology, the totality of microperceptions is the *unconscious*. For us, as for Leibniz, the unconscious is a locus of experience beyond conscious awareness, not simply an empty hole in the mind:

> Incidentally there are a thousand signs that make us judge that there are at every moment an infinity of perceptions in us, but without apperception and without reflection, that is to say, changes in the soul itself of which we are

> unaware, because these impressions are either too miniscule [*petites*] and too numerous, or else too integrated [*unies*] such that they have no sufficient distinguishing features, but joined to others, they do not cease to have an effect and to make themselves felt at least confusedly in the composite whole [*l'assemblage*]. It is thus that custom leads us to take no notice of the motion of a windmill or of a waterfall when we have lived in the vicinity for some time. [...] All attentiveness requires memory, and when we have not been advised, so to speak, to pay attention to certain of our own present perceptions, we let them pass on without reflection and even without noticing them. But if someone should immediately advise us and cause us to notice, for example, some sound that we have just heard, we remember it and we are aware that we had earlier had some impression of it. Thus they were perceptions of which we were not immediately aware, apperception coming only in the case of having been advised after some interval, however small it may be. [...] These micro-perceptions are thus more efficacious than we think. It is they who form this *je ne sais quoi*, these tastes, these images of the qualities of the senses, clear in the composite whole [*l'assemblage*] but confused in their parts, these impressions that surrounding bodies make on us and that contain the infinite, this link that each being has with the whole rest of the universe. We can even say that as a result of these microperceptions the present is pregnant with the future and laden with the past [...] and that in the least of substances, eyes as penetrating as those of God could read all the sequence of things in the universe.
>
> *(1703/1990, pp. 41–42)*

Now the final all-important question concerns the actual *content* of intramonadic experience. As we have seen, every monad is a locus of experience; but of experience of what? Since inert matter has no true existence in Leibniz' ontology, the answer can only be: of other monads. It follows that *the sole possible content of monadic experience is the relationship of that monad with all other monads in the created universe*:

> 56. [...] every simple substance has relations that express all the other [simple substances], and [it] is in consequence a perpetual living mirror of the universe.
>
> 57. And just as one and the same city viewed from different sides appears completely different and is, so to speak, perspectively multiplied, it happens in the same way that through the infinite multitude of simple substances, there are, so to speak, as many different universes, which are, however, merely the perspectives of one single universe according to the different *points of view* of each monad.
>
> *(1714/1996, pp. 254–255)*

It is striking that Leibniz too employs the mirror metaphor in speaking of the constitution of the self; it is also curious that Leibniz' use of the metaphor is significantly different. For Freud, Lacan, and Winnicott, the mirror is the other, while for Leibniz, both the self and the other are mirrors of each other. The ultimate point of this appears to be that the only defining content of an individual, the only true content of the self, is its perspective on a particular relationship; the self has no content other than this. In our own metapsychological terminology: the sole content of the mind is the totality of its relationships with objects, and it has no content, no individuality, other than this.[2] To speak crudely, individuals are defined by their particular "take" on the totality of their relationships with others. Relationships exist first; the existence of separate and distinct individuals is contingent upon the existence of relationships. The individual is, so to speak, a precipitate of an object relationship. It is not an isolated, separate unit that somehow must establish a connection with a hard external reality at the expense of its narcissism. Put differently, minds are always already "outside." An "inside" only forms gradually and over time as an artefact, so to speak, of the experience of certain types of relationships. The self is an *achievement*, the active product of a definite process, and not an immediate raw given.

To sum up, then, I find that the structure of the self is characterized by three essential features: (1) the mind is possessed of an essential epistemic limitation that prevents it from thinking its own states; (2) this epistemic limitation is overcome through the intervention of the other, in comparison with and in contrast to which the self is gradually and continually defined; (3) the essential content of the mind is object relationships, while the content of the self consists of a particular individual perspective or point of view on these object relationships. One's own individuality is, so to speak, the implied dimensionless point to which the totality of object relationships in the mind refer. One obvious and important conclusion is that every possible form of self-knowledge is ultimately relational. Self-reflection is a type of stripped-down object relationship. There is always a tacit fantasy of an audience, an implied fantasy of another's view of one's own self. This is, after all, what self-reflection is: the ability to look at oneself as if one were another, i.e. the ability to see oneself from the imagined point of view of an imagined other.

For this conceptualization of the nature of the self, for the above-mentioned reasons, I will reserve the term *the dialectical structure of the self.*

## Notes

1 For the sake of clarity, and as a concession to traditional terminology, I will here remark in passing that the processes of objectification and imagination correspond roughly to what is commonly called the interplay between *projection* and *introjection*, while the activity of symbolization corresponds roughly to something that has no traditional name in psychoanalytic theory, but that we could call "introspection," for lack of a better word: the ability to call an experience by its own correct name. Note that meanings of the terms "projection" and "introjection" are extremely inexact in current usage; for example, sometimes projection is a pathological process that we expect will diminish in the course of a successful analysis, and sometimes it merely denotes the cognitive processes by which we perceive the external world, in which latter case it overlaps with the concept of reality-testing. Furthermore, even the distinction between projection and introjection is disturbingly vague; for example, Ferenczi (1909/2014) thinks that transference is a

phenomenon attributable to introjection, whereas most contemporary analysts, if asked to make a choice, would probably see transference as a *projective* phenomenon.

2 This conception has a striking resemblance to the 3rd-century Mahayana doctrine of Indra's net, but my scholarship is inadequate to the task of further exploring the connection.

## References

Ferenczi, S. (1909/2014). Introjektion und Übertragung. In S. Ferenczi, *Schriften zur Psychoanalyse I* (pp. 12–47). Frankfurt am Main: S. Fischer Verlag GmbH.

Freud, S. (1912b/1997). Ratschläge für den Arzt bei der psychoanalytischen Behandlung. In S. Freud, *Schriften zur Behandlungstechnik* (pp. 169–180). Frankfurt am Main: S. Fischer Verlag.

Freud, S. (1912c/1997). Zur Dynamik der Übertragung. In S. Freud, *Schriften zur Behandlungstechnik* (pp. 157–168). Frankfurt am Main: S. Fischer Verlag.

Harding, D. E. (1986/2004). *On Having no Head. Zen and the Rediscovery of the Obvious.* Carlsbad, CA: Inner Directions Publishing.

Hegel, G. W. (1807/1988). *Phänomenologie des Geistes.* Hamburg: Felix Meiner Verlag.

Heidegger, M. (1929/1976). Vom Wesen des Grundes. In M. Heidegger, *Wegmarken* (pp. 123–175). Frankfurt am Main: Vittorio Klostermann.

Hume, D. (1738/1969). *A Treatise of Human Nature.* London: Penguin Books.

Kohut, H. (1977). *The Restoration of the Self.* New York: International Universities Press.

Kojève, A. (1947). *Introduction à la lecture de Hegel.* (R. Queneau, Ed.) Paris: Éditions Gallimard.

Lacan, J. (1949/1999). Le stade du miroir comme formateur de la fonction du Je telle qu'elle nous est révélée dans l'expérience psychanalytique. In J. Lacan, *Écrits 1* (pp. 92–99). Paris: Éditions du Seuil.

Leibniz, G. W. (1703/1990). *Nouveaux essais sur l'entendement humain.* Paris: Flammarion.

Leibniz, G. W. (1714/1996). Principes de la philosophie [Monadologie]. In G. W. Leibniz, *Principes de la Nature et de la Grâce. Monadologie. et autres textes*1703–1716. (C. Frémont, Trans., pp. 241–263). Paris: Flammarion.

Lipton, S. D. (1988). Further Observations on the Advantages of Freud's Technique. *The Annual of Psychoanalysis*, 16: 19–32.

Plato. (1992). *Republic* (2nd ed.). (C. Reeve, Ed., & G. Grube, Trans.) Indianapolis and Cambridge: Hackett Publishing Company.

Plato. (2000). *Timaeus.* (D. J. Zeyl, Trans.) Indianapolis and Cambridge: Hackett Publishing Company.

Schopenhauer, A. (1851/1988). Transscendente Spekulation über die anscheinende Absichtlichkeit im Schicksale des Einzelnen. In A. Schopenhauer, *Parerga und Paralipomena I* (pp. 203–224). Zürich: Haffmans Verlag.

Sembera, R. (2007). *Rephrasing Heidegger. A Companion to "Being and Time".* Ottawa: University of Ottawa Press.

Winnicott, D. W. (1967/1999). Mirror-role of Mother and Family in Child Development. In D. W. Winnicott, *Playing and Reality* (pp. 111–118). Hove and New York: Brunner-Routledge.

Wittgenstein, L. (1922/1990). *Tractatus Logico-Philosophicus.* London and New York: Routledge.

# 14

# WHERE DO WE THINK?

The question that this chapter addresses is of fundamental importance to our attempt to understand the nature of the mind, despite any initial impressions we may have of its strangeness. The question is of course the title of this chapter: where do we think? – or, to put the question in the form in which it occurs in Winnicott's paper on the subject (1949/1975): why do we think that we think with our heads? The problem is simple to understand and difficult to resolve. When asked, most of us would reply that we do indeed think with our heads. When, however, we look for arguments to justify this commonplace opinion, we find ourselves rapidly at a loss. It is not hard to imagine that very young children, upon being told by their parents that they think with their heads, may well be completely puzzled how that could possibly be the case. One wonders about the type of explanations invoked by the parents should children happen to express doubt about this state of affairs. Perhaps it is something of which children have to be convinced rather than something that is obviously the case, like eating with one's mouth or hearing with one's ears?

In any event, here is the simplest formal explanation of the issues involved that I have been able to come up with. Begin with any arbitrary thought – say, the thought of an apple. The thought of an apple is a thought of something that has a certain texture, colour, smell, and taste. This much is clear; but it is also clear that the thought of an apple does not itself have a texture, colour, smell or taste. One can have a thought of a red apple, but that thought is not itself red. In short, the thought of an apple is not itself an apple (as is patently obvious). Now it is also clear that a thought of a physical thing is not itself a physical thing, i.e. a thought qua thought has none of the properties of things that are extended in space, that is to say, no position, orientation, size, shape, or any other spatial quality. A thought qua thought therefore has no location, since it cannot possibly be possessed of any quality that would permit us to specify its location qua thought. Why, then, do we persist in believing that we think with our heads?

It is clear that in the case of our physical senses no such problem exists, for the information furnished by our senses is physical in nature and can be assigned a definite place in the body. All major sensory organs furnish us with information about the part of the body that is doing the sensing. That is to say, there is direct testimony offered by the sensory experience itself regarding its spatial location. To continue the example from the last chapter, although one can technically not see one's own eyes, it is clear from the perspective of vision that one's eyes and not one's fingertips are doing the seeing. One can also block one's eyes with one's eyelids or other opaque and semi-opaque objects and convince oneself that one's eyes are in fact doing the seeing; and similar experiments are possible with all the other physical senses. Now it is evident that nothing whatsoever of this sort is possible with the mind. *If* it be possible to attribute a location to thoughts at all, it can only be done through indirect testimony. For example, one can observe a certain correlation between events in other people's brains and alterations in their thinking – intoxication and brain injury are perhaps the crudest and most obvious examples – but there is nothing in thinking itself, as there would be in seeing, hearing, tasting, or any other sensory experience, that would imply a particular physical locus of the experience of thinking. I know that it is the current fashion to consider the brain as the organ of thought, but if this is indeed the case (and I am not completely convinced that it is), it is, I think, abundantly clear that the brain cannot be the organ of thought in the same way that the eye is the organ of sight, or in the way that the stomach and intestines are the organs of digestion. That is to say, thoughts may well be *dependent on* the brain for their existence (though I think that even this is far from proven) but they cannot be said to be *in* the brain in any conceivable sense of the preposition "in." This much Winnicott understood, but he did not see, or was not able to see, the considerable philosophical can of worms that this forces us to open. More detail on this subject will be given in the course of the present chapter.

Now the first point to consider is that there is no compelling reason to link the experience of thinking with the experience of the head. While it is unlikely that there have ever been people who, under normal circumstances, would opt to believe that they do not see with their eyes, smell with their noses, hear with their ears, and so on, there are, and have always been, people who do *not* think that they think with their heads. The philosopher Aristotle, for example, believed the brain to be an organ whose purpose was to cool the blood, while he reserved the special privilege of being the organ of thinking and feeling for the heart. This would not have been possible if the act of thinking as such provided any immediate information regarding its physical locus. The belief that the heart is the physical centre of the personality is apparently also shared by other cultures; consider the following dialogue between an indigenous American and a German-speaking Swiss:

> "Look," said Ochwiä Biano, "at how cruel the whites look. Their lips are thin, their noses pointy, their faces are furrowed with wrinkles and twisted, their eyes have a fixed gaze, they are always searching for something. What are they

> searching for? The whites always want something, they are agitated and restless. We don't know what they want. We don't understand them. We think that they're crazy."
>
> I asked him why he thought whites were all crazy.
>
> He replied, "They say that they think with their heads."
>
> "Well, naturally. Where do you think then?" I asked, astonished.
>
> "We think here," he said, and pointed to his heart.
>
> *(Jung, 1961/1997, p. 251)*

Since the heart has entered our cultural treasury as a symbol of emotion, this belief at least may not strike us as particularly alien, but we may find ourselves rather at a loss when we begin to ask *why* the heart has this particular significance for Aristotle, for the indigenous American in the dialogue, and for contemporary popular Western culture. We can perhaps speculate that the motion of the heart within the breast is so exquisitely attuned to emotional states that cultures with an unsophisticated grasp of physiology may easily mistake it for the cause of these very emotions. This type of argument has a certain basic validity; we can certainly say that we breathe with our diaphragm and lungs because we move them when we breathe. In the case of the heart, however, it is clear that a mental cause is being confused with a physical effect, so that the latter is taken to be the cause of the former. Such confusions are common even in our own day; witness the suggestion of some popular psychologists that smiling can induce happiness or that slowing the breath can induce calmness. In any case, even if we grant this argumentative strategy a certain basic plausibility under certain restricted circumstances, it is clear that there can be no such speculative origin of the belief that we think with our heads, for the brain does not perceptibly pulsate in time with our thoughts. There must therefore be some other origin of the belief that we think with our heads.

Another apparently plausible reason for believing that we think with our heads is the fact that five of our main senses (sight, hearing, smell, taste, and the sense of balance) have their locus in the head, while the remaining sense, the sense of touch, is spread out over the surface of the entire body. Still, this argument could only suggest that the head is an important centre of experiencing or sensing, but does not necessarily lead to the notion that the head is the centre of thinking. What does thinking have in common with sensing as such? We could also argue that thinking is a fantasized reproduction of the sound of one's own voice (Plato, *Sophist* 263e; *Theaetetus* 189e; Ryle, 1949/2000, pp. 36–40) along with a fantasized hearer (Lothane, 2007, p. 267). Since the mouth and ears are both engaged in the act of speaking, and a definite position can be assigned to the voice, we could argue that this gives rise to the notion that we think with our heads. But this argument too is untenable, for closer scrutiny suggests that in fact it is an argument in favour of the belief that we think with our mouths and ears; there would be no compelling reason to displace the activity in question from these two physical areas to an imagined space a couple of centimetres below the apex of the skull. As well, the argument, if valid, would imply a cultural consensus regarding the location of thought that, as we have seen, does not in fact exist. Any argument for the localization of thought processes based on bodily sensations of whatever sort falls prey to the same criticism; see my remarks on Winnicott's speculative origin of the belief later on in this chapter.

If one is curious enough to inquire among one's contemporaries regarding their own personal reasons for believing that they think with their heads, one establishes quickly enough that there is something like an official position on the matter, one that can more or less be paraphrased in the following way: "I think that I think with my head because that's where the brain is, and it's the brain that thinks." It is worthy of passing mention that at least one prominent scientist found this line of argument unconvincing (Feynman, 1992, p. 333). In any event, what I find so striking about this answer is that, for most people, it can only be a matter of faith. I mean that there is an obvious difference between the results of a scientific theory and the immediate testimony of one's own senses, and it is an odd thing when the former usurps the latter. The fact that science has found it convenient to localize thought processes in the brain does not in any way imply that we must experience them there, given that thoughts do not localize themselves. Should the Greeks have experienced their brains as organs for cooling the blood because that is what Aristotle said they were? For most of us it is a matter of faith that the earth orbits the sun as well as revolves around its own axis at incredible speeds, and for most of us it is a matter of faith that this cool liquid we call "water" is in fact really dihydrogen monoxide, i.e. a compound of two elements that are gaseous at room temperature. Nevertheless, if people began to tell us that as a result of being enlightened by the discoveries of science they now experienced the earth's motion and the gaseousness of water, we would probably conclude that they were either being disingenuous or that they were delusional. In other words, there is a clear difference between an inferred scientific fact and a concrete personal experience, and we may expect the former to provide a framework for the contextualization of the latter but not to replace it. Yet when it comes to the mind, in our culture a different set of rules seems to apply.

Consider that the argument can be generalized. Most of us believe that we see with the eyes, but we could argue that the true locus of seeing is not in the eyes, but in the brain. After all, the image on the retina is flat and upside-down. Nerve fibres from the retina presumably carry information to the brain, where a number of bio-cognitive functions process the information from the retina such that it appears to us as a right-side-up visual image characterized by shape, colour, and so on. If we accept this belief, we could argue that no organ is the locus of its own experience, so that we would be forced to surrender our belief that we see with our eyes, smell with our noses, and feel with our skins; instead we would have to say that we accomplish all these sensory tasks by means of the brain. Yet it seems most peculiar, even in the light of our relatively sophisticated knowledge of physiology, to claim that we taste cheesecake, for example, with the brain and not with the tongue. We do not, after all, consume cheesecake by spooning it into the brain. Why, then, should any similar claims be made for thinking? If clients were to begin using phrases of this sort, phrases that attribute their own personal agency to their brains, we would quite rightly suspect that some sort of disavowal of their own experience was taking place, and we would begin looking for the motivation behind this characteristically schizoid defence mechanism. From the psychoanalytical point of view, to claim that one's experiences are being had by the brain and not by oneself is not all that different from claiming that God, Martians, Jim Morrison, or any other external source is doing one's thinking on one's own behalf; the same, incidentally, is true of the claim that a third party, "libido," is doing one's loving on one's own behalf. It is all too clear in such cases that there is a hidden motive for the disavowal of one's own experiences and one's own responsibility for their contextualization.[1]

The fact that we do not, broadly speaking, expect scientific theories to alter the nature of our own immediate experiences leads to another horrendous philosophical can of worms, namely the problem of what to do when our immediate experiences are in fact contradicted by the results of science, or, in other words, the problem of the contradiction of primary experience by secondary experience. I am not so sure that there is any immediate solution to this problem. In my view, the sophisticated philosophical systems of Leibniz and Schopenhauer have come closest to offering a real conceptual solution, but I do not wish to enter so deeply into metaphysics within the context of our present investigations. Ultimately, the question has little practical significance to the analyst, and what is important is that the analyst avoid making certain types of errors in interpretation. In this spirit I offer the following critical remarks.

In the first place, it is a common tendency (as we saw above) to subordinate primary experience to secondary experience. To return to the example quoted above, we might feel that we have to claim that our senses are wrong in telling us that the earth is stationary because science tells us that the earth is rotating about its own axis and hurtling about the sun at an incredible velocity. This line of thought leads us to become budding Cartesians, doubting all the evidence of our senses, because there is no sensory experience that is absolutely certain. Thus we have to renounce our primary experience and rely on scientific secondary experience as a corrective.

This attitude, however, is based on a widespread misunderstanding and a misinterpretation of the facts. Our senses tell us exactly what they might be expected to tell us under the circumstances, i.e. that there is no perceptible alteration in the earth's motion, not that the earth is either "still" or "in motion." Secondary scientific experience, when fully and properly elaborated and understood, should not conflict with or contradict primary pre-scientific experience but rather provide an additional framework for its contextualization. Unless and until we arrive at a similar result in the case of the body and the mind we can be reasonably sure that our scientific understanding of the issues is incomplete; and we can be sure that our understanding of the mind–body problem *is* scientifically incomplete, because we still do not know how a chemical event in the brain becomes an experience in the mind and vice versa – *if* that is indeed what happens, which is not at all certain.

Even such an excellent author as Gabbard in his comprehensive overview of psychodynamic psychiatry (2005) can do no more than juxtapose paragraphs on psychobiology with paragraphs on psychoanalysis; it is all too clear that there is no real conceptual link between the two separate disciplines.

In the second place, the fundamental style of argument employed in scientific theories that attempt to place the locus of thought in the brain appears to me to be flawed. I cannot enter into individual theories in any great detail, but they all boil down to a certain type of fallacious argument that can be crudely summarized in the following way: "There are changes in the brain; there are changes in the individual's thoughts; so the individual's thoughts are made by the brain, they are in the brain, the brain makes them, and they are nowhere but in the brain." I do not think that I have done any real injustice to neuroscience with this argumentative paraphrase, and if I am right in thinking this, the number of things that are wrong with it fairly boggles the mind. For one thing, it is common to hear people assert "depression is caused by certain definite chemical changes in the brain" when the same evidence equally well allows the conclusion "certain definite chemical changes in the brain are caused by depression." For another, the fact that intact thinking requires an intact brain does not guarantee the truth of the statement that the brain makes thoughts or that thoughts are in the brain in any real sense. Consider the following similar argument: "I hear a voice coming from a radio; I smash the radio and the voice stops; therefore the radio made the voice, the voice was in the radio, and it was nowhere but in the radio." In other words, the fact that intact thinking requires an intact brain in itself does not exclude the possibility that the brain is a medium of thought and not its originator; this latter conclusion requires something else that has not been provided by the biological sciences and likely cannot be provided by them at all, for it is likely not at all true. Consider the following observation from § 17 of Leibniz' *Monadology*, in my opinion as perennially true today as it was when Leibniz first wrote it down:

> We are, moreover, obliged to confess that Perception and what is dependent on it is inexplicable by mechanical causes, that is to say by form and motion. Imagining that there is a machine whose structure makes it think, feel, and have perceptions, we could conceive it enlarged so as to conserve the same proportions such that we can enter into it as we can enter into a windmill. This posited, by visiting it inside we will find nothing but parts that push each other, and never something that could explain a perception. Thus it is in simple substance [in the mind] and not in the composite or in the machine [in the physical body] that one has to seek it [i.e. perception]. Also, in simple substance there is nothing but this that we can find, namely perceptions and their alterations. Also, it is in this alone that all the internal actions of simple substances can consist.

That is all that I find it appropriate to say here regarding the obvious philosophical weaknesses of the various neuroscientific attempts to resolve the mind–body problem. I want to return now to our previous line of investigation, namely the origin of the fantasy that we think with our heads. Earlier I argued that there was no inherently compelling reason to link the mind with any particular part of the body; now I want to return to the question of why we nevertheless seem to be inclined to do so. As I hope I have convincingly shown, neuroscience may occasionally be used as an excuse to link the experience of thought with the head, but cannot be the final reason for this tendency. In considering the same problem, Winnicott argued that the link between thinking and the head was an artefact of the pressure exerted on the infant's head by its passage through the cervix during the process of birth, but even if one finds this plausible, it nevertheless implies a cross-cultural consensus that does not appear to exist (not to mention somewhat peculiar consequences for those infants delivered by Caesarean section). I personally am inclined to see the localization of the mind in particular areas of the body as a cultural artefact with perhaps some underlying basis in physiological experience. It does not seem possible under normal circumstances to localize thinking in completely arbitrary parts of the body. It is hard to imagine a cultural consensus that one thinks with one's ankles, but relatively easy to imagine one in which this role is attributed to the diaphragm or belly (Sekida, 2005, pp. 33, 83–90; Winnicott, 1971a/2002, p. 53; Winnicott, 1988, pp. 77–78).

I think that Winnicott comes much closer to the mark in the following passage:

> The question has to be asked why the head should be the place inside which the mind tends to become localized by the individual, and I do not know the answer. I feel that an important point is the individual's need to localize the mind because it is an enemy, that is to say, for control of it. A schizoid patient tells me that the head is the place to put the mind because, *as the head cannot be seen by oneself*, it does not obviously exist as part of oneself.
>
> *(1949/1975, p. 247)*

It does not take much effort to recognize the similarity with Harding's headless man (1986/2004). However, the really important lesson to be learned from the passage is that an individual's localization of the mind in the body is the result of a fantasy, and not of some compelling factual necessity. There does not have to be one universal fantasy that determines the location of the mind for every single individual. There are, however, in addition to Winnicott's client's fantasy, a number of very common fantasies about the mind and head that are easily recognized. Winnicott mentions the fantasy that the will can exercise the same sort of control over the mind that it can exercise over body parts, and notes that this is a powerful motivation for the localization of the mind in the head: the client can then attempt to control the mind through head-banging and other similar actions. Another common fantasy stems from the fact that the mind consists of everything that can be felt by you but not by others. It is the part of you that makes you the person you are and not some other person, so it is whatever is most private about you, the private part *par excellence.* This fantasy can be further linked with the male genitalia by means of the symbolism of the "head," or with the female genitalia by linking mental space with the receptive space of the female body. Of course, cultural and physiological experiences will help overdetermine these fantasies; as we have already noted, the chest and heart react with great sensitivity to emotional states, while the head is relatively non-reactive to them. Abstract thought, which typically does not arouse strong emotional responses, is thus more likely to be localized in the head than in the heart and chest. The mind can also be experienced as the best place to put anything that does not fit in anywhere else, so that it becomes the ultimate *fourre-tout* for everything non-physiological. Again, since the head is a part of the body that can be seen by others but not directly by oneself, the head may become a symbol for the mirroring relationship with the infant's primary caretaker, who is the infant's initial source of information about the infant's own mental states. We must also not forget the importance of the face as a source of information about the infant's and caretaker's individual mental states, which may in fantasy lead to the belief that something behind the face is responsible for what appears upon the face. The face is thus experienced as the primary inter-face between one's own thoughts and the thoughts of others. It is, perhaps, this early experience of having one's thoughts "read" and of "reading" others' thoughts that gives rise to later adult theories of telepathy and thought-transference along with their various paranoid derivatives.

Now our fundamental aim in considering all these issues is really to answer the following all-important question: what *is* the mind insofar as it is an object of study of psychoanalysis? I am completely in agreement with Winnicott in answering that the mind is "the *imaginative elaboration of somatic parts, feelings, and functions*, that is, of physical aliveness" (p. 244), in short "the imaginative elaboration of somatic experience" (p. 253) as such. For Winnicott's phrase "imaginative elaboration" we can substitute our own term "contextualization," and we can also leave out the qualifier "somatic," because it is an obvious given that all experience is first and foremost experience of the body, i.e. of physical states along with all the information that is conveyed to us through the senses. I do not mean by this to deny that there may well be something like "innate ideas" in the human mind; I think that the question of the existence of innate ideas is irrelevant to the analyst in any case. But as Kant pointed out – and here I am in complete agreement with him – even if there are innate ideas or "categories" of whatever nature, it is, and can only be, in sensual experience that they are first given to us and that we make our first acquaintance with them (*Critique of Pure Reason* B75/A48). If I read Winnicott rightly, he seems to think that this is a radical thesis, but it really is quite trivial and evident. What else are we supposed to have primary experiences of, if not the information provided to us by our own bodies? This idea is expressed in unforgettable poetic detail by Nietzsche in his *Thus Spoke Zarathustra*, in the section entitled "Von den Verächtern des Leibes" ("Of the Despisers of the Body") (Nietzsche, 1883–91/2007, pp. 39–41), to which I refer those with a deeper interest in the subject.

So in short, for us the mind is *the totality of fantasies about bodies and their relationships with their corresponding objects* (Aulagnier, 1975/2007, p. 59; also see Part II of Spinoza's *Ethics*, where the human mind is presented as the idea of the body).

Originally, of course, these will consist of fantasies of body parts such as the mouth, rectum, genitals, and so on and their relationships with the corresponding aspects of the primary caretaker. In the course of successive stages of elaboration and contextualization these slowly develop into fantasies about relationships between whole people; and finally, in the latter stages of contextualization, these become abstract thoughts that can be used as the basis of various scientific and philosophical systems. It will be recalled that in Chapter 2, I pointed out that even in the most abstruse scientific speculations there is always an underlying fantasy (that, of course, may or may not be pertinent for the actual content of the science in question). Fantasy is thus finally seen to be the fundamental bedrock of the human mind, the fundamental element from which all other mental entities are ultimately derived. Compare this conclusion with the discussion of Schafer's position in Chapter 2.

The results of our inquiry into the nature of the mind have important consequences for our understanding of the nature of psychoanalytic knowledge. Our metapsychological system necessarily leads to a drastic restriction of the sphere of psychoanalytic knowledge and a decisive modification of its claims to validity. No longer can we see psychoanalysis as a sort of fundamental super-science, as some early psychoanalysts were inclined to do. While psychoanalysis still has important contributions to make in many different spheres of human knowledge, it can never replace or even correct any particular discipline taken on its own terms; for the proper sphere of psychoanalysis is no more and no less than the *study of human fantasy*. We defined a fantasy in Chapter 11 as a primeval image of the relationship between the self and the other, typically existing at a low level of contextualization; by "primeval image" and "low level of contextualization" I mean that fantasies are images about whose truth or falsity no decision has yet been taken. In this light it is, I think, abundantly clear that psychoanalysis proper, in studying fantasies, is in no position to decide which of them is true or false. I do not mean by this that it is impossible to arrive at a reasonable degree of certainty, in taking into account clients' biographical statements, about the truth of their childhood experiences. I do mean that psychoanalysis works primarily at disentangling the unconscious fantasies about childhood experiences and should allow clients to make up their own minds about the truth or falsity of their memories. I also mean that from clients' fantasies about their minds and bodies we do not necessarily discover anything about how their minds and bodies actually work. Consider the following account by a scientist experimenting with a sensory deprivation tank:

> A week or two after, I was thinking a great deal about how the brain works compared to how a computing machine works – especially how information is stored. [...] When I went into the tank that week, and had my hallucination, I tried to think of very early memories. [...] When I got a very early memory – let's say from my home town of Far Rockaway – then immediately would come a whole sequence of memories, all from the town of Far Rockaway. If I then would think of something from another city – Cedarhurst, or something – then a whole lot of stuff that was associated with Cedarhurst would come.

> And so I realized that things are stored according to the *location* where you had the experience.
>
> I felt pretty good about this discovery, and came out of the tank, had a shower, got dressed, and so forth, and started driving to Hughes Aircraft to give my weekly lecture. It was therefore about forty-five minutes after I came out of the tank that I suddenly realized for the first time that I hadn't the slightest idea of how memories are stored in the brain; all I had was a hallucination as to how memories are stored in the brain! What I had "discovered" had nothing to do with the way memories are stored in the brain; it had to do with the way I was playing games with myself.
>
> *(Feynman, 1992, pp. 334–335)*

I think this quotation explains with sufficient clarity what I mean when I say that nothing can be learned from fantasies about the way the body or brain actually function. To put the matter crudely, unless analysts are doing something they shouldn't, they are not touching, examining, or otherwise inspecting their clients' physiology, and therefore are not getting any information about it. They are listening to them talk for the purpose of contextualizing their unconscious fantasies, and from this process nothing can be learned about biological realities. We can learn a lot about how clients *experience* their biological realities, but this is something entirely different that need not correspond to biological facts in any straightforward way:

> [...] if one is listening to another person talking, one may either *(a)* be studying verbal behaviour in terms of neural processes and the whole apparatus of vocalizing, or *(b)* be trying to understand what he is saying. In the latter case, an explanation of verbal behaviour in terms of the general nexus of organic changes that must necessarily be going on as a *conditio sine qua non* of his verbalization, is no contribution to a possible understanding of what the individual is saying. Conversely, an understanding of what the individual is saying does not contribute to a knowledge of how his brain cells are metabolizing oxygen. That is, an understanding of what he is saying is no substitute for an explanation of the relevant organismic processes, and vice versa.
>
> *(Laing, 1960/1990, pp. 21–22)*

And so the most we can say about Freud's structural model of the mind, as we saw in Chapter 2, is that it is a good description of clients who share Freud's fantasy that the mind is a nation at war with itself, that the currency of this nation is "libido," and that the mind is not really a nation, but in fact a machine. It tells us nothing about actual neurological or physiological processes, or about biological "drives" in any meaningful sense of the word, and it is therefore impossible, from the information at the analyst's disposal, either to make inferences regarding the biological basis of mental operations or to correlate them with actual neurological events.

All of this should really have been obvious to analysts from the very beginnings of the discipline. We are reminded that one of the earliest discoveries regarding hysterical paralysis, for example, was that there was no actual correspondence between the paralysis and the actual real pathways in the body. From the very beginning, then, it should have been clear – and often enough was clear, to the early Freud at least – that fantasy, and not reality, is the true subject matter of psychoanalytical investigation. What is important from a psychoanalytical point of view is not biological reality, but the manner in which biological reality is subjectively experienced by the client. Therefore biological reality lies wholly outside of the scope of psychoanalytical inquiry as such (Loewald, 1973/2000, p. 92). This conclusion is particularly important in the light of the fact that biology, whether in the guise of heredity or else in the guise of supposed neurological correlates to extreme psychological states such as trauma or severe depression, is all too frequently invoked as a convenient means of explaining the failure of analytic interventions. In my view the invocation of biology as a principle of explanation runs a real risk of encouraging intellectual slothfulness, especially since often enough in an analytic context there is no really adequate biological explanation of the facts that require an explanation (e.g. sexual orientation, human destructiveness, predisposition to certain types of mental illness). Given that this is the case, as it usually is, how different is invoking the name "biology" as an explanation from invoking the name "God" or "fate" or "Luna in Scorpio" as an explanation? To be completely intellectually honest, we should not really invoke biology before our repertoire of analytic explanations is completely exhausted and it is absolutely certain that there is no deficiency in our analytic understanding, and where a really complete biological explanation exists; and how often is this how matters really stand?

It may, in this context, be found useful to consider the following passage from Freud's essay "Psychische Behandlung (Seelenbehandlung)":

> "Psyche" is a Greek word and its German translation is "soul." Psychical treatment hence means "treatment of the soul." One could thus think that what is meant is: treatment of the morbid phenomena in the life of the soul. But this is not the meaning of this term. Psychical treatment wishes to signify, rather, treatment originating in the soul, treatment – of psychic or bodily disorders – by measures which influence above all and immediately the soul of man.
>
> *(Bettelheim, 1984, pp. 73–74)*

It is, to say the least, curious that this essay in particular was subjected to some rather interesting treatment by the editors of the *Standard Edition*. Bettelheim, whose translation I have used, is extremely critical of the official translators' choice of words, a criticism with which I can only agree, and Lothane (2007) has called attention to the fact that some rather shaky reasons were found to backdate this paper from 1905 to 1890. In any case, what Freud meant by "psychical treatment" is clear. We can add the following for still greater clarity. The biological aspect of a given psychological problem either can or cannot be influenced by purely psychological interventions; if it cannot, then psychoanalysis is not appropriate; if it can, then psychoanalysis, being a purely psychological intervention, does not need to concern itself with the biological basis of its efficacy any more than editors need to concern themselves with the mechanics of typesetting or bookbinding. Putative modifications to cerebral tissue (or the lack thereof) are of no interest to someone trying to effect psychological changes by psychological means; and except for the very crudest cases (e.g. massive brain damage) it is not at all clear to what extent modifications to cerebral tissue can or cannot limit the efficacy of purely psychological interventions. Of course some MDs with analytical training may, for example, combine the use of prescription medication with analytical treatment, but this is a case where a doctor who *happens* to also be an analyst is combining two fundamentally unrelated treatment approaches. So long as this is in the client's best interests, so much the better; but we must not allow the coincidence that the MD in question happens to be an analyst mislead us into thinking that there is some essential connection between the two disciplines. To put it neatly and succinctly: an editor is not a typesetter or bookbinder, just as a guitarist is not a luthier, although in some cases for the sake of convenience it may well be useful to have several distinct and unrelated areas of expertise combined in one person.

What consequences do these ongoing reflections have for the nature of our own metapsychological enterprise? One could perhaps put the matter in this way: a system of metapsychology is – at least in its inception – really an elaborate system of fantasies about other people's fantasies. This is not to say that no system of metapsychology can be a better descriptor of other people's fantasies than another, however. A description of fantasies is something that can be more or less true or false, even if the truth value of the fantasies themselves is in question. I only mean to emphasize the necessarily subjective element in metapsychological reflection, and to underline the necessity of embracing it. An absolutely neutral metapsychological system of the sort proposed by Stolorow and Atwood (see Chapter 2) is simply not possible. As well, there is no reason to mourn the apparent loss of breadth of the discipline. The gain in clarity is, in my opinion, well worth the restriction of the scope of our discoveries. I will take the liberty of repeating the quotation from Kant's *Critique of Pure Reason* that I cited in Chapter 1: "It is not enrichment but deformation when one allows the boundaries of the sciences to flow into each other" (*Critique of Pure Reason*, B VIII–IX).[2]

## Notes

1 As we have seen, there *is* a point in infant development when the primary caretaker is doing the thinking on the infant's behalf, and this gives us an important clue regarding the precise motive in any given case.

2 It should be noted that this entire chapter is merely a preliminary treatment of an extremely complex subject that will be addressed in a more conclusive way in Chapter 18. It would be impossible to address the subject at more length in the present chapter without introducing unnecessary complications.

## References

Aulagnier, P. (1975/2007). *La violence de l'interprétation.* Paris: Presses Universitaires de France.

Bettelheim, B. (1984). *Freud and Man's Soul.* New York: Vintage Books.

Feynman, R. P. (1992). *"Surely You're Joking, Mr Feynman!" Adventures of a Curious Character as Told to Ralph Leighton.* London: Vintage.

Gabbard, G. O. (2005). *Psychodynamic Psychiatry in Clinical Practice.* (4th ed.) Arlington, VA: American Psychiatric Publishing, Inc.

Harding, D. E. (1986/2004). *On Having no Head. Zen and the Rediscovery of the Obvious.* Carlsbad, CA: Inner Directions Publishing.

Jung, C. G. (1961/1997). *Erinnerungen, Träume, Gedanken.* Zürich and Düsseldorf: Walter-Verlag AG.

Kant, I. (1996). *Kritik der reinen Vernunft 1.* (W. Weischedel, Ed.) Frankfurt am Main: Suhrkamp.

Laing, R. (1960/1990). *The Divided Self. An Existential Study in Sanity and Madness.* London: Penguin Books.

Leibniz, G. W. (1714/1996). Principes de la philosophie [Monadologie]. In G. W. Leibniz, *Principes de la Nature et de la Grâce. Monadologie. et autres textes 1703–1716.* (C. Frémont, Trans., pp. 241–263). Paris: Flammarion.

Loewald, H. W. (1973/2000). Some Considerations on Repetition and Repetition Compulsion. In H. W. Loewald, *The Essential Loewald. Collected Papers and Monographs* (pp. 87–101). Hagerstown, MD: University Publishing Group.

Lothane, Z. (2007). The Power of the Spoken Word in Life, Psychiatry, and Psychoanalysis – A Contribution to Interpersonal Psychoanalysis. *The American Journal of Psychoanalysis* 67: 260–274.

Nietzsche, F. (1883–91/2007). *Also Sprach Zarathustra.* (G. Colli, & M. Montinari, Eds.) Munich: Deutscher Taschenbuch Verlag.

Plato. (1992). *Theaetetus.* (B. Williams, Ed., & M. Levett, Trans.) Hackett Publishing Company.

Plato. (1993). *Sophist.* (N. P. White, Trans.) Indianapolis and Cambridge: Hackett Publishing Company.

Ryle, G. (1949/2000). *The Concept of Mind.* London: Penguin Books.

Sekida, K. (2005). *Zen Training. Methods and Philosophy.* Boston and London: Shambhala.

Spinoza, B. (1992). *The Ethics. Treatise on the Emendation of the Intellect. Selected Letters.* (S. Feldman, Ed., & S. Shirley, Trans.) Indianapolis and Cambridge: Hackett Publishing Company.

Winnicott, D. W. (1949/1975). Mind and its Relation to the Psyche-Soma. In D. Winnicott, *Through Paediatrics to Psycho-Analysis* (pp. 243–254). London: The Hogarth Press and the Institute of Psycho-Analysis.

Winnicott, D. W. (1971a/2002). Playing. Creative Activity and the Search for the Self. In D. W. Winnicott, *Playing and Reality* (pp. 53–64). Hove and New York: Brunner-Routledge.

Winnicott, D. W. (1988). *Human Nature.* New York and London: Routledge.

# 15

# REPETITION AND TRAUMA

At first glance it may appear that despite the exhaustiveness of our ongoing investigations, important aspects of a metapsychological system have been neglected, for example the theory of dream formation, the theory of defences, an account of the "drives," and so on. In the present chapter I am going to argue that this is only an appearance, and that in fact our system is perfectly capable of dealing with all the aforementioned phenomena with relative ease.

I think that it is most convenient to begin with the theory of defence. What little I have to say on the subject has already been said in Chapter 6. I will content myself with a brief summary of the essentials. It is common knowledge that to begin with, Freud employed one catch-all term to designate any and all forms of defence: *Verdrängung*, literally "driving" or "fending off," normally rendered as "repression." Since the essence of all possible forms of defence is to prevent an experience from being thought (or in more Freudian language, to prevent some mental image from becoming conscious), the advantages to using one single term are obvious. One then simply needs to adduce a description of the exact processes at work in each individual case – so to speak, a detailed account of the *how*, i.e. "reaction-formation," "conversion into the opposite," "denial," "displacement," "dissociation," "splitting," and so on, the forms of which, after all, are, and must be, endless in number – without needing to add repeated descriptions of the *what*.

In contrast to this simple and straightforward approach, the contemporary tendency with regard to understanding defences seems to have been guided by the mistaken belief that to catalogue is to understand. This gives rise to intricate hierarchical arrangements that seem more intended to rank people according to their supposed level of maturity than to explain anything about the actual nature of defence. The defences themselves are so protean in form that there are hardly any obvious principles on which a really informative classificatory scheme could be based. Attempting to classify them according to the basic operations of the mind is as futile as attempting to derive the totality of possible English words from the various permutations of the 26 letters of the alphabet.

It will be recalled that the purpose of the core mental process is contextualization, i.e. the processing of an experience in order to accommodate the demand that it makes upon the mind for work. A contextualized experience is one that can be recognized as that experience which it is, one that has been prepared to become part of a coherent life history, or else one that can be genuinely dismissed if there is no longer any need for it to play a role in one's own self-understanding. Accordingly, I conceive of defence as a specific type of failure in contextualization. I define a *defence* as an attempt at dismissing an experience without the necessary degree of imaginative elaboration demanded by the experience in question. To speak metaphorically, it is an attempt to replace digestion by evacuation, by vomiting out (or otherwise expelling) an experience that insists upon digestion (Bion, 1962/1977, p. 84). If an act of contextualization does not have this specific character, such as healthy laughter, altruism, and reasoning – in short, any constructive management of experience – I do not call it a defence, but a mode of contextualization. Defence always constitutes a premature attempt at dismissing. Contextualization without this character is not a defence but a healthy coping strategy.

A contextualized experience – whether its ultimate fate be either integration or dismissal – is a clear experience. As we saw in Chapter 8, the clarity of an experience consists in its adequacy and in its distinctness. We also saw that an adequate experience is one that can be remembered, while a distinct experience is one that can be felt. A defence is a type of failure in contextualization, and as such can consist either in a forced diminution of adequacy, i.e. an attack upon memory; or in a forced diminution of distinctness, i.e. an attack upon feeling. Thus all defences involve one of two fundamental acts: *forgetting* or *numbing*. Other than this basic classification I do not believe that any other classificatory scheme is possible or even desirable.

In passing it should be added that the apparent fragmentation of objects we encounter in dreams (and in everyday life as well) may often be the result of an original lack of synthesis of the child's experiences rather than of the operation of a defence in the proper sense. Thus for example, there is not just one father-image, but a multiplicity of images, each corresponding to one significant aspect of the child's original relationship with its father, that become active in very specific types of situations. This is the artefact of an original "splitting" of images, but I see this as a defect in processing: the relationship is just too complex for the child to take in all at once, so it is taken in according to very specific themes, like specific roles in a play. These experiences then become lodged in the mind, where they function as the basis for the bewildering multiplicity of ways in which one and the same person can be encountered in dreams (and in everyday situations).

It is worth adding that in contrast to healthy contextualization the ultimate cause of defence is always the underlying presence of a "bad" object that forbids the thinking of the offending experience; healthy contextualization is by extension always a function of a protective and supportive "good" object. The unconscious always has a threatening character because thinking it imperils a relationship: the object will abandon you (or worse) if you go ahead and think the unthinkable. Thus the ultimate motive of defence is *the fear of the loss of a relationship and the desire to protect it.* This is an immediate consequence of our theory as it was presented in the last few chapters.

We can now transition to a far more challenging and far more interesting task, namely the formulation of a theoretical account of the so-called "drives." I find it most convenient to do this by means of a discussion of the most fundamental "drive" whose existence Freud was able to establish: the repetition compulsion. As is well known, in sections II and III of *Beyond the Pleasure Principle* Freud identified four types of unpleasurable repetition that contradict the theoretical predictions of a conceptual system based on the pleasure principle: (1) dreams (and presumably flashbacks) in post-traumatic stress disorder; (2) the repetition of traumatic events in children's play; (3) the repetition of past conflicts in the transference; (4) the "daimonic" experience of a personal "destiny," i.e. a characteristically recurring unpleasant personal experience.

Freud's stratagem for resolving this contradiction is peculiarly interesting: first, pleasure is conceptually stripped of any positive content and equated with the absence of excitation (the so-called "constancy" or "Nirvana" principle). This is necessary because, second, it permits Freud to define the drives as "conservative" in nature. If a drive actually had a positive aim – if the goal of sexuality, for example, were really positive sexual pleasure – its general strategy would be to maximize the opportunities for pleasure through continual expansion, and so it would constantly be in search of new and novel experiences. It would be a progressive and creative developmental force instead of a "conservative" – that is to say: repetitive – one. Repetition would then be inexplicable.

Stripping the drives of any positive content thus allows Freud to see a drive not as striving for new and novel experiences of satisfaction, but as an attempt merely to disenburden the organism of tension. This is the only way that repetition can be made an essential aspect of a drive, which is then defined as "an urge, inherent to an animate organism, to restore an earlier condition" (1920/1997, p. 246), i.e. the tensionless, excitationless state before the biological need arose at all. Redefined in this way, drive action simply becomes a sort of complicated detour on the way to inertness and motionlessess, which is its true aim. Rather like the force of gravity, the aim of a drive is to make sure nothing gets off the ground, and that whatever does happen to get off the ground gets brought back there as soon as possible. A drive, Freud assures us, is thus an impulse to turn the living into the dead – or, more accurately: an impulse to turn the living self into a dead self.

It is striking that Freud, having undertaken such complex conceptual contortions in order to explain the phenomenon of repetition, appears to overlook, or at least minimize, the inherent periodicity of the drives themselves, i.e. the reoccurrence of biological needs such as breathing, eating, sleeping, and sexual activity at more or less regular intervals; but in any case yet more paradoxes abound. Freud's redefinition of drive activity as the activity that attempts to *do away* with desire necessarily entails that *drives can no longer be understood as the sources of desire*. What then *is* the source of desire? No answers are forthcoming; we are sadly presented with yet more patent absurdities of a pseudo-metaphysical – one is almost tempted to say pseudo-theological – nature. Over and above the fact that this conceptual strategy allows Freud to redefine sexuality, or the drive to produce new life through biological reproduction, as a manifestation of the death drive, or the urge to turn life into death, it is notable that Freud characterizes the drives as "conservative" in nature, when in fact the more appropriate, but presumably more embarrassing, term from his own technical vocabulary would not be "conservative" but "regressive." This alone is a sufficient clue that some peculiar conceptual alchemy is at work behind the scenes; but yet more obvious indications abound in the work, such as the following passage from section V:

> If we may assume that experience shows us that without exception all life dies for *internal* reasons [!], returns to the inorganic, we can then only say: *the goal of all life is death* [...].
>
> *(1920/1997, p. 248)*

It is difficult to take this passage seriously enough to justify the effort of criticism, so I will content myself with a passing reference to the many, obviously absurd pseudo-biological myths Freud invents in this paper in lieu of proper psychoanalytic explanation as well as a brief mention of the quasi-religious character with which Freud endows the sex and death drives. One final passage from the first paragraph of section II is worthy of citation for the value of its irony in the context of our 21st-century understanding of such matters:

> The terrible war that has just come to an end [WW I] caused a great number of such disorders [PTSD] and at least put an end to the temptation to explain them in terms of organic damage to the nervous system through the influence of mechanical violence.
>
> *(1920/1997, p. 222)*

Repetition compulsion indeed.

As is so often the case, however, Freud's work contains a germ of brilliant and invaluable insight marred by faulty and incomplete articulation of thought. Let us set to work making good the omission. I want to begin with a passage from George Santayana that points us in the direction of a useful fundamental principle:

> Progress, far from consisting in change, depends on retentiveness. When change is absolute there remains no being to improve and no direction is set for possible improvement: and when experience is not retained, as among savages, infancy is perpetual. Those who cannot remember the past are condemned to repeat it.
>
> *(1948, p. 284)*

It is of course the last sentence that I find most pertinent to our task, but I want to give it a more concrete meaning in the light of the principles of the present system of metapsychology. This I propose to do in the following way. Instead of postulating the existence of a hypothetical mental force or "drive," we can account for the phenomenon of repetition in terms of the epistemic structure of the mind itself. As we saw previously in Chapter 6, experience is constantly flowing into the mind from the id. The core mental process has the task of contextualizing this experience so as to help relieve the demand for work that experience places upon the mind. The act of contextualization has two basic strategies for handling the flood of experience: dismissing and elaborating. It will be recalled that dismissing is only possible in the case of relatively trivial experiences, while any experience above a certain minimal threshold of insistence will require the more sophisticated operations of elaborating – to wit, the activity of objectification, imagination, and symbolization. In the case of this class of relatively intense experiences, it is only after elaborating has succeeded that genuine dismissing (i.e. an appropriate response to the experience) can take place.

We also saw earlier that a defence is a failure in contextualization. In other words, it is an attempt at premature dismissing. More broadly, it is a refusal to think an experience that demands thought. Now it is clear enough that the refusal of contextualization does not eliminate the original experience that impinges upon the mind. That experience simply continues to exist, and exerts a continual demand on the mind for some sort of response. To return to the explanatory metaphor we introduced in Chapter 6, all of the defences boil down to trying to deal with the fact that one is sitting on a tack by ignoring it. Obviously this strategy is doomed to failure. It is thus clear that the defences, as such and by definition, never succeed over the long term. Despite individual or cultural fantasies, it is not possible to deal with reality by failing to think about it. Eventually, if the defence in question is inflexible enough that proper contextualization of the offending experience never ensues, then, once the proper conditions are met, *the defence unavoidably and inevitably breaks down.* Over the long run, defensive strategies are always futile; their victories, such as they are, are always temporary and always Pyrrhic. This is all in stark contrast to Freud, who mistakenly believed that there was such a thing as "successful" repression and that it had "failed" in the case of the "neurotic."

For our own purposes of explaining the repetition compulsion, we can, in the light of this knowledge, slightly modify Santayana's motto into the following principle: "those who cannot think past experience are condemned to repeat it" – for the simple reason that an experience that cannot be thought can never become a past experience, but remains eternally present, eternally active, eternally impinging upon the mind, and therefore eternally and unconsciously repeated in contemporary thought, word, and deed. It is not, after all, possible to disenburden oneself of experience by refusing to think it. The repetition compulsion so-called is, therefore, not a "drive" as such, but an inherent property of the human epistemic constitution. Whatever cannot be thought must be repeated.

Having arrived at this insight, it is natural to inquire into the possibility that the other "drives" so-called may also consist in something a little more complicated than the mere mental equivalent of a physical force. Perhaps they too can be seen to be anchored within the information processing function of the mind. In my opinion, the true nature of the drives can be brought to light if we study their operation within another framework, namely the operation of the mechanism of traumatic response.

The history of the psychoanalytic study of trauma is interesting in itself, for to me at least it seems to consist of alternating phases in which trauma is studied and understood, followed by phases in which the predominant sentiment is perplexity and in which everything that previously was learned appears to have been entirely forgotten. This is evident even in the works of Freud; in 1910, Freud could confidently write:

> It is only the experiences of childhood that provide an explanation for the vulnerability to later traumatic experiences, and only through the discovery and making conscious of these almost routinely forgotten memory traces that we acquire the power to do away with the symptoms.
>
> *(1910/1955, p. 43)*

By 1920, only ten years later, this fundamental insight was apparently forgotten in the unholy confusion of *Beyond the Pleasure Principle* and its speculative biological religion. One thinks, of course, of the influence of World War I on Freud's thought; but in my opinion these new observations should have confirmed Freud's earlier convictions and not have introduced any new and unnecessary confusion. In any case, a similar pattern appears to recur throughout the later developments of psychoanalytic thinking on the subject. As far as I can tell from our contemporary preoccupation with alterations in nervous tissue, we appear to be regressing to the type of thinking that was cutting edge before the time of Charcot and the great debate on the nature of "railway spine." Of course, no one should underestimate the power of horrific experiences to cause suffering; I wonder, though, if investigations into the nervous system really do encourage analysts to be more empathetic with their clients' sufferings, or if they do not rather have precisely the opposite effect. Surely the proper task of the analyst is not to study client physiology, but rather to study the mind? And when we do this responsibly, the facts are clear: regardless of whether one lays the causative accent on present or on past experience – and where one places the accent may well differ in different cases – traumatic response always involves a link between at least two experiences, one present experience and one or more past experiences, and without this characteristic and defining relationship a traumatic response in the proper sense is simply not observed.

To put it clearly, if crudely: if an overwhelming experience is going to make you crack, it is going to happen along preexisting fault lines that were laid down in childhood. It will not, and cannot, create an entirely new defect with no prior historical background, and that for the same reason that a chain subjected to excessive tension snaps at the link that is already the weakest. It is a purely semantic quibble whether the ultimate cause of the chain's snapping was the application of tension or the presence of a weak link. It depends on whether one understands "cause" as "occasioning incident" (efficient cause) or as "latent potentiality" (material cause). And why should we exclude the obvious possibility of multiple causal factors?

It seems to me quite clear that nothing is added to our understanding of these matters by a study of psychophysiology except an additional statement of the intractability of severe trauma, of which everyone is aware in any case; it also seems to me quite clear that identifying and recognizing the unique and defining mental structure of traumatic response in no way necessarily entails any risk of neglecting the causal significance of the present experience, something of which many contemporary analysts appear to be afraid. Furthermore, a proper comprehension of trauma requires a model that explains traumatic responses to relatively mild present experiences as well. We should not let our current preoccupation with war neuroses blind us to the fact that the traumatic response is a clearly defined, and dare I say easily observable, mental structure that is present in many other situations than war, catastrophe, and violent assault.

In what precise mental structure, then, does traumatic response to experience consist? I suggest that traumatic response consists of four distinct elements:

1. a present experience that is subjectively experienced as overwhelming regardless of its actual intensity, which may be greater or lesser in different cases;
2. a past uncontextualized (or inadequately contextualized) experience;
3. the presence of a defensive mechanism (ultimately: the presence of a "bad" or deficient object) that actively prevents the contextualization of the past uncontextualized experience (or else the presence of a deficient object that is not equal to the task of contextualization); and
4. an associative link between the present and past experience such that the inability to contextualize the past experience entails, for the individual in question, the concomitant inability to contextualize the present experience (which contributes to the subjective experience of being overwhelmed in the first place).

The mind, as a result, emphatically refuses to think the present experience, rejecting it with the same vigour as it rejects the past experience. Since the refusal to think creates widespread confusion regarding the actual state of affairs, it is unclear to the traumatized individual whether the perceived threat is internal or external, in the past or in the present, fantasy or reality. In fact it is both: but this fact is concealed from the traumatized individual, whose capacity to think is overwhelmed by having to fight a war on two fronts without even a clear notion of where the battle lines are to be found. As a result of the interference with the core mental process, the present cannot become the past: it is reacted to as if it were continually present – and this is as true of the past uncontextualized experience as it is of the present uncontextualized experience.

The failure of the mind to contextualize its experience in trauma parallels the experience of the nightmare in healthy individuals, for nightmares are dreams that have failed to contain nocturnal experience through contextualization and so have failed in their task of safeguarding the condition of sleep. It is not, therefore, a mere metaphor to assert that in effect the severely traumatized individual is living a nightmare from which not even sleep can afford any escape. Consider the following quotation:

> During the war in Afghanistan, CNN interviewed a man whose wife had been killed by an American missile. "Now that I have no wife," he said, "I have no mind." Being confronted by this sudden catastrophic loss had destroyed the widower's mind, leaving him without the ability to think.
>
> *(Boulanger, 2005, p. 21)*

The application of our theory to this and similar events is immediately obvious and can be left to the imagination of the reader. I will only add that much of the rest of Boulanger's article struggles, in my view not entirely successfully, with the phenomenon of the misapprehension of objects in response to trauma (failures in reality testing, or what she calls "the state of psychic equivalence"). The corresponding explanation is particularly straightforward within the present system of metapsychology.

Now as I have already said, we must not allow the more dramatic forms of trauma to blind us to the fact that the traumatic response is a fundamental – and therefore, to some extent, "normal" – idiosyncrasy of the core mental process and its manner of working. Nowhere is this more evident than in Freud's original theory of dreams. If we consider the basic theory, it becomes clear to us that Freud has an essentially traumatic theory of dream formation: the impingement of the day residues (*Tagesreste*) upon the mind reawakens unfinished business from childhood that erupts into the mind during sleep. The dream – if it succeeds – elaborates and contextualizes the past experience to the point where true dismissing becomes possible. Dream formation thus is seen to be a particular variation of traumatic response, with this important difference: the mind is ultimately able to overcome its own resistance to thinking to the point that the amorphous, inchoate, uncontextualized experience is contextualized to the degree that at least some symbolization becomes possible, even if only in the form of a dream. "It was only a dream" is the first step towards genuine dismissing. The dream succeeds in thinking the unthinkable; in the various traumatic disorders, we witness a failure of this adaptive response that is characteristically experienced as "mindlessness."[1]

With the aim of sparing ourselves having to go into more detail than is absolutely necessary, I think it will be sufficient if I merely state in passing that the mechanism of traumatic response is entirely normal, and if I cite as commonplace examples, in addition to dream formation, the experiences of puberty and of falling in love. In the case of puberty, early experiences of helplessness in the face of the demands of the body are re-experienced, while in the case of falling in love, early erotic object relationships are brought to life again. Of course, as we saw with dreams, some form of spontaneous remission (though not without decisive sequelae) is the usual outcome, so we tend not to think of these experiences as "traumatic" in the usual sense, although the same fundamental process is at work.

The specifically traumatic character of puberty and falling in love is dependent on past experiences that we do not usually characterize as necessarily "traumatic" in the proper sense, namely the experiences of early childhood. This is partly due to an equivocation in the meaning of the adjective "traumatic." In the strict sense, an experience should only be characterized as traumatic when it evokes the full quadripartite response described above. A properly traumatic experience in this sense should be strictly distinguished from an *overwhelming* experience, in which some or all of the four elements of traumatic response may be lacking. Thus in order to understand the psychogenesis of susceptibility to trauma, it is important to consider that infancy as such is overwhelming by its very nature, i.e. experience makes a constant demand on the core mental process that commonly exceeds the naïve and inexperienced child's capacity for contextualization. This necessarily results in failures in contextualization. In traditional terminology: childhood repressions are both universal and unavoidable.

Even where there is no positive neglect or abuse, the child's own inability to deal with childhood can be experienced as a positive presence, and so as something deliberately inimical to the child. We are familiar with the Kleinian notion that an infant cannot experience the lack of a breast as a mere absence; rather, we believe the infant experiences lack as the presence of an internal tormentor (hunger pangs). Along these lines the child's failures in contextualization give rise to the fantasy of a "bad," oppressive object that forbids the thinking of the overwhelming experience (or type of experience) in question. Because of this it can sometimes be difficult to determine the exact origin of the "bad" objects and the degree to which actual parental failure is responsible for their existence. They exist, of course, as fantasies; yet their mere presence implies some degree of actual parental failure, since they would not exist if the parents had been able to contextualize the child's experiences on the child's behalf, as is their responsibility.

In any event, it is true to say that the seeds of traumatic response are sown in childhood, since it is in childhood that two of the requisite elements of traumatic response are generated, namely past uncontextualized experience along with the defensive mechanism that prevents the future contextualization of that particular experience (or type of experience). Keeping in mind our basic principle that whatever cannot be thought must be repeated, it is clear that the inherent inadequacy of the child's mind to deal with experience gives rise to a sort of "imprinting" phenomenon that is almost certainly responsible for the "stickiness" of the oldest and most primeval experiences of the child. This is why sexual identity and orientation, along with the disorders of the same, including the various perversions, are typically experienced as so "deeply rooted" and as so resistant to any sort of influence. This should not be misunderstood; the innocence of the child is such that even positive experiences such as healthy identification may be overwhelming and so result in "imprinting."

Finally, it can safely be asserted that the "trauma" of early childhood, i.e. the superabundance of overwhelming experiences, only ceases when the core mental process is finally able to deal with most of the demands made upon it by the body and by the world; and this ushers in the so-called "latency period," which – ideally – should not be understood as a literal biological event, but as a developmental phase in which the child's information processing ability is more or less adequate to the task of being a child. In less ideal cases, of course, this involves learning from its parents that it is dangerous to have certain thoughts.

## Note

1 An additional parenthetical comment for the sake of clarity: in chapter 8 of the *Introductory Lectures*, "The Dreams of Children," Freud says: "A difference between latent and manifest dream [content], a distortion of the latent dream thoughts, can thus also be found in the case of these simple children's dreams, [namely] the conversion of thought into experience" (1916; 1933/2007, p. 142). In fact I would say the exact opposite: the dream is the conversion of experience into thought. Freud's terminology is faulty: the raw given is much closer to an "experience" than a "thought." Experience is what we start with; a "thought," like a "thing," is a derivative experience, the result of an experience that has undergone some degree of contextualization. He also errs along similar lines in thinking that the intrapsychic, in its pure form, appears *as* something intrapsychic. A desire is something that *befalls* one, hence an experience; a thought is only possible after elaboration and contextualization of the raw given has taken place. It would be still more correct to say that the dream turns experience into action rather than thought proper; as such the dream is the *primeval form of acting out.*

## References


Bion, W. R. (1962/1977). Learning from Experience. In W. R. Bion, *Seven Servants.* New York, NY: Jason Aronson, Inc.

Boulanger, G. (2005). From Voyeur to Witness: Recapturing Symbolic Function After Massive Psychic Trauma. *Psychoanalytic Psychology* 22(1): 21–31.

Freud, S. (1910/1955). Über Psychoanalyse. Fünf Vorlesungen, gehalten zur zwanzigjährigen Gründungsfeier der Clark University in Worcester, Mass., September 1909. In S. Freud, *Gesammelte Werke* (Vol. VIII, pp. 3–60). London: Imago Publishing Co., Ltd.

Freud, S. (1916; 1933/2007). *Vorlesungen zur Einführung in die Psychoanalyse Und Neue Folge.* Frankfurt am Main: S. Fischer Verlag.

Freud, S. (1920/1997). Jenseits des Lustprinzips. In S. Freud, *Psychologie des Unbewußten* (pp. 217–272). Frankfurt am Main: S. Fisher Verlag.

Santayana, G. (1948). *The Life of Reason or the Phases of Human Progress Vol. 1: Introduction and Reason in Common Sense* (2nd) ed. New York: Charles Scribner's Sons.

# 16

# THE MOTOR OF THE MIND

The phenomenon of repetition, is, as we have seen, not a fundamental "drive," as Freud postulated, but an idiosyncrasy of the core mental process that can metaphorically be understood as a type of "mental indigestion." If there is any fundamental need of the human mind it is the need for understanding of experience. This may sound strange to a dynasty of psychoanalysts accustomed to thinking in terms of the drive-defence model, but strange or not, it is an insight that is necessitated by the observable facts.

Some psychoanalysts see the concept of drives as so central to psychoanalytic theory that they simply cannot imagine a metapsychology in which drives are understood as derivative entities. According to their point of view, human beings experience themselves as driven by forces that are beyond their control. Therefore there must actually be forces that they cannot control that impel them to perform actions that they do not wish to do. An extreme form of this argument can be found in Green (2000). The substance of Green's argument is that chemical castration can prevent pedophilic behaviour, therefore pedophilic behaviour is caused by a drive.

This argument, however, succumbs to a two-pronged counter-argument with a formal aspect and a material aspect. With regard to the formal aspect, Green's argument is deficient in that its premises do not guarantee the truth of its conclusions. To make this clear, consider the following argument, which has an identical form as Green's: aspirin can suppress the pain of headache, therefore the pain of headache is caused by a drive. This is patently absurd.

Now it may well be that there are certain drugs that interfere with the subjective feeling of sexual desire, but it is not at all clear whether a psychological experience of this sort can straightforwardly be equated with the inhibition of a biological drive. Even if we grant that it can, a further problem arises, since Green's argument simply takes on another invalid form: cutting out the tongue prevents the coprolalia associated with Tourette's syndrome, therefore the tongue is the cause of Tourette's syndrome. It is clear that one needs a tongue to present the symptoms of Tourette's syndrome (unless one learns sign language, I suppose) but in no sense can the tongue be conceived as their cause, although one requires a tongue to speak. Similarly, it is clear that a pedophile requires sexual desire for the purposes of sexually assaulting a child, and when this is absent due to castration, chemical or otherwise, sexual assault cannot occur in this form. But this in no way implies that the ultimate cause of sexual assault is sexual desire.

This leads neatly into the material aspect of the counter-argument. No one with even a passing acquaintance with the issue can possibly believe that the ultimate motive for sexual assault, whether of an adult or of a child, is frustrated sexual desire. As Green must know, the ultimate motive of sexual assault is the need to exercise absolute power and absolute control over another human being through cruelty, humiliation, and torture, and the origin of this need is to be sought in the perpetrator's own object world. Compounded with psychopathic sadism, sexual assault has the same basic structure as all perverse acts, namely the attempt magically to undo the perpetrator's own past victimization through erotic acting out and role reversal. Not only is Green's argument void of explanatory power, it brings us back to a 19th-century view of sexual assault as the product of untamed desire and of the aggressor as a passive victim of his own sexual desire, rather than as a psychopath who very actively twists his own sexual desire into a means to an end, namely to obliterate the psychotically threatening image of his own powerlessness by sexually assaulting an innocent human being.

The responsibility for sexual assault must be laid squarely with the perpetrator. Any attempt to blame some putative "drive" for its occurrence is a disavowal of personal responsibility that flies in the face of the obvious fact that the vast majority of men and women have sexual desires, but only a tiny minority are sexual criminals. Sexual assault is the acting out of a twisted object relationship. Here the theoretical emphasis must be placed on the relationship, which is unique to the criminal – not on the desire, which is common to all.

I have four more general points that I wish to adduce as a general criticism of drive theory. The first – as shocking as this idea may seem – is that biological needs, as such and without qualification, are entirely irrelevant to the psychoanalytic enterprise. What is relevant is the relational matrix in which biological needs are embedded. This can be made quite clear if we consider biological needs that are usually ignored by psychoanalysts, for example the need to breathe. The need to breathe plays no significant role in classical psychoanalytical theory despite the fact that it is even more urgent than the needs for sex, food, and the like. This can only be explained by the fact that certain bodily needs have a definite social significance, and therefore an ultimate emotional meaning, that others do not. Consider the following:

> Freud taught that sex and aggression were the two most powerful drives in the human psyche. He was wrong, of course. If you go for two days without sex

> and water, you will go for the water first when you get the chance. At the same time, he was very right. It's not that sex and violence are the two most powerful human drives, it's that sex and violence *are the two areas where what we have been told is "right" and what we feel can have the greatest conflict.* How we resolve these conflicts greatly defines our personality.
>
> *(Miller, 2008, p. 153) [italics mine]*

If for some reason our society suddenly decided to make breathing as significant to child-rearing as is, say, toilet training, we would probably find that breathing suddenly would be psychoanalytically significant in a way that it was not before (Guntrip, 1971, p. 35). This shows that biological needs of whatever sort are originally entirely neutral and only acquire meaning within the network of relationships. Perhaps future analytic work with asphyxiophiles will make this even clearer.

The second is that drive theory is entirely devoid of explanatory power. If we observe tremendous aggression and self-destructiveness, as Freud did in his patients, partly as a result of the two world wars, it tells us nothing to say that there is a supposed "death drive" that is supposedly responsible for the manifestation of these phenomena. It would both be simpler and more honest to invoke the traditional explanation and to say, "The Devil made them do it." I am reminded of Nietzsche's criticism of Kant to the effect that Kant did not actually explain the existence of a priori knowledge, he simply invented a new faculty that was supposed to explain it (*Beyond Good and Evil* § 11). To me, a proper explanation is supposed to account for the initially unfamiliar in terms of the familiar; accounting for the obscure in terms of the still more obscure is an attempt to avoid explanation, not to provide it. I am strongly inclined to agree with Nietzsche that such replies belong to the realm of comedy, and that – to borrow his phrase – it is high time to ask, "Why is belief in the drives *necessary*?"

My third point. Drive theory is often invoked as the only satisfactory way of explaining the subjective experiences of compulsion and conflict, but in point of fact that is precisely what it does *not* explain. Forces do not struggle against each other, they simply operate. Gravity does not struggle against an opposing force to pull an object to the earth, it either can or cannot do so, and if all the variables are known, there is no doubt with regard to the outcome. Struggle and conflict only occur when actual agents are involved, i.e. people in relationships striving with and against each other, and not when it is a case of the operation of mere forces or "drives." An inner struggle is always a struggle against an object, i.e. a fantasy involving persuasion or coercion: I want to, but you won't let me; I don't want to, but you're making me, and so on. There can never be a struggle against a biological need without the intervention of an object. Therefore the struggle is best understood as a struggle with the object, and not with the biological need.

My fourth and final point. We also need to take into account that a biological drive, in the proper sense of the term, is characterized by a "for" structure. So for example, hunger is a need *for* food just as the urge to breathe is a need *for* air. Love and aggression, however – Eros and Thanatos so-called – are characterized by a *with* ... *because* ... structure: in love *with* mother *because* she feeds me, angry *with* father *because* he takes mother away, and so on. In other words: a true biological drive has no true object in the strict psychoanalytical sense of the term, and this is its defining character. When an object is involved, the urge in question is either not a biological drive at all, or else it is a biological drive upon which an object relationship has been overlaid. Properly speaking, only object relationships are of any interest to psychoanalysis; inquiry into biological drives, if it has any place at all, would be the exclusive concern of an entirely different discipline, namely biology.

It would be most unfortunate if the reader were to misunderstand my rejection of drive theory as a rejection of the essentially passionate nature of human mental life. I hope that I have made it adequately clear that my objection to drive theory is based on weaknesses in its explanatory strategy. It is of no use to us if for every observable human action we hypostasize a mental entity that is supposed to be responsible for that action. It is as if we were asked to explain how a clock tells time and answered that a clock has an inherent horary drive that compels it to count the passage of the hours. What is required instead, in the case of a traditional mechanical clock for example, is an outline of how the mainspring and other parts in the movement of the clock interact to make the clock do the work that it does for us. Similarly, in the case of the mind, it is of no use to us if we posit the existence of some hypothetical force called Eros along with its evil twin Thanatos and then, like caricatures of idle mediaeval scholars, get into arguments about the nature of beings whose very existence is, to say the least, highly speculative. It may be of use to us, however, to provide a type of explanation that accounts for the significance that biological needs can acquire for the mind and for the driving effect that they can have on mental life. How, in other words, can the mind be pressed into the service of the body? What is the responsibility of the mind towards the biological reality with which it is partnered?

In order to answer this question I need to introduce another psychoanalytic construction, but one whose verisimilitude is strongly reinforced by the general postulates of our metapsychological system. I begin with our postulate of the infant's original mindlessness, as introduced in Chapter 11 and further qualified in Chapter 12. In those chapters we used the term "mindlessness" to denote the as yet minimally developed capacity for contextualization as a result of the minimal involvement of objects in the process of contextualization at the beginning of life. As far as we can tell, intrauterine existence makes no demand whatsoever upon the nascent mind for work. This is not to say that there are no intrauterine experiences at all, but it is likely that whatever experiences there are can all adequately be dealt with by summary dismissing. The nascent mind either does not think at all, or simply refuses to, and this is entirely adequate to its needs.

As Winnicott has suggested (1949/1975), the first real demand for work that is made upon the mind is occasioned by the experience of birth. The experience of birth is the first experience any of us have of an independent, uncontrollable external demand. It is thus the first intimation of an object, and everything we know or can reasonably hypothesize about the experience suggests that it is an extremely "bad" object that is created as a result. Owing to the infant's as yet undeveloped capacity for contextualization, the experience of birth leaves a permanent imprint on the infant's mind. This experience is the primeval cataclysmic "Big Bang" that thereafter never can be completely erased. It remains as a first, shattering experience that forever after leaves the individual vulnerable to fear and anxiety. This is so much the case that anxiety in later life is best described as the fear that the mind will fail to think, i.e. the fear that experience will prove just as overwhelming to the mind as it did during the act of birth. Anxiety is therefore rooted in the experience of maternal failure, since the core of the mind is patterned after the child's primary caretaker, and the cataclysm of birth is in a sense the very first experience of the failure of the mother to contain the child.

In time, of course, exhaustion supervenes, and the horrors of birth and breath yield to the infant's first exhausted sleep outside the womb. But the analysis of myth and legend, as well as hypotheses drawn from the examination of the mental life of adults, suggest that the event has momentous consequences. First, the period antecedent to birth is retroactively recast as an existence in Eden, as a lost Golden Age. It is frequently symbolized as an existence outside of time altogether, which makes sense in light of the fact that the infant's first experience of time is likely to be the cyclical recurrence of hunger, which is of course not experienced in the womb. Second, the period following birth is recast as a fall from grace, as a period of toil and trouble, and of progressive and inevitable decline. In other words, the experience of birth gives rise to the original split between the "good" and "bad" object. The experience of the "good" object through breastfeeding and satiation along with the comforting of the infant's physical malaise gives rise to an approximation of the intrauterine state; this is the source of its "goodness." Paradoxically enough, however, its very "goodness" entails its "badness," since the experience of the continual recurrence of hunger reveals it to be essentially impermanent and therefore essentially unreliable. Thus there may even arise an aversion towards the "good" object, a disinclination towards it or even a sense of positive resentment towards it, owing to its inability to produce lasting and permanent satisfaction, i.e. the relativity of its "goodness." This is equivalent to a resentment of having to undertake the burden of existence at all (Aulagnier, 1975/2007, pp. 63–66). None of this could have arisen within the original "good" environment, the womb, in which there is presumably a total or near-total absence of desire. It would perhaps not even be going too far to say that life itself gives our little philosopher a firsthand lesson in Buddhist ontology.

It will be noted that up to this point I have spoken of the experience of birth rather than of the birth trauma. This is a consequence of the very technical and very specific definition of trauma that I introduced in Chapter 15. I think that in any case there can be no doubt that the experience of birth is an overwhelming event that sows the seeds of later trauma. It can fruitfully be compared to the seed crystal around which the whole mental lattice crystallizes, or else with the grain of sand that gives ultimate shape to the pearl in the oyster.[1]

In this context I am concerned with a very specific type of traumatic response to the experience of birth, one that I will describe in the following terms. There can be little doubt that the experience of birth is an overwhelming event (in the technical sense of the phrase introduced in Chapter 15). It is a cataclysmic experience that completely exceeds the infant's capacity for information processing. As a result, the experience persists in the unconscious. In a very real sense, this experience will never be completely contextualized, since the infant's capacity for thought at this point is so limited that the impressions left in the mind are so incredibly inchoate and unformed that by their very nature they cannot be conceived or put into words in any real sense. This is probably why humans tend to resort to myths when they speak of their earliest beginnings: no other narrative mode is able to reflect the essential ineffability and uncertainty of our earliest experience of life.

Now with the uncontextualized experience of birth along with the essential incapacity of the infant's mind to think this experience, we have two of the four elements required for a traumatic response. The remaining two elements are supplied by the needs of the body. When, for example, hunger arises, the infant is all too easily overwhelmed by this new, as yet unfamiliar sensation (compare the discussion of Winnicott's notions of infant experience in Chapter 6). The ensuing distress is all too similar to that experienced by the infant during the birth experience. What we have, in short, is a full-blown traumatic response; and anyone in doubt about this needs only to listen to a child cry and ask what we would need to be feeling in order to produce similar noises. Over time, of course, the ministrations of the infant's primary caretaker ease the infant's sufferings, and the infant's mind begins to recognize what hunger is and how it is dealt with. Hunger pangs eventually become more or less routine, at least if the infant's caretaker succeeds in being good enough at the work of mothering, and at this point pleasure-seeking becomes a possibility among the infant's various motivations. What is most important for our theoretical enterprise, however, is the realization that *bodily needs initially only have a driving effect through retraumatization, i.e. through the reawakening of the birth experience – i.e. the reactivation of the primeval experience of distress.*

Now the phenomena of desire and aversion manifested in our example are well known, seemingly too well known to require any further examination; but this is only an appearance. The operation of desire and aversion in mental life gave rise to Freud's notion of the pleasure principle, which was later distilled into the constancy (or "Nirvana") principle. But the question we need to ask ourselves is: what is the central motive behind the operation of desire and aversion? Do they really function in order to keep the level of excitation in the organism at a minimal level? Or are they limited expressions of some other, more central process?

In answering this question we must insist upon our basic insight that all experiences are originally unconscious, i.e. uncontextualized, and in order for an experience to be experienced at all, whether as pleasurable or as painful, it must, to however minimal an extent, first be thought (contextualized). Once an experience has been contextualized as pleasurable or as painful, *then* various reactions to that fact can take place, including defensive reactions and other reactions in conformity with what Freud calls the "pleasure principle" or the "constancy principle." But without a prior, primeval disclosure of the experience in question, no reaction of any sort to that principle is possible. The mind cannot defend itself against anything that has not first been *actively recognized* as a threat. Therefore the primeval mental act, being prior to the pleasure and constancy principles, is not itself subject to these principles, since the primeval mental act – what I call the core mental process, or *thinking* – may well result in the thinking of an *unpleasurable* thought. Otherwise said: thinking, even in its embryonic forms, is *not* governed by the pleasure or constancy principles because it may well result in pain or in increased excitation. *The deliberate avoidance of thinking – defence – is a later, acquired response.*

Thinking in itself and as such *is* the response to a demand placed on the mind for work, but the nature of this demand is *not* to experience pleasure and avoid pain. Its nature is something else entirely; what it is, we shall see in Chapter 17. For now I will merely point out that (in contrast to Freud's later beliefs) the work accomplished by the core mental process also has nothing to do with repetition as such; as I explained in Chapter 15, repetition phenomena are themselves contingent on the core mental process, appearing only when there is a failure of this process (the traumatic response). *Thus the primeval principle of mental functioning is the need to know, whether or not what is known is pleasurable or painful, whether or not it increases the level of arousal in the organism or decreases it; and repetition is incidental, not essential, to its functioning.*

In order to avoid a possible misunderstanding it should be noted that by using the word "thinking" I have something rather different in mind than what we usually mean by the term. I use the word "thinking" as a convenient technical term to refer to the activity of the core mental process, i.e. the activity of contextualization. This is a spontaneous act (in Kant's sense of the term), i.e. it is not necessarily a conscious, voluntary, willed action, but something as independent of the personal will as the various metabolic processes of the body. Just as the body automatically undertakes the multitude of complex biological acts that are necessary to sustain life, the mind automatically undertakes the basic functions that are necessary to maintain its own life (Loewald, 1972/2000, pp. 145–146). What interests us here is the possibility of deeper insight into these basic functions.

Let us briefly review the territory we have covered so far in order to make sure that a somewhat complicated line of argument is completely clear. It is, I think, beyond a reasonable doubt that the infant's experience of birth is an experience of unfathomable distress. I have also explained the distress caused by bodily needs as a reactivation of the birth experience by means of the traumatic response. I think it is perfectly reasonable to assume that the infant has strong feelings of aversion to the birth experience and to the experience of biological needs (e.g. hunger) and does everything within its limited abilities to be rid of them. Insofar as this is the case, Freud's description of the operation of the pleasure principle is perfectly valid. Furthermore, Freud, in his attempt to explain the various phenomena of repetition, felt the need to introduce a supposedly more fundamental principle, the repetition compulsion; he then attempted to account for the pleasure principle as an aspect of the repetition compulsion (the attempt to reproduce the intrauterine state). In the present system of metapsychology, however, the phenomena of repetition are understood as incomplete attempts to process uncontextualized experiences, i.e. as manifestations of the traumatic response. In other words, I do not doubt that phenomena of repetition do in fact occur (it would be pointless to do so), but I do not think it is to the repetition compulsion that mental activity should be reduced. What I think Freud overlooked, however, is that in order both for the phenomena of repetition and for the phenomena that he understood as drive activity to take place, something else that is prior to both of these is required, something that we can describe as *the basic openness of the mind to experience.*

It is a central tenet of the present system of metapsychology that experience is not simply passively given to the mind. Rather, from the very beginning, experience is an active product, an active creation, of the dialectical structure of the self. Just as the products of vision are not simply given to the eye, but are in fact the results of extremely complicated spontaneous cognitive acts that involve the processing and recognition of colour, shape, distance, depth, and the like, experience itself is the result of a no less complicated array of psychological processes, *some* aspects of which our metapsychology strives to identify and to explain. Just as the basic task of the visual apparatus is to see, the basic task of the mind is to experience. Just as it makes no difference to the eye as such whether what is seen is pleasant or unpleasant, it makes no difference to the mind as such whether what is thought is pleasant or unpleasant. Of course, at a *later* stage of contextualization, owing to the presence of a persecutory or inadequate object world, individual perceptions may be both retroactively erased from the eye as well as from the mind. It would be sheer folly to doubt this. But we are nonetheless compelled by the facts to recognize that these defensive phenomena are *derivative* phenomena whose appearance is necessarily contingent upon a *prior* disclosure of the very experiences they attempt to suppress. Thus the fundamental phenomenon that makes defence at all possible is the basic disclosure of experience to the mind, or, in different terms, the basic need of the mind for experience (Heidegger, *Being and Time* § 7A; Sembera, "The Phenomenon-Concept in *Being and Time* and its Meaning for Hermeneutic Phenomenology," no date). This insight has two important consequences:

1. The "drives" are all merely *occasional* causes of human action. The real cause of human action is the attempt to process the birth experience. This alone is the real cause of human responsiveness to need.
2. Since the need for understanding – the need to think experience – is indifferent as such to pleasure or pain, neither the pleasure principle nor the constancy principle are adequate to describe its manner of working. Another principle must be invoked: *the fundamental need is to think.*

When I say the fundamental need is to think, this is equivalent to saying that the basic human need is to preserve psychic coherence and integrity in the face of the threat of psychic disintegration. Otherwise stated, in less traditional, and perhaps more accurate, terms: the one fundamental task set before every human individual by virtue of the very conditions according to which individuals can come into being at all is the solving of the riddle of one's own existence. This is the one true "drive" that impels to action; this is the true riddle of the sphinx of which all other human pursuits – ranging from the formation of infantile sexual theories to the pursuit of pleasure, and all the rest – are merely partial and limited aspects. Underlying all human pursuits, as their common ground and motivation, we see this attempt to answer the one single fundamental question: "*Why am I here?*"

The mind of the infant poses this question from the moment it is faced with the shattering experience of birth; perhaps its ability to feed and grow are the answers it finds. The mind of the adult poses this question and perhaps finds answers in the ability to love and work. The mind of the senior looks ahead to the cataclysmic moment of death, and perhaps finds answers in wisdom. *This* is the fundamental existential need that makes all human virtues desirable, all as possible viable answers to this fundamental human question.

## Note

1 In this context it may not be superfluous to add that although the idea of the significance of the birth experience is of course inspired by Otto Rank (1924), I have found his detailed interpretations so implausible and improbable that I have made no use of them in what follows.

## References

Aulagnier, P. (1975/2007). *La violence de l'interprétation*. Paris: Presses Universitaires de France.

Green, A. (2000). The Intrapsychic and Intersubjective in Psychoanalysis. *Psychoanalytic Quarterly* 69: 1–39.

Guntrip, H. (1971). *Psychoanalytic Theory, Therapy, and the Self.* New York: Basic Books.

Heidegger, M. (1927/1977). *Sein und Zeit.* (F.-W. v. Herrmann, Ed.) Frankfurt am Main: Vittorio Klostermann.

Kant, I. (1996). *Kritik der reinen Vernunft 1.* (W. Weischedel, Ed.) Frankfurt am Main: Suhrkamp.

Loewald, H. W. (1972/2000). The Experience of Time. In H. W. Loewald, *The Essential Loewald. Collected Papers and Monographs* (pp. 138–147). Hagerstown, MD: University Publishing Group.

Miller, R. (2008). *Meditations on Violence: A Comparison of Martial Arts Training & Real World Violence.* Wolfeboro, NH: YMAA Publication Center.

Nietzsche, F. (1886/1993). Jenseits von Gut und Böse. In F. Nietzsche, G. Colli, & M. Montinari (Eds.), *Jenseits von Gut und Böse. Zur Genealogie der Moral* (3rd ed., pp. 9–243). Munich: Deutscher Taschenbuch Verlag.

Rank, O. (1924). *Das Trauma der Geburt und seine Bedeutung für die Psychoanalyse.* Leipzig, Vienna and Zurich: Internationaler Psychoanalytischer Verlag.

Sembera, Richard. "The Phenomenon-Concept in Being and Time and Its Meaning for Hermeneutic Phenomenology." Unpublished paper, Ottawa, n.d.

Winnicott, D. W. (1949/1975). Mind and its Relation to the Psyche-Soma. In D. Winnicott, *Through Paediatrics to Psycho-Analysis* (pp. 243–254). London: The Hogarth Press and the Institute of Psycho-Analysis.

# 17

# FROM METAPSYCHOLOGY TO METAPHYSICS

The conclusions of the last chapter are, perhaps, conclusions at which it is unsurprising that a philosopher should arrive; but this can be no argument against their essential correctness, as we saw in Chapter 2. In any case they indicate the true nature and potential of the psychoanalytic enterprise, which I see as essentially and profoundly humanistic in orientation. No one could doubt that psychoanalysis from its very inception had an important relationship with questions of human freedom and culture, but what is perhaps somewhat less openly acknowledged is that what I may call the "humanistic" aspect of psychoanalytic theory has always existed in a very peculiar sort of alliance with its (pseudo-) scientific aspects. To put it clearly, if bluntly: in the forms in which science and humanism exist and are conceptualized within psychoanalysis, and despite all pretensions to the contrary, they can have nothing to do with each other, and can only be mutually antagonistic. Attempting to disentangle the history of this enmeshment is a wearisome and, in terms of practical consequences, one suspects, a futile task. Nevertheless I will content myself with a few remarks on the shifting historical attitude of psychoanalysis towards humanism and the sciences for the sake of bringing to light an aspect of this relationship that I think has been insufficiently appreciated in the past.

Wherever there is an intellectual discipline with an emphasis on a central founding figure, there is usually a concomitant blindness to errors and omissions in that central figure's works. For example, thanks to the considerable reputation that Aristotle enjoyed for millennia, until very recently his works were considered to be systematic, authoritative treatises that methodically addressed every aspect of reality and everything worth knowing within the limits of human experience – and this despite the obvious patchwork character of the Aristotelian corpus. The entire body of surviving Aristotelian writings is now considered by most scholars to represent in essence lecture notes, either taken down by Aristotle himself for his own use, or, more likely, compiled and edited by his students based on the notes they took during his classes. Those of us with teaching experience certainly know what it would mean if the only surviving record of our opinions and thoughts were to be redacted notes taken down by our own students, and I think we can be forgiven for feeling that this might just be a fate worse than complete obscurity.

A mischievous commentator might be tempted to say that the reader who knows Freud only in Strachey's English translation is hardly in a better position than the reader of Aristotle armed with the belief that he is working with complete, systematically composed treatises; but in any case I am for the moment more interested in an aspect of Freud's writings that I think is evident in both the German originals and their highly redacted English translations. Freud's works are replete with contradictions and inconsistencies, but perhaps the most significant of them all is the tension between the humanistic and (pseudo-) scientific inclinations in his writings. In the early published Freud, at the time, say, of the writing of *The Interpretation of Dreams* (1900/1996), the humanistic strain appears to be dominant. This Freud reprimands the physicians of his day for neglecting psychological causes and overemphasizing physical causes; he challenges the scientific orthodoxy of his times; he expresses a fundamental belief in the power of human reason and insight; his basic values include freedom, responsibility, and self-determination: as I noted in Chapter 5, *The Interpretation of Dreams* reads as if it were partly intended to be an instruction manual for interpreting one's own dreams. To anyone who admires this early Freud, whom I shall call Freud #1, the later Freud, or Freud #2, can only come as a bitter disappointment. This Freud #2, the Freud of the so-called "cultural" writings, instead of reprimanding physicians for reducing everything to physical causes, tries to outdo them at their own game; he is concerned to shoehorn his own psychological insights into what he perceives to be the scientific orthodoxy of his day, regardless of how grotesque the fit; far from believing in human reason and insight, he assures us that "cultural repression" is an absolute precondition of social cohesion – something that Freud #1 would have found absurd and would not under any circumstances have accepted; and far from positing human freedom as a basic value, Freud insists that everyone who wishes to practise analysis responsibly must be analyzed by him or by someone whose analytic lineage can be traced back to him, creating a widespread dependence of both would-be analysts and of individuals with mental health issues on a small côterie of supposedly well-trained specialists with transferential connections to himself. From this point of view the psychoanalytic movement certainly does appear as a "quasi-political movement," one that was prevented from developing to its true potential and from benefiting humanity to the fullest possible extent because of the many fatal personal limitations of its own founder, including ambition, greed, and destructive envy.

It is clear, then, that one of the central tasks facing modern psychoanalysis – should it wish to develop itself into an academic discipline, into a practical healing technique that can be learned and taught like any other – is to liberate itself from the personality cult that Freud established in order to limit the access of the general public to psychoanalytic knowledge and thus to cripple its own possibilities for development.

In popular depictions of psychoanalysis it is common to find the corpus of Freud's writings designated as the one thing all psychoanalysts of whatever stripe share in common; it would hardly be an exaggeration to say that acknowledgement of the privileged status of Freud's writings is more or less the *sine qua non* of recognition as a "genuine" psychoanalyst. This should give us pause, because in fact it is one obvious characteristic not of a science or of an academic discipline, but of a religion. In physics, for example, despite Einstein's monumental influence upon the subject, no physicist is characterized by an acceptance of the privileged status of Einstein's writings. One can well doubt whether the average physicist ever encounters Einstein's original papers, since these are now of merely historical interest. That a similar process – the dissemination of ideas along with a concomitant de-emphasizing of their original written form – has not occurred within psychoanalysis is a strong indication that its historical development has not followed the typical path of a "science" in any but the loosest sense of the word.

In this regard it would one day be most instructive to compare psychoanalysis with Zen Buddhism, though not in the casual way that this has been done in the past: I mean with a view to what I may call their common foundational myths. Many historical forms of Zen Buddhism also acknowledged the existence of a single, self-illuminated founder for whom an "exceptional position" within the structure as a whole was claimed; they were organized according to real or imagined lineages such that every full member of the hierarchy could claim some direct relation to the original founder and his authority; they insisted upon years of personal training with "qualified" teachers – i.e. ones who supposedly could trace their lineage back to the original founder – as a precondition for full membership; and their fundamental organizational principles appeared to be derived from the fantasy that correct organizational teachings are contained in a particular sort of "mind" understood to be a thing that could be transmitted from person to person through certain types of personal contact.

I think it is important to bear in mind when considering both movements and religions that one of the chief functions of a personality cult, or of any "cult of genius" in the widest sense, is to secure such a privileged position for the founder that average members feel relieved of both the responsibility of actually following in the founder's footsteps and of the guilt at failing to do so. Only such an exceptional individual could attain to such an exalted status, or so it is believed; why then trouble oneself with the attempt? What else can one expect but failure?

In any event, as much as we may deplore the essentially religious manner in which psychoanalytic organizations appear to have developed, it cannot be denied that psychoanalysis as an academic discipline does have some relevance to questions that it has traditionally been considered the responsibility of religion and philosophy to answer, largely because there has hitherto been nowhere else to address them. I now propose to summarize the findings of our metapsychological inquiry regarding some of these important issues before going on in the next chapter to address some of their purely metaphysical implications.

The definitive appreciation of the meaning of psychoanalysis for *ethics* has yet to be written; by "ethics" I do not mean what is usually designated by this term in our society, to wit: academic reflections on what the law should or should not be extended to allow people to do; rather, I am concerned with the implications of psychoanalysis for personal responsibility in the everyday act of decision making. Consider the following quotation:

> Until Freud, sincerity could be defined as saying what one believed. Since Freud this is no longer a sufficient definition. The difference between what I say and what I believe assumes a new dimension, namely that of my unconscious belief or my unconscious striving. If in pre-Freudian time a man was convinced that he punished his child because it helped the child's development he would have been quite honest, as long as he really believed that. After Freud the critical question has become whether his belief is not simply a rationalization of his sadistic wishes – that is to say, that he has pleasure in beating the child and only uses as a pretext the idea that such punishment is for the benefit of the child. In fact one might ethically prefer the one who is at least honest enough to admit his real motive; he would not only be more honest but less dangerous. There is no kind of cruelty and viciousness which has not been rationalized individually or in history as being motivated by good intentions. Since Freud, the sentence *I meant well* has lost its function as an excuse. Meaning well is one of the best rationalizations for acting badly, and nothing is easier than to persuade oneself of the validity of this rationalization.
>
> [...] Freud's discovery is not yet so generally accepted that people are instinctively critical of statements of good intentions or stories of exemplary behavior, nevertheless the fact is that Freud's theory is a critical theory [...]. Freud did not accept statements at face value; he looked at them skeptically even when he did not doubt the conscious sincerity of the person speaking. But conscious sincerity means relatively little within the whole of somebody's personality structure.
>
> Freud's great discovery, with its fundamental philosophical and cultural consequences, was that of the conflict between [conscious] thinking and being. But he restricted the importance of his discovery by assuming that essentially what is repressed is awareness of infantile sexual strivings and that the conflict between [conscious] thinking and being is essentially that between [conscious] thinking and infantile sexuality.
>
> *(Fromm, 1988, pp. 22–23)*

To begin with the last part of the citation: the primary motive of repression – or, as we would say, of the refusal of the mind to think – is *the fear of one's own personal responsibility and its ultimate consequences, i.e. its implications for the object world* (Heidegger, *Being and Time* §§. 39–40; Sembera, 2007, pp. 108–17). In this light it is clear that Freud's system of metapsychology is in fact a very accurate description of one particular type of mind, one that has a strong inclination towards one particular defence strategy, namely reduction to part-objects. Instead of existing in a world of people, the individual described by classical Freudian metapsychology exists in a world of "objects," i.e. of means towards ends. That such a stripped-down, depopulated environment can only be the product of a defensively motivated laying waste to the environment is conveniently overlooked, for this is part of the attempt to escape the complex ethical burden that existence itself imposes upon each and every individual.

It may be objected, though only by someone who has not carefully followed the arguments of the previous chapters, that the "infantile" state of mind is purely "narcissistic" and as such people can have no existence for infants except as the "drive objects" of classical theory. To this I reply that even intrauterine existence is not a truly "narcissistic" state, since this state can only exist at all when suitable conditions for its maintenance are provided by someone else on the infant's behalf. Far, then, from being a state in which another is absent, or a state of complete psychic self-sufficiency, it is rather a state completely permeated with the other, a state that continually testifies, however mutely at first, of its own complete dependence upon the other. There is no real escape, and never has been any, from the interpersonal network into which we are born and which crystallizes as the activity of the mind. Others are everywhere; they permeate the entire universe of experience, both conscious and unconscious.

Returning to the passage cited above, one could, perhaps, soften the tone of Fromm's criticism by claiming that psychoanalytic knowledge is after all not truly universal knowledge, but there is no way of escaping the ultimate conclusion that those who *have* been exposed to psychoanalytic knowledge, namely those who have benefited from psychoanalysis as clients, as well as those who have trained in psychoanalysis, psychoanalysts themselves – have thereby bound themselves to an ethical standard that is unique and without parallel in all of world history. Those who have never learned to see cannot be faulted if they stumble or bump into others; those who have learned to see can only stumble and bump into others if they are not paying attention or if they deliberately shut their eyes, and so are always and everywhere deserving of censure.

Psychoanalysis thus makes ethical demands upon the practitioner of an entirely novel and unique sort that cannot be compared with the ethical demands of other helping disciplines. Whereas the latter only apply to the individual to the extent of professional practice, the former are binding upon every single aspect of the individual's life, both personal and private. In this respect psychoanalysis does indeed have more in common with a religion than with an ordinary course of professional training, though with this difference: historically, religions have not been in possession of knowledge of the unconscious, and therefore have at least a superficial excuse if they have consistently failed to meet their own ethical standards. Psychoanalysis, on the other hand, *is* in possession of knowledge of the unconscious and of methods for making it conscious, and therefore has no excuse for failing to meet its own ethical standards. In terms of the therapeutic process, we may borrow a leaf from Jung and metaphorically state that psychoanalysis has this common with alchemy, that the state of grace of the operator (to use traditional mediaeval terminology) is vital to the success of the *magnum opus*, and that without it no work can be accomplished and all effort is in vain, even when all the requisite steps for the preparation of the Philosophers' Stone have been exactly and correctly followed to the letter.

In short, we are not so far from Plato's similar conclusions regarding philosophical knowledge in the *Meno*: it appears that psychoanalysis can indeed be learned, because there are some people who clearly can practise it; but it also appears that it cannot be taught, because it is not a mere procedure or technique that can be transferred from person to person, but a concrete practice with essential and intimate links to the internal ethical state of the practitioner – *i.e. one can only acquire psychoanalytic knowledge and practise psychoanalysis to the extent to which one accepts responsibility for one's own unconscious and takes active steps to establish and maintain a continual state of adequate relative self-knowledge throughout the whole of one's life and in all of its aspects, and succeeds in doing so.*

The mention of the subject of ethics naturally leads to the question of the possibility of freedom of choice, or, in other words, to the problem of free will so-called. Of course it is impossible in such a limited space adequately to address a problem that has bedeviled thinkers of all persuasions for more than two millennia, but there are two important points that I feel need to be made, particularly in light of Freud's generally quite casual treatment of the subject.

First, in *The Uncanny*, Freud speaks of

> all the unfulfilled possibilities of the shaping of [one's] destiny that fantasy still wants to hold on to, and all ego-strivings that could not assert themselves because of unfavourable circumstances, as well as all the suppressed [*unterdrückt*] decisions of will, which have given rise to the illusion of free will.
>
> *(1919/1994, p. 259)*

This rather offhanded treatment of an extremely important subject is all the more puzzling in the light of Freud's peculiar choice of words: he employs *unterdrückt*, "suppressed," where one would more naturally expect *verdrängt*, "repressed." In any event, I understand the passage to be based on a line of thought that runs something like the following: begin with the fundamental assumption that an unconsciously determined decision is not free; since all decisions have some unconscious determinants, no decision is free; therefore free will is an "illusion."

The fundamental assumption that underlies the argument is, however, rooted in a basic misunderstanding of the concept of freedom. It is more correct to say that a decision is free when it proceeds from one's true nature, and not free when it is forced upon one by circumstances, by authorities, or by an inadequate, neglectful, punitive, or hostile object world. In the words of Spinoza:

> That thing is said to be free which exists solely from the necessity of its own nature, and is determined to action by itself alone. A thing is said to be necessary or rather, constrained, if it is determined by another thing to exist and to act in a definite and determinate way.
>
> (Ethics *Part I, Def'n 7)*

Freedom, in other words, does not consist in the absence of determinants, but in the absence of compulsion: a decision made by flipping a coin may indeed be free of determinants from one's personal psychopathology, but we would hardly take this as an example of free choice for the simple reason that free choice does not mean arbitrary or random choice. The term "free choice" can therefore only mean a decision that reflects who one really is and what one truly wants. Freedom does not require freedom from oneself, but only a relative independence from alien interference.

This makes it evident that the free/unfree dichotomy does not straightforwardly dovetail with the conscious/unconscious dichotomy, as Freud's words would seem to imply. Generally speaking, it is of course more likely that an unfree decision will be predominantly determined by unconscious (i.e. repressed) factors, and that a free decision will be predominantly determined by conscious (or preconscious) factors, but all decisions, whether free or unfree, have both conscious and unconscious determinants. In the strictest terms, however, the difference between a free and an unfree decision does not consist in whether the decision is conscious or unconscious, or whether it is arbitrary and random on the one hand or completely determined on the other. If a decision is based on a correct understanding of one's own internal states, regardless of any other factors that decision is free; to the extent that a decision is based on an incorrect understanding of one's own internal states, that decision is unfree. The opposite of "free" is neither "unconscious" nor "determined" but "compelled"; and it is immaterial whether that compulsion proceeds from a bad object or from a good object, or from any other source. In still more basic terms: a free decision is made on the basis of what one really knows one really wants for oneself; an unfree decision is not.

Insofar as we consider freedom an ethical value, the aforementioned considerations make it all the more evident why the supreme ethical value is, and can only be, self-knowledge. Only those who know themselves can be themselves, and only those who can be themselves are free.

Second, in *The Question of Lay Analysis*, Freud remarks that:

> All our social institutions are tailored to persons with a unitary, normal ego that one can either classify as good or evil, that either performs its function or is disabled by a much more powerful influence. Thus the legal alternative: responsible or not responsible. All these decisions are not suitable for neurotics. [...] Were the neurotics who withdrew from military service malingerers or not? They were both. [...] Neurotics complain about their illness, but they capitalize upon it with all their might, and when one wants to

> take it from them, they defend it like the proverbial lioness defends her cub without there being any sense in reproaching them for this contradiction.
>
> *(1926/1997, p. 312)*

Although we can safely dismiss the implication that everyone who avoids military service for reasons of psychological illness is in some sense a malingerer, the passage does touch upon an extremely thorny issue, namely the complications that the concept of the unconscious introduces for the issue of legal and ethical responsibility. We might perhaps state the problem in this way: we know from clinical practice that there is a strong link between early child abuse and criminal and antisocial behaviour in later life. That is to say, from a psychoanalytic point of view antisocial and criminal acts are very often attempts on the part of psychologically damaged individuals to deal with their own intolerable mental states by acting out apparent solutions in the real world. To take a banal example, many child abusers were themselves victims of abuse as children, and the ultimate aim of their crimes is to obliterate the torment of the mental image of themselves as helpless victims and to allow them to experience themselves as powerful abusers. But if criminals were themselves originally victims, to what extent can they be blamed for their actions later in life? In more abstract terms: having established the conditions under which a decision is free or unfree (the presence or absence of compulsion), it is now important to inquire into the conditions under which one can be said to be *responsible* for a particular decision.

I find it convenient to begin this inquiry with a distinction between *responsibility* and *accountability*. One can, indeed must, be held accountable for actions for which one is not responsible. Common sense suggests, however, that lack of responsibility can be a mitigating factor. I mean for example that if Alzheimer's disease causes someone to be violent, it makes sense to restrain, but not to jail or otherwise punish, that particular person.

I think I can say that traditionally psychoanalysts felt a certain temptation to equate responsibility with conscious decision and lack of responsibility with unconscious decision. As we saw in our prior discussion of freedom, however, this is no longer possible. I think that it is most in accord with our natural use of the term if we see responsibility as proceeding along a continuum beginning with totally free decision and ending at a point where there is totally unfree decision. In other words, I see responsibility as essentially another word for freedom.

Thus prepared, we are better equipped to return to our original question, which we can now frame in the following terms: although it is clear that the criminally violent must be held accountable for their actions, to what extent are they truly responsible for them? To what extent do they freely choose to be what they are?

It will be seen that this question is closely linked to the problem of whether there is or is not an innate human need for violence, a "death drive" or "Thanatos" so-called. I have already pointed out the inadequacies of drive theory as an explanatory strategy in Chapter 16, but there I left the question of the nature and number of the traditional psychoanalytical drives more or less open. Here, however, I will go one step further and demonstrate that there is no such thing as a "death drive" in any meaningful sense. Consider the following:

1. Any true drive (i.e. biological need) is necessarily linked with an experience of satisfaction or at least satiation when its aim is achieved. Thus the sex drive is commonly satisfied by the orgasm, the hunger drive by food, and so on. It is, however, a matter of common experience that there is no such moment of satisfaction when aggression is expressed. Even the clinical sadist has to forge an artificial link with the orgasm in order to obtain a semblance of actual pleasure from destructiveness, and any satisfaction derived from the act is related to the fantasy of triumphing or vanquishing, not to destructiveness itself.
2. If there were really an innate need for aggression, we would expect destructive people to count among their number many whose childhood experiences were pleasant, happy, and marked by indulgence; and we would expect healthy and satisfied adults also to be destructive individuals. Yet it is again a matter of common knowledge that the exact opposite is actually the case.
3. The "death drive" theory is sometimes touted as a means of explaining how it is that apparently "normal" people can commit atrocities during times of war. The problem with this explanatory strategy, however, is that it tends to blind us to the question of what "normal" really means. In this particular case an obviously false assumption is being made that, when applied to the human population, "normal," "numerically preponderant," and "healthy" are more or less convertible terms.

For my part, I believe that wars of all stripes are the loud and public manifestation of a silent and private disgrace, namely the widespread proliferation of unrecognized, unacknowledged, and frequently culturally sanctioned child abuse of a physical and/or psychological nature. That the average and expectable home environment even in our supposedly civilized Western society is most often woefully inadequate, at best, should be clear to every psychoanalyst, if not to every human being of discerning judgement; there is a reason why group phenomena – of which society at large is but one example – are as blind, disordered, and destructive as they commonly are. It is because in groups people behave as they do in families. The so-called riddle of wartime violence disappears when we realize that average individuals are psychopathic in many well-defined and culturally approved areas of their lives, not the least of which is our typical treatment of animals. War simply provides the opportunity for our normal psychopathic state to express itself openly. One might even go so far as to say that there is nothing less in need of an explanation than wartime atrocities. To borrow a phrase from von Clausewitz, war is simply the continuation of everyday life by other means.

It follows from all this that the single most important thing to be done for the betterment of society as a whole is to secure a widespread improvement in child-rearing techniques, and it is hardly an understatement to say that until this is done the world will not know peace.

At the beginning of life, then, just as we are all born mindless – with the potential for thought but lacking the means – we are all born *unfree*, and remain so until someone else makes it possible for us to be free. By engaging the rest of our own abilities, talents, and skills we can expand and elaborate upon that initial grain of freedom, but always and only within the limits dictated by the structure of our object world. Freedom, then, is limited both by our own nature and by the object world, but it can be increased over time – by knowledge, which transforms the object world by bringing it into consciousness where it becomes subject to change (contextualization). Increasing our freedom also increases our responsibility, i.e. our moral and ethical burden, something in which ethical individuals delight, because to bear the burden of oneself is to be oneself. It is in this that, to me, true wisdom consists.

In conclusion – and to finally give a direct and unequivocal answer to our main question – we are free to the extent that the object world allows us some ability to understand and to respond to our inner states accurately and appropriately and to the extent that we have the inner resources available to make use of this ability. Thus everyone who suffers child abuse but does not become a criminal as a result has had some lingering experience of a good, reliable person somewhere, or has some internal resources to draw on, e.g. critical intelligence, in order to cope with the abuse. In this way the individual has managed to retain some capacity for freedom. Where these two – internal and external goodness – are utterly lacking, the person becomes a criminal because "identification with the aggressor" so-called (really: driving away an intolerable mental image by means of magical ritual) is the only option for psychic survival. In short: no one who *can* choose otherwise than to become a criminal fails to do so (compare Plato's *Meno* 77b–78c).

This is, of course, an extreme case, and the vast majority of us know at least some goodness and therefore have at least some freedom. With freedom comes the moral obligation to do everything in one's power to increase it. One should never forget that the original capacity to be free is not itself a matter of free choice, and that it is not granted everyone in the same measure, although we all can be held responsible, to the degree that we are free, for failing to increase our freedom (Matthew 25:14–30; Luke 19:12–27). Thus, as difficult as it may be, it is well for one to say in considering even the most twisted criminal: "There but for the grace of God go I."

## References

Freud, S. (1900/1996). *Die Traumdeutung*. Frankfurt am Main: S. Fischer Verlag.

Freud, S. (1919/1994). Das Unheimliche. In S. Freud, *Psychologische Schriften* (pp. 243–274). Frankfurt am Main: S. Fischer Verlag.

Freud, S. (1926/1997). Die Frage der Laienanalyse. Unterredungen mit einem Unparteiischen. In S. Freud, *Schriften zur Behandlungstechnik* (pp. 275–349). Frankfurt am Main: S. Fischer Verlag.

Fromm, E. (1988). *Greatness and Limitations of Freud's Thought*. Chicago: Meridian.

Heidegger, M. (1927/1977). *Sein und Zeit.* (F.-W. v. Herrmann, Ed.) Frankfurt am Main: Vittorio Klostermann.

Plato. (1981). *Meno* (2nd) ed. (G. Grube, Trans.) Indianapolis and Cambridge: Hackett Publishing Company.

Sembera, R. (2007). *Rephrasing Heidegger. A Companion to "Being and Time".* Ottawa: University of Ottawa Press.

# 18

# WHERE DO WE LIVE?

I have tried throughout this book to confine the discussion of purely philosophical topics to an absolute minimum, preferring for the most part to use philosophy as an instrument to address difficult points of psychoanalytic theory, but we have reached a point in our investigations when this is no longer possible. In the end it is impossible to ignore the fact that the mind is by its very nature linked with the body, and so the nature of the mind cannot be grasped without some understanding of this link. In Chapter 14 I dealt with this issue in a preliminary way, going only so far as to point out that the mind as such is not a physical thing and therefore is entirely lacking in physical properties: it has neither extension in space nor any physical location, nor does it have any physical relation to any physical object whatsoever, including the body, to which it is only linked in fantasy. Accordingly, in Chapter 14 I defined the mind as "the totality of fantasies about bodies and their relationships with their corresponding objects." For the sake of completeness one could of course add the clause "along with the fantasy-making activity itself," i.e. the work of contextualization, which is the activity of the core mental process. While this definition is more or less adequate for the practical work of psychoanalysis and psychotherapy, it sheds no light on the relationship between the apparently immaterial and disembodied mind and the material and physical body that it nevertheless in some way possesses, and this so intimately and necessarily that one's own body figures in some form in virtually every single individual experience that one has. How is this possible?

This problem is, of course, known to the wider philosophical tradition as the mind–body problem, the essentials of which it may be useful briefly to summarize. To put it in very concrete first person terms, on the one hand it is difficult to understand how the alcohol in my glass, which is a physical thing, becomes the euphoria in my mind, which is, qua experience, neither a physical thing nor any conceivable aspect of a physical thing. On the other hand I have a similar difficulty in understanding how the notion in my mind, which is a thought, becomes my writing on paper, which is, qua physical thing, neither a thought nor any conceivable aspect of a thought. So the infamous mind–body problem really boils down to a conceptual difficulty – not a real difficulty, it is to be noted – in connecting thoughts with things, and vice versa. We know that physical states do influence mental states in some non-trivial sense of the term "influence," and vice versa. What we fail to understand is *how* this takes place.

One obvious strategy when faced with two apparently irreconcilable elements is to try to do away with one of the pair. This is the common strategy shared by both Materialism and Idealism. The former is the reduction of thoughts to things; the latter is the reduction of things to thoughts. The fact that both these formulations sound so peculiar is already a hint that neither approach works particularly well in the end.

The central weakness of the materialist approach is that it never explains precisely how a chemical can give rise to an experience. In basic terms, Materialism fails to explain how a physical thing can apparently become something utterly unlike a physical thing, namely a thought, while actually remaining a physical thing all the time. Or if you like, it never explains how a chemical process can wake up and say (bark, chirp, chatter) "I." The best Materialism has done so far is to offer a sort of rough correlation between thoughts and things in the nervous system or elsewhere in the body, but when it comes to the actual explanation of the effects of things on thoughts, metaphor is relied upon. Alcohol supposedly fuddles our wits because it "interferes" with the transmission of electro-chemical impulses across our synapses. Proponents of this style of explanation simply cross their fingers and hope that the biochemical "interference" with our synapses is ultimately the same as the cognitive "interference" with our thoughts; but this is relying on a purely verbal resemblance to do the work of crossing the ontological breach between mind and body. It is to pretend that metaphor can do the same work as explanation. Would we conclude that anxiety is the stretching of a spring simply because we use the same word "tension" to describe both states? (Chapter 1)

There are, of course, also the various materialist evasions of the problem, such as behaviourism, epiphenomenalism, and the like. In essence, these are theories of how to avoid the issue with a clear conscience. Their common strategy is to argue that thoughts just do not influence physical things at all, which is clearly absurd. If I insult someone and that someone flushes with anger, I do not consider it an adequate explanation to maintain that said person was "conditioned" to respond to a particular series of sonic units with a particular physiological reaction, nor do I consider it an adequate explanation to claim that the kinetic energy in the sound waves I emitted, after entering into the brain via the eardrum and then meandering for some distance through various electro-chemical pathways, was eventually transformed (according to the principle of conservation of energy) into tachycardia and into the dilation of subcutaneous facial capillaries. Surely we have to take the insult itself and as such into account?

The other form of philosophical reductionism, Idealism, attempts to redefine all experiences of physical things as experiences of thoughts. Perhaps the clearest exposition of this point of view can be found in the opening sentences of § 1 of Schopenhauer's masterwork *The World as Will and Representation*:

> "The world is my representation": – this is the truth that is valid for every living and knowing being; although humans alone can bring it into reflective abstract consciousness: and should they really do this, then they have achieved philosophical illumination. Then it is clear and certain to them that they know no sun and no earth; but always merely an eye that sees a sun, a hand that feels an earth; that the world that surrounds them only exists as representation, i.e. completely only in relation to something else, [namely] that which represents, which they themselves are.
>
> *(1818/1988, p. 31)*

Criticisms of Idealism tend, broadly speaking, to rally around various shibboleths of common sense, and while I think that common sense by and large gets far more credit than it actually deserves, it has to be admitted that Idealism does have its problems. The elimination of a shared physical world makes it difficult to explain how different people can have the same shared experiences, so that one either has to introduce some form of *deus ex machina* that is responsible in some way for ensuring the fundamental agreement of the shared content of shared experiences between different individuals – whence the transcendent "God" of Descartes, Leibniz, and especially Berkeley (Chapter 10) – or else collapse into the position that only one's own mind is known with certainty, which is a polite way of saying, "I know that I exist, but I'm not so sure about all of you." A more extreme variant of this latter position, "I know that I exist and I know that none of you do," is known to the philosophical tradition as *solipsism* (Chapter 13), about which two things bear mentioning: first, solipsism only exists as a theoretical position that is most frequently used to illustrate the conceptual difficulties of Idealism. There has never been one single solipsist in the entire history of Western philosophy. Second, in some form or another, solipsism is a theoretical problem for every skeptical system, not just for Idealism. In this connection it is interesting to note that Schopenhauer himself concedes in § 19 of *The World as Will and Representation* that solipsism (which he calls "theoretical egoism") is irrefutable; since, however, it could only be found as a "serious conviction" in a "madhouse," it is less in need of a refutation than a "cure," and so we can treat it "as a small border fortress that can never be taken, but whose garrison can never leave, for which reason one can simply pass by and leave it behind without any danger" (1818/1988, p. 157). As true as this may be in practice, we are, I think, justified in continuing to feel a certain unease at leaving this particular fortress unconquered in our wake. Resorting to invective when arguments fail us is a time-hallowed tradition that is as old as Aristotle, but it seems to me that for this issue in particular – the existence of a plurality of individual consciousnesses – we should have some better solution than invective.

Any theory that aspires towards a satisfactory resolution of the mind–body problem should therefore in the first place attempt to avoid the weaknesses of both Idealism and Materialism, which is to say:

1. it has to allow for shared experience and exclude solipsism as a theoretical possibility;
2. it has to explain the apparent two-way communication between mind and body without simply eliminating one in favour of the other.

It will be seen that the problem as a whole really has two distinct aspects: the *intersubjective* aspect, or the problem of communication between individuals, and the *intrasubjective* aspect, or the problem of communication between different regions (for lack of a better term) of the same individual.

Within the relatively restricted scope of this essay I cannot present the entire course of argument that has led me to adopt the following solution. Such a presentation would be better suited to a formal treatise of ontology, which this book cannot aspire to be. In the present context I think it should suffice if we adopt a slightly lower formal standard that we can call a *heuristic* criterion of truth.

The application of a heuristic criterion of truth can be illustrated in the following way. If, for example, we are faced with an initially meaningless cipher and then, after some experimentation, find that applying a certain substitution of letters allows us to translate the original into a meaningful message, we can reasonably safely assume that we have indeed found the correct solution to that cipher, particularly in the absence of any other functional solution. Even more simply: if we find that applying a particular key to a particular lock allows us to open that lock, then we can assume that we have the correct key in our possession, particularly in the absence of any other functioning key. A heuristic criterion of truth is perhaps not the ideal – one can always imagine a cipher with several meaningful solutions, or a lock that can be opened by several keys, which leaves us in a quandary as to which (if any) is the actually intended meaningful solution of the cipher, or which (if any) is the key that was actually made to fit the lock. For most everyday practical purposes, however, a heuristic criterion of truth is perfectly adequate, and so for the immediate purposes of this essay it will also be sufficient if we arrive at a solution that is possible, workable, and suggestive of further meaningful lines of investigation.

It is also important – to me at least – that the solution be possessed of a certain elegance and even grace, for lack of a more precise and concrete term. The simplest way of opening a lock is to smash it with a sledgehammer; but I prefer the gentle easy glide of the key turning in the lock. This is in my opinion the true essence of that aesthetic principle generally known to the lay public as "Occam's Razor" and that is so often incorrectly paraphrased as "the simplest explanation is the best."

In this spirit I now wish to direct the attention of the reader towards the phenomenon known as the *lucid dream*. I have no way of knowing how many of my readers have actually experienced a lucid dream, or how clearly those among my readers who have had them can remember them, for which reason I will go into the matter in some detail. A lucid dream is a dream in which dreamers are aware that they are dreaming. The degree of this awareness is variable; sometimes the awareness is merely recalled in the morning like any other aspect of any other dream; and sometimes it attains the immediate intensity of a conscious experience in everyday waking life. It is with this latter – and I think relatively rare – type that I am principally concerned, because it is the type that is the most philosophically instructive.

For those who would like to experience lucid dreams for themselves, I unfortunately have no advice; in myself the phenomenon has been infrequent enough, and the most intense lucid dreams I have had appeared more or less spontaneously as a result of regular meditation practice over a number of years and as a result of psychological changes that were occurring in me at that time. In any case the ability is not one that I would either encourage or discourage anyone from developing. For those who would like some acquaintance with the general emotional landscape of these and similar regions of the mind I can recommend the reading of Philip K. Dick's *Ubik* (1969/2002), which deals with essentially the same philosophical issues in a purely literary context.

As stated above, in the course of my entire life, to the best of my recollection, I have had only a handful of lucid dreams that exhibited the full intensity of conscious experience. The sample size being relatively small, it would be difficult to arrive at reliable statements about dreaming in general and about lucid dreaming in particular. Still, what is important in the present context is to ascertain the extent of the active role of the mind in producing conscious experience. Our question is: "Is the mind capable of producing an experience that for all intents and purposes is indistinguishable from ordinary everyday waking experience without the assistance of physical objects in an external physical world?" I want to address this question by quoting a short record of one of my own lucid dreams:

> *Thursday July 8, 2004. A Biographical Note.* About two weeks ago, in the last week of June, I had an extremely vivid lucid dream. The dream began with a scene in which I was driving a car up a very steep hill, perhaps in [...] Park? The area was vaguely familiar from my childhood. Then I was standing on some rocky cliffs [...] looking down upon a marvellous river. The area reminded me vaguely of the creek at [...] my old junior high school. The entire scene glowed with vivid, surreal colours – emerald green for the trees, aquamarine blue and arctic white for the crashing waves below. I was thrilled beyond words.
>
> But then the dream changed and seem to become a long sequence of banal events involving a lot of travelling, driving around, pointless, hectic searching, and so on. I found myself in a hotel room rather like the one I stayed at during the [...] job interview. All this time in the dream it seemed that I heard a distant voice muttering "This is only a dream," over and over, with a resigned tone, as if it all had to be gotten over with. I just had to wait until the sequence of events in the dream played itself out.

But all of a sudden, the thought flashed into my head: "Well, if this is a dream, and I find it tedious and banal, then why don't I just wake up?" And suddenly I was conscious within the dream itself. I realized I was dreaming and decided to use the opportunity to experiment. The first thing I did was to very carefully become aware of my surroundings. In retrospect, my memory seemed to be a little weak – I knew who I was and that I was dreaming, but not much else. A lot of my usual memories seemed to be disabled. But I was able to become aware of a whole network of thoughts in the "background," as if they were part of the scene in the hotel room. It was like a battery of telegraph operators all relaying messages to each other. It seemed to me that this was the mental activity that created the scenery of the dream, an activity of which I was only peripherally aware. Watching this background mental activity, it seemed obvious to me that in dreaming, we always know that we are asleep. This knowledge is just temporarily suppressed in order to subject the dream-ego to the experiences of the dream, for whatever ultimate purpose.

Then I focussed on the objects in the hotel room. They were perfect in every respect, from shading to colour and texture. The texture of the carpet and the details of the radiator – rust, peeling paint, and so on – were perfect. The scene was absolutely indistinguishable from a real world experience. I reflected that had I not known I was dreaming, there would be no way to distinguish the dream from reality. The simulation was flawless. It puzzled me that one part of me was apparently undertaking all the work involved in generating the scenery, and yet my conscious self within the dream was only very peripherally aware of the process by which the scene was generated. I could neither explain nor understand it; I only understood that it was a production of a part of myself.

Finally, I decided to attempt to change the scenery by force of will. I thought of causing [...] to appear in the dream. I immediately thought this to be an utterly stupid use of the lucid state, but then I began, it seemed, to drift back into sleep within the dream state itself. I knew that if I succumbed, the banal sequence of events would resume, and I would become the same will-less spectator I had been before waking up. I needed to think of something shocking in order to retain my grip on wakefulness. So I focussed my will and the scene began to blur and change. But suddenly, my consciousness "widened" in an odd sort of rush – like the aperture of a camera suddenly being opened fully. I can only explain the sensation by saying that parts of my conscious mind which had previously been disabled were suddenly enabled – there was a "widening" and "complexity-increasing" effect, and I woke up to a morning scene with [my wife shaking me awake] – but with absolutely no interruption in the flow of consciousness like there normally is when one wakes from a dream. I had quite literally already woken up in the dream state.

[...]

The peculiar attentive focus in the dream seems to have been the result of my meditation practice – in the dream I felt myself relaxing and just watching

> my thoughts, just as one does in meditation, and this is probably the effect which caused me to become conscious in the dream. The implication seems to be, though, that everyday life might just be produced in analogy to a dream, and that it might be possible to wake from this dream. But this means that there are uncharted and unsuspected depths to our everyday experience that are lurking in the background – our everyday experience is, in fact, a sort of dream – and the reality behind it might just be utterly different from what we think it is.

To begin, some words about the traditional interpretation of lucid dreams. In 1909 Freud added a few brief paragraphs to *The Interpretation of Dreams* (pp. 543–545) in which he attempted to assimilate lucid dreaming to the wish fulfillment theory; the brevity of his remarks suggests that he did not consider the existence of lucid dreaming to pose any real challenge to his ideas regarding the nature and function of dreams. In brief, for Freud lucidity occurs (1) to avoid unpleasant outcomes in the dream, e.g. to prevent the experience of anxiety; and (2) to gain pleasure from the sense of control over the dream. In other words: Freud conceded the existence of lucidity as a phenomenon, but treated it as an aspect of wish fulfillment, and so like any other manifest content of a dream.

There can be absolutely no doubt about the essential correctness of this analysis, so far as it goes; my own account begins with an exhilarating vivid natural scene that was clearly pleasurable (compare the beginning of the second of Berkeley's *Three Dialogues*) and my own satisfaction at being able to conduct my philosophical investigations of the dream was quite evident. There can also be no doubt that in this dream at least the emergence of lucidity served the immediate purpose of breaking off the beginning of a nightmare; for reasons of personal discretion I have of course edited my account to keep the latent dream content private, but I will mention that the hotel room in the dream was associatively linked with a series of thoughts that was highly disturbing to me at the time. These and later experiences have led me to believe that the unconscious motivation of a lucid dream is the denial of some distressing reality. This defensive strategy is mirrored in the dream as a denial that one is dreaming. The lucid dream cries, "I can't believe my eyes!" or "This can't be happening!" These are not mere statements of fact, but expressions of desire. The surface meaning "this can't be happening" carries the deeper meaning "I don't want this to happen," just as the surface meaning "I can't believe my eyes" carries the deeper meaning "I don't want to believe my eyes." For this reason I suspect, but cannot prove, that lucid dreams may be more common in those with primal scene experiences in infancy. In any case, the essentially defensive function of lucidity along with its origin in denial is absolutely clear.

Of course the psychoanalytical meaning of a lucid dream in itself says nothing about its philosophical implications, which are varied and interesting. In a lucid dream the experiences of the mind, the body, and the apparently external physical world are all just as they are in waking life. Other than the knowledge that one has that one is dreaming, there are absolutely no internal criteria that could be used to distinguish the dream experience from waking experience. The experience of physical objects is just as it is in waking life; every detail is perfect; and I have no doubt that given a lucid dream of sufficient length and consistency, a physicist could perform a series of experiments and formulate a system of physics that would describe the behaviour of objects in the dream world just as well as our modern physical theories describe our own apparently real waking world. Perhaps the resulting theories in both cases would even be identical.

It is important to note that despite the obvious wish fulfillment in the dream my mind was still able to generate a perfect simulacrum of the waking world. Whether it did or did not do so at the behest of a wish, it remains true that it *was* able to do so; and this is the all-important point as far as our present investigation is concerned.

Let us consider matters a little more closely, beginning with the internal perspective of the lucid dream. In the lucid dream there is an experience of the mind and of the stream of consciousness along with an experience of the body and of the external physical world, just as there is in everyday waking life. It exhibits the same broad division into mind and matter as does the waking world. And yet in the lucid dream there is a clear awareness that one is in fact dreaming, i.e. there is definite knowledge of a *third* that is not the mind because it is producing the experience of a mind within the dream, and that is also not a physical thing because it is producing the experience of physical things within the dream. It is, again, a *third* possibility that, with respect to the internal dream perspective, is neither material nor mental, but carries all the information we need to construct the experience of a mental and material world (Chapter 9). As well, again with reference to the internal perspective of the dream, this third is unknown and unknowable. We can be certain that it is there and that it is responsible for the many and varied dream experiences because we know that we are dreaming, and yet we can neither know what it is nor understand how it functions because it is this itself that is responsible for producing the phenomena of knowledge and understanding within the dream. It is something = X of whose existence we can be certain and yet of which we can have no real knowledge because knowledge is one of the artefacts of its activity; it is something that precedes and surrounds the act of knowledge, and which makes knowledge possible in the first place. This X remains, and must remain, in the background of the dream in order for us to have the dream experience of a mental and material world, from the perspective of which world it is uncontextualized and uncontextualizable, being a third that is neither matter nor mind, and therefore does not fit into the possible regions of experience.

Now our specific term for the totality of the uncontextualized is the *unconscious*. In Chapters 4 and 7 we mentioned in passing Bion's notion that processes analogous to the dream work are constantly occurring, both during the dream state and throughout waking life; and in Chapter 6 we saw that the core mental process, or the activity of contextualization – the process that converts uncontextualized unconscious primary experience into contextualized conscious secondary experience – is a continual, unceasing process that transcends and permeates every possible phase of our experience. In other words, it is my contention that our waking life, with its division into the realms of matter and mind, self and other, is produced and sustained by processes analogous to those that are active in the lucid dream, to wit: a universal process appearing to our investigations as the core mental process (the activity of contextualization) that surrounds, permeates, and ultimately creates the totality of human experience by elaborating and articulating the information carried in the unconscious into the experience of our everyday waking world. In short: the difference between waking life and the lucid dream or even the regular non-lucid dream is more a difference of coherence and duration, and not a radical difference in kind (compare Schopenhauer's *The World as Will and Representation* § 5).

In comparing waking life with a dream in this way it is perhaps not superfluous to mention that my aim is not to undermine the reality of the waking world in any sense, rather I mean to emphasize the active creative role that the marvellous creative power of the mind plays in producing experience of whatever sort. Let us proceed to investigate this power from the perspective of waking life rather than from that of the lucid dream. If the results of our investigation are essentially correct, then the answer to the question "Where do we live?" is neither "in the physical world" nor "in the mental world"; the answer can only be: in the unconscious. The unconscious is the apparently empty, apparently unknown, ever mysterious womb of experience. All we are comes from it; all we see is seen in it. To use the language of Spinoza: it is an infinite substance possessing infinite attributes expressing infinite essence. To us, two broad regions of this infinite substance are accessible: the world of mind and the world of matter. The unconscious is the repository of uncontextualized primary experience; it carries all the information we need to construct a world of matter and of mind; it conceals itself qua totality of the uncontextualized in order to show itself in us, through us, and to us, remaining in the background all the while, inaccessible and unknown and yet powerfully and creatively active, forming a negative horizon for the work of contextualization, much as the paper is inaccessible and unknown in the course of the act of reading and yet forms the backdrop against which the letters of the writing can appear at all. One of its names in Sanskrit is *śūnyatā*; the *Upanishads* call it *Brahman*; Spinoza calls it *deus sive natura*; I call it the *unconscious*. All are different names referring to the different paths by which it is possible to arrive at the same destination.

From the unconscious the process of contextualization elaborates the experience of the two realms of matter and mind in a fashion analogous to translating the same primary text into two radically different and unrelated languages. The realm of matter consists of an apparently endless chain of efficient causes that apparently stretch into infinity in both directions of time; the realm of mind consists of a similar infinite chain composed instead of final causes. This implies that body and mind are ultimately one and the same experience that is narrated according to two different and distinct themes (Chapter 9). As well, from this point of view the core mental process, corresponding to the *Ātman* in the system of the *Upanishads*, is not something that takes place within our heads, or even within our individual selves: it is a universal and impersonal cosmic process. It creates and sustains the myriad individual viewpoints that exist within the vast sea of experience and therefore transcends all individuality. The core mental process is prior to all contextualization of an individual self, prior to the emergence of personality (individual perspective) and therefore it is common to all, the shared basis of a shared physical world and of shared experience. As the universal source of contextualization, it is the source of the differentiation of experience into different individuals and into different regions within the same individual (mind and body). It tells us all one and the same story – the tale of the unconscious – articulated and expressed (contextualized) according to different sets of narrative rules: mind and body, self and other. It is the fundamental activity of the cosmos manifesting itself as the infinite experiences of infinitely many individuals in an infinite world.

When, then, we recall our conclusion in Chapter 16 to the effect that the fundamental need is to think, we will have relatively little difficulty in understanding the cosmos as the process of the self-revelation of the unconscious in, through, and for the unconscious; or, to employ the poetically powerful, if antiquated, language of the Christians: the cosmos is God knowing Himself through Man. In fact we have never left the unconscious: it is our true home. It is where we live.

To return to the philosophical issues for the sake of which we pursued this line of metaphysical thinking:

1. *The intersubjective problem.* There *must* be a real external impulse acting upon the mind, i.e. a truly independent primary caretaker, or else the mind could never form to begin with. The dialectical structure of the self implies the real independent existence of persons outside of the immediate sphere of one's own mental life. And yet communication between these separate and apparently isolated minds is still possible because they have a shared identity in the unconscious that produces a shared experience in a shared world. In clinical terms, there must be a truly independent external reality with which the object can be compared and in the light of which it can be known and corrected, or else we would all be prisoners in our own skulls, eternally unable to verify any of our fantasies, and eternally at the mercy of the unreal.

   It is, perhaps, not insignificant that the English word "matter," which is the primary content of the external world, is etymologically derived from the Latin *materia*, which in turn is derived from *mater*, meaning "mother."
2. *The intrasubjective problem.* Body and mind are, as we have seen, the same thing viewed in two different ways, from two different viewpoints, according to two different sets of rules. The laws of physics fail to describe a certain class of experiences, namely the experience of the mind. At the same time, the experiences to which the laws of physics do apply, physical things, are ultimately non-different from their mental equivalents. Both the material and mental realms are patterns within the unconscious. Similarly, the entries in an encyclopedia are ordered alphabetically while the rest of the text is not. All, however, are part of the same book and do not differ except with regard to their arrangement within the whole.

Having answered our questions regarding the nature of the mind and its place within the totality of experience, our investigation has reached its conclusion.

From an individual perspective, the unconscious is the totality of uncontextualized experience. What is uncontextualized has no position in space or time. This being the case, we cannot say that it did or did not begin, was or was not there at any specific point. For all we know it may well have originated in a past life; or, to employ the popular vocabulary of our times, that it is "biologically determined."

From a universal perspective (*sub specie aeternitatis*) the unconscious is a brightly shining void that only emerges into space and time – only becomes contextualized experience – by being given to us in, through, and as the self, and as we saw, that primarily means as the history of our interactions with others. Knowledge of the unconscious is mediated through an external world. Thus the fundamental process of experience – the act of world-creation – is the process of manifestation-as-other for the sake of illumination-of-self. When we are aware of all three terms of this process – the ground of being, its manifestation, and its withdrawal into the place of emergence – the mind, the world, and the self – we can be said to have attained wisdom. *Then the ego knows its place in the grand scheme of things*. It knows where it is and can remain there. It becomes *ethical* in the true, original sense of the word:[1] to know where one is, to know one's place, and to remain there.

The unconscious projected outwards into the heavens is "God" in the sense of traditional religion. Hypostasized and located within a part of the body, it is the "id" qua totality of biological drives. Assigned its proper place within the individual, it is the True Self or Buddha-mind. *In fact we have never left the unconscious*; all experience is a form of dream; we dream constantly; we can never be born into it or die out of it. We can only worship it by being it, which is functionally equivalent with being ourselves.

## Note

1 *Êthos* in Greek originally meant "the place one is usually to be found," "habitat"; also see Book IV of Plato's *Republic*.

## References

Berkeley, G. (1988). *Principles of Human Knowledge/Three Dialogues*. London: Penguin Books.

Dick, P. K. (1969/2002). Ubik. In P. K. Dick, *Counterfeit Unrealities* (pp. 337–510). New York: SFBC.

Freud, S. (1900/1996). *Die Traumdeutung*. Frankfurt am Main: S. Fischer Verlag.

Plato. (1992). *Republic* (2nd ed.). (C. Reeve, Ed., & G. Grube, Trans.) Indianapolis and Cambridge: Hackett Publishing Company.

Schopenhauer, A. (1818/1988). *Die Welt als Wille und Vorstellung. Erster Band*. (L. Lütkehaus, Ed.) Zurich: Haffmans Verlag.

Spinoza, B. (1992). *The Ethics. Treatise on the Emendation of the Intellect. Selected Letters*. (S. Feldman, Ed., & S. Shirley, Trans.) Indianapolis and Cambridge: Hackett Publishing Company.

# EPILOGUE

> Will they ever forget their hurts and their sorrows or will they gradually build for themselves escapes and resistances? To keep these hurts seems to be the nature of human beings and from this their actions become twisted. Can the human mind never be hurt or wounded? Not to be hurt is to be innocent. If you are not hurt you will naturally not hurt another. Is this possible? The culture in which we live does deeply wound the mind and heart. The noise and the pollution, the aggression and competition, the violence and the education – all these and more contribute to the agony. Yet we have to live in this world of brutality and resistance: we are the world and the world is us. What is the thing that is hurt? The image that each one has built about himself, that is what is hurt. Strangely these images, all over the world are the same, with some modifications. The essence of the image you have is the same as of the man a thousand miles away. So you are that man or woman. Your hurts are the hurts of thousands: you are the other.
>
> *(Krishnamurti, 1991, pp. 22–23)*[1]

## Note

1 Content reproduced with permission. Permission to quote from the works of J. Krishnamurti or other works for which the copyright is held by the Krishnamurti Foundation of America or the Krishnamurti Foundation Trust Ltd has been given on the understanding that such permission does not indicate endorsement of the views expressed in this publication. For more information about J. Krishnamurti (1895–1986) please see: www.jkrishnamurti.org.

## Reference

Krishnamurti, J. (1991). *Krishnamurti's Journal.* Madras: Krishnamurti Foundation India.

# SELECTIVE INDEX